AF530471

India's Social Sector and Millennium Development Goals

India's Social Sector and Millennium Development Goals

Issues, Challenges and Policy Measures

Anupam Hazra

RAWAT PUBLICATIONS

Jaipur • New Delhi • Bangalore • Hyderabad • Guwahati

ISBN 978-81-316-0579-0

© Author, 2013

No part of this book may be reproduced or transmitted in any form or by any means, electronic or mechanical, including photocopying, recording or by any information storage and retrieval system, without permission in writing from the publishers.

Published by
Prem Rawat for **Rawat Publications**
Satyam Apts, Sector 3, Jawahar Nagar, Jaipur 302 004 (India)
Phone: 0141 265 1748 / 7006 Fax: 0141 265 1748
E-mail: info@rawatbooks.com
Website: www.rawatbooks.com

New Delhi Office
4858/24, Ansari Road, Daryaganj, New Delhi 110 002
Phone: 011 2326 3290

Also at *Bangalore, Hyderabad* and *Guwahati*

Typeset by Rawat Computers, Jaipur

Printed at Chaman Enterprises, New Delhi

To

My dearest *'Dadubhai'* Late Shri Tarakeshwar Mondal

Contents

List of Tables

Acknowledgements

I owe a sincere debt of gratitude to my dearest mother Smt. Manju Hazra, the most admired person in my life, my father Shri Debnath Hazra and my sweet 'Didibhai' Smt. Annapurna Mondal for their blessings and to my affectionate brother Shri Nirupam Hazra for his incessant encouragement to initiate this literary venture. I am also grateful to Ms. Subhashree Sanyal for supporting me unconditionally towards successful completion of this book. Lastly, I would like to thank all my critics for their constant criticism which has always been the source of inspiration for me to put more sincere and concerted efforts towards my academic endeavours.

Anupam Hazra

Preface

Countries across the globe today are fanatical about development and in the current era of sustainable development, the issue of achieving the Millennium Development Goals (MDGs) has been gaining special attention of the development experts, academicians, researchers and policy makers as MDGs are considered to be the most comprehensive framework for tracking the overall growth of a nation across the globe. A cursory look at the Millennium Development Goals (MDGs) makes it evident that the first six goals fall under the broad purview of social sector which puts an intense focus and concerted efforts on tackling the issues of poverty alleviation and hunger reduction (Goal 1), universalization of primary education (Goal 2), women empowerment (Goal 3) and health sector development (Goals 4, 5 and 6) to ensure a sustainable growth across the globe. So, social sector development lies at the heart of Millennium Commitments which has come to acquire a very important and new salience in the literature and practice of sustainable development and an inadequate attention on social sector may jeopardize any country's overall progress towards MDGs.

In recent years, India has emerged as one of the most progressive nations in the world in terms of its booming economy, and also making waves in the fields of science and technology, nuclear energy, etc. India has attracted global attention for rapid economic growth; global multinationals and growing industries have changed the face of India with people being employed in corporate sector, having a fairly high standard of living and an increased purchasing power. In the current context of development, the Indian economy is regarded among the fastest growing economies in the world – but what about social sector progress? Trends of growing expenditure on social sector by the government in the recent years reflect the emphasis on the social sector. Available statistics and different development reports make it quite evident that over the years, India has made substantial progress in key human development areas such as health, education and purchasing power. Sustained and high economic growth in the post-reform period reduced the poverty ratio significantly. Noteworthy improvement has also been noticed over time in literacy rates leading to a decline in the absolute number of illiterates. But this just shows the glorious side of the story. But, as far as the context of MDG Commitments is concerned, India's overall performance in social sector growth has been mixed in the last decade. The mid-term appraisal of India's 10th Five-Year Plan expresses concern that while some progress has been made in education and health indicators over time, India continues to lag far behind levels achieved by East Asian and Southeast Asian countries and there still remains huge room for improvement in making primary education, food, basic health care services available and accessible to its entire population.

Although all relevant MDG indicators of social sector have moved towards their 2015 targets, their performances have been uneven. To understand this variation, it is important to analyse the reasons of the slowing down of the infant mortality rate, the apparent plateauing of chronic hunger rate, the rise in youth unemployment rate, and most important of all what factors work in accelerating the pace of rural poverty reduction. First, the recent statistics and reports explore that the proportion of people living in poverty in India is decreasing but the number of poor Indians is increasing. The paradox of India is that the growth has been instrumental in reducing poverty rates, but poverty rates have not fallen fast enough to reduce the total number of poor people. This is because population is growing faster than the poverty rate reduction. While urban India has made progress in poverty reduction, its rural counterpart is unlikely to meet the goal without significant additional policy efforts and resources. So, for India, rapid economic growth does not have a substantial impact on rural poverty reduction and, at the same time, India is having a new opportunity also to harness the economic growth and reduce poverty through employment creation and social protection schemes. Strong, sustained and shared growth must be the key priority for future macro-economic policy and, at the same time, without inclusive growth it will be difficult to significantly reduce poverty. Secondly, for India, ensuring food for all still remains a distant dream. The country achieved self-sufficiency in food grain production in the 1970s and has sustained it since then; but the achievement of food grain security at the national level did not percolate down to households, resulting into high chronic food insecurity among the poor. Though India is one of the largest producers of food grains in the world, yet millions of people struggle to get two square meals a day and an equal number are undernourished. While efforts need to be made to increase production and productivity of food grains, providing access to the needy remains a major challenge. Thirdly, as far as the issue of primary education is concerned, while the country continues to make advancements towards primary school enrolment, this growing enrolment rate is yet to translate into increased primary education completion rates. This slow progress demonstrates the importance of improving the quality of education rather than aiming solely for the quantitative target. Fourthly, Indian women have made progress in more or less every sphere of life. India continues to maintain its positive trend towards progress in gender equality and women's empowerment, especially in political arena, and this becomes much more evident when we notice the mounting number of women representatives in the panchayat system in rural India as well as their dominance and increasing participation in national-level politics, diminishing gender disparity in primary school enrolment, etc. But maternal mortality rate (MMR), the most common measure of maternal health, domestic violence, female foeticides, etc., continues to be high and is still regarded as a normal phenomenon – which aptly reveals the fact that gap still exists in the process of empowering women in India. Last but not the least, though in recent years significant progress has been observed in health sector but India has still to go a long way in improving the major health indicators and tackling the challenge of making basic health care facilities available and accessible for its population. Improvements in health indicators such as maternal mortality and infant mortality rates have been much slower than expected. There is widespread undernutrition among women and children, and maternal and child health still remain areas of concern especially for rural India. On the other hand, limited positive changes have been perceived in the quality of life of the rural poor. Rural India still struggles for its basic necessities of life such as basic health care facilities, access to food, education, safe drinking water, proper sanitation, etc. In spite of some improvement in nutritional status at the national level, nearly half of the rural children are suffering from malnutrition. However, improvements in stemming the HIV/AIDS pandemic have been significant in both preventing new infections and making antiretroviral treatment available to infected people.

Much time has passed since the world leaders came together and agreed on the essential eight global Millennium Development Goals (MDGs) – the most prominent global parameters for assessing any country's overall growth and progress that have to be achieved by 2015. Now, with less than three years remaining to the target date of 2015, this assessment is of utmost importance as it will help countries identify the targets that require concerted efforts for achievement of the MDGs. While the full achievement of the MDGs may still elude us for years to come, the goals and targets of the MDGs are already fast becoming irrefutable and irrepressible global norms with a compelling legitimacy – and once again failure to achieve them will not constitute just accidental lapses, but an unmistakable symptom of leadership failure.

In spite of significant investments and concerted efforts, it appears to be quite exigent for the country to achieve its Millennium Commitments, particularly in its social sector arena, which are expected to be attained by 2015. This book basically focuses on India's approach and current state of progress in the context of social sector which has received a major boost through the country's Millennium Commitments and simultaneously has made an attempt to explore the emerging issues and challenges of this sector that have been instrumental in jeopardizing India's journey towards its Millennium Commitments. Each of the sectoral agenda such as poverty, food insecurity, primary education, women empowerment and basic health care has been analysed with the dynamics of its contemporary scenario as well as with the suggestive measures which may determine the future course of action and may guide the Indian policy makers to tackle the particular issue on a priority basis for ensuring a sustainable growth in social sector.

Acronyms

AAY	Antyodaya Anna Yojana
ACT	Artemisinin Combination Therapies
ADB	Asian Development Bank
AEP	Adolescence Education Programme
AIDS	Acquired Immune Deficiency Syndrome
AIE	Alternative and Innovative Education
ANM	Auxiliary Nurse Midwife
API	Annual Parasite Incidence
ARI	Acute Respiratory Infection
ASER	Annual Status of Education Report
ASFR	Age-Specific Fertility Rates
BPL	Below Poverty Line
BRGF	Backward Regions Grant Fund
CADA	Command Area Development Agency
CBO	Community-Based Organization
CCS	Country Cooperation Strategy
CED	Chronic Energy Deficiency
CFC	Chlorofluorocarbon
CHC	Community Health Centre
CIP	Central Issue Price
CLR	Computerization of Land Records
CMR	Child Mortality Rate
CSO	Civil Society Organization
CSRE	Crash Scheme for Rural Employment
CSSM	Child Survival and Safe Motherhood
CSS	Centrally Sponsored Scheme
DAC	Development Assistance Committee
DDP	Desert Development Programme
DDT	Dichlorodiphenyltrichloroethane

DES	Dietary Energy Supply
DGHS	Director General of Health Services
DISE	District Information System for Education
DM & HO	District Medical and Health Officer
DOTS	Directly Observed Treatment Short Course
DPAP	Drought Prone Areas Development Programme
DPEP	District Primary Education Programme
DWCD	Department of Women and Child Development
DWCRA	Development of Women and Children in Rural Areas
EAG	Empowered Action Group
EAS	Employment Assurance Scheme
EBB	Educationally Backward Blocks
ECCE	Early Childhood Care and Education
EFA	Education for All
EGS	Education Guarantee Scheme
EMCP	Enhanced Malaria Control Project
EPI	Expanded Programme on Immunization
ESD	Education for Sustainable Development
EVBDCP	Enhanced Vector Borne Diseases Control Project
FAO	Food and Agriculture Organization of the United Nations
FCI	Food Corporation of India
FFW	Food for Work
FYP	Five-Year Plan
GDI	Gender Development Indicators
GNI	Gross National Income
GDP	Gross Domestic Product
GER	Gross Enrolment Ratio
GHI	Global Hunger Index
GKY	Ganga Kalyan Yojana
GNP	Gross National Product
GOI	Government of India
GPI	Gender Parity Index
HADP	Hill Area Development Programme
HCR	Head Count Ratio
HDI	Human Development Index
HH	House Hold
HII	Health Information of India
HIPC	Heavily Indebted Poor Countries
HIV	Human Immunodeficiency Virus

HMIS	Health Management Information System
HPI	Human Poverty Index
IAS	Indian Administrative Service
ICDS	Integrated Child Development Services
IDD	Iodine Deficiency Disorders
IDU	Injecting Drug Users
IEC	Information, Education and Communication
IFPRI	International Food Policy Research Institute
IGNOAPS	Indira Gandhi National Old Age Pension Scheme
IHD	Institute for Human Development
IHSP	India Health System Profile
IIPS	International Institute for Population Sciences, Mumbai
ILO	International Labour Organization
IMCP	Intensified Malaria Control Project
IMNCI	Integrated Management of Neonatal Childhood Illness
IMR	Infant Mortality Rate
IRDP	Integrated Rural Development Programme
ISHI	India State Hunger Index
ISM & H	Indian Systems of Medicine and Homoeopathy
IWDP	Integrated Wasteland Development Programme
JGSY	Jawahar Gram Samridhi Yojana
JSS	Jan Shikshan Sansthan
JRY	Jawahar Rozgar Yojana
JSY	Janani Suraksha Yojana
KGBV	Kasturba Gandhi Balika Vidyalaya
LBW	Low Birth Weight
LDC	Least Developed Countries
LHV	Lady Health Visitors
M&E	Monitoring and Evaluation
MCH	Maternal and Child Health
MDGs	Millennium Development Goals
MDMS	Mid-Day Meal Scheme
MDT	Multi-Drug Therapy
MFAL	Marginal Farmer and Agricultural Labour Development Programme
MGNREGA	Mahatma Gandhi National Rural Employment Guarantee Act
MGNREGS	Mahatma Gandhi National Rural Employment Guarantee Scheme
MHRD	Ministry of Human Resource Development

MMR	Maternal Mortality Rate
MPCE	Monthly Per Capita Expenditure
MPI	Multidimensional Poverty Index
MPR	Mixed Recall Period
MPW	Multipurpose Worker
MSSRF	MS Swaminathan Research Foundation
MS	Mahila Samakhya
MWCD	Ministry of Women and Child Development
NAC	National Advisory Council
NACO	National AIDS Control Organization
NCMH	National Commission for Macroeconomics and Health
NER	Net Enrolment Rate
NFBS	National Family Benefit Scheme
NFE	Non-Formal Education
NFFWP	National Food for Work Programme
NFHS	National Family Health Survey
NFSM	National Food Security Mission
NGO	Non-Governmental Organization
NHP	National Health Policy
NIPCCD	National Institute of Public Cooperation and Child Development
NLEP	National Leprosy Eradication Programme
NLRMP	National Land Records Modernization Programme
NMCP	National Malaria Control Programme
NMEP	National Malaria Eradication Programme
NOAPS	National Old Age Pension Scheme
NPCB	National Programme for Control of Blindness
NPE	National Policy on Education
NPEGEL	National Programme for Education of Girls at Elementary Level
NPNSPE	National Programme of Nutritional Support to Primary Education
NPP	National Population Policy
NREGP	National Rural Employment Guarantee Programme
NREP	National Rural Employment Programme
NRHM	National Rural Health Mission
NSAP	National Social Assistance Programme
NSSO	National Sample Survey Organization
NTCP	National Tuberculosis Control Programme
NVBDCP	National Vector Borne Disease Control Programme

OBCs	Other Backward Classes
ODA	Official Development Assistance
ODP	Ozone Depletion Potential
OECD	Organization for Economic Cooperation and Development
OPHI	Oxford Poverty and Human Development Initiative
OPV	Oral Polio Vaccine
PCPNDT	Pre-Conception and Pre-Natal Diagnostic Techniques
PDS	Public Distribution System
PF	Plasmodium falciparum
PHC	Primary Health Centre
POA	Programme of Action
PPI	Pulse Polio Immunization
PPP	Public Private Partnerships
PPP	Purchasing Power Parity
PMGSY	Pradhan Mantri Gram Sadak Yojana
PMTCT	Prevention of Mother-To-Child Transmission
PRIs	Panchayati Raj Institutions
PROBE	Public Report on Basic Education
PSK	Prarambhik Shiksha Kosh
RCH	Reproductive and Child Health
RLEGP	Rural Landless Employment Guarantee Programme
RMK	Rashtriya Mahila Kosh
RMP	Rural Manpower Programme
RNTCP	Revised National TB Control Programme
RPDS	Revamped Public Distribution System
RTE	The Right to Education Act
SAARC	South Asian Association for Regional Cooperation
SC	Scheduled Castes
SCs	Sub-Centres
SFDA	Small Farmer Development Agency
SGRY	Sampoorna Grameen Rozgar Yojana
SGSY	Swarnjayanti Gram Swarozgar Yojana
SHG	Self-Help Group
SIDA	Swedish International Development Agency
SITRA	Supply of Improved Toolkit for Rural Artisans
SPR	Slide Positivity Rate
SRA & ULR	Strengthening of Revenue Administration and Updating of Land Records
SRS	Sample Registration System

SSA	Sarva Shiksha Abhiyan
STIs	Sexually Transmitted Infections
STs	Scheduled Tribes
TB	Tuberculosis
TBC	Tuberculosis Control India
TPDS	Targeted Public Distribution System
TRYSEM	Training of Rural Youth for Self-Employment
TSC	Total Sanitation Campaign
TT	Tetanus Toxoid
UFM	Under-Five Mortality
UEE	Universalization of Elementary Education
UGC	University Grants Commission
UIP	Universal Immunization Programme
UNAIDS	United Nations Programme on HIV/AIDS
UNCTAD	United Nations Conference on Trade and Development
UNDP	United Nations Development Programme
UNICEF	United Nations Children's Fund
UN	United Nations
URP	Uniform Recall Period
VEC	Village Education Committees
WCP	Women Component Plan
WEF	World Economic Forum
WFP	United Nations World Food Programme
WHO	World Health Organization
WPA	World Population Awareness
WPC	Women Component Plan
WTO	World Trade Organization

1 Viewing India's Social Sector from MDG Lens

Some Reality Bites

On 8 September 2000, during the UN Millennium Summit held in New York at the United Nations headquarters, 147 heads of state and 189 nations made themselves committed towards improving the lot of humanity across the globe with an aim to make the entire human race free from the clutches of abject and dehumanizing conditions of extreme poverty, by signing the Millennium Declaration at the dawn of a new Millennium. The Millennium Declaration consolidated a set of eight interconnected and time-bound development promises into a global agenda in the form of the Millennium Development Goals (MDGs) – representing the most determined universal efforts towards achieving sustainable development across the globe by 2015 and signifying an unprecedented global consensus to address the overriding concern of human deprivation as represented by income poverty and the inadequacy of enabling opportunities for all. The MDGs constitute an internationally agreed framework composing of eight goals and 18 targets, for directing the entire global efforts towards the ultimate goal of poverty elimination by ensuring a situation of sustainable human development across the world and a global parameter complemented by 48 technical indicators for assessing the overall global progress towards achievement of the eight development goals (Table 1).

The MDGs have been tremendously successful in galvanizing political leaders, civil society organizations, private sector actors, the media and donors in the pursuit of human development. These have also succeeded in bringing into focus the key development issues for all countries worldwide, providing a momentum to the

Table 1 *The Millennium Development Goals: Targets and Indicators*

Goals and Targets	*Indicators for Monitoring Progress*
Goal 1: Eradicate extreme poverty and hunger	
Target 1: Halve, between 1990 and 2015, the proportion of people whose income is less than one dollar a day	1. Proportion of population below $1 (PPP) per day[a] 2. Poverty gap ratio (incidence × depth of poverty) 3. Share of poorest quintile in national consumption
Target 2: Halve, between 1990 and 2015, the proportion of people who suffer from hunger	4. Prevalence of underweight children under-five years of age 5. Proportion of population below minimum level of dietary energy consumption
Goal 2: Achieve universal primary education	
Target 3: Ensure that, by 2015, children everywhere, boys and girls alike, will be able to complete a full course of primary schooling	6. Net enrolment ratio in primary education 7. Proportion of pupils starting grade 1 who reach grade 5 8. Literacy rate of 15–24 year olds
Goal 3: Promote gender equality and empower women	
Target 4: Eliminate gender disparity in primary and secondary education preferably by 2005 and to all levels of education no later than 2015	9. Ratios of girls to boys in primary, secondary and tertiary education 10. Ratio of literate females to males of 15–24 year olds 11. Share of women in wage employment in the non-agricultural sector 12. Proportion of seats held by women in national parliament
Goal 4: Reduce child mortality	
Target 5: Reduce by two-thirds, between 1990 and 2015, the under-five mortality rate	13. Under-five mortality rate 14. Infant mortality rate 15. Proportion of 1 year old children immunized against measles
Goal 5: Improve maternal health	
Target 6: Reduce by three-quarters, between 1990 and 2015, the maternal mortality ratio	16. Maternal mortality ratio 17. Proportion of births attended by skilled health personnel
Goal 6: Combat HIV/AIDS, malaria and other diseases	
Target 7: Have halted by 2015 and begun to reverse the spread of HIV/AIDS	18. HIV prevalence among 15–24 year olds pregnant women 19. Condom use rate of the contraceptive prevalence rate[b] 20. Number of children orphaned by HIV/AIDS[c]

Cont'd...

...Cont'd

Target 8: Have halted by 2015 and begun to reverse the incidence of malaria and other major diseases	21. Prevalence and death rates associated with malaria 22. Proportion of population in malaria risk areas using effective malaria prevention and treatment measures[d] 23. Prevalence and death rates associated with tuberculosis 24. Proportion of tuberculosis cases detected and cured under directly observed treatment short course (DOTS)

Goal 7: Ensure environmental sustainability

Target 9: Integrate the principles of sustainable development into country policies and programmes and reverse the loss of environmental resources	25. Proportion of land area covered by forest 26. Ratio of area protected to maintain biological diversity to surface area 27. Energy use (kg oil equivalent) per \$1 GDP (PPP) 28. Carbon dioxide emissions (per capita) and consumption of ozone-depleting CFCs (ODP tons) 29. Proportion of population using solid fuels
Target 10: Halve, by 2015, the proportion of people without sustainable access to safe drinking water	30. Proportion of population with sustainable access to an improved water source, urban and rural
Target 11: By 2020, to have achieved a significant improvement in the lives of at least 100 million slum dwellers	31. Proportion of urban population with access to improved sanitation 32. Proportion of households with access to secure tenure (owned or rented)

Goal 8: Develop a global partnership for development

Target 12: Develop further an open, rule-based, predictable, non-discriminatory trading and financial system Includes a commitment to good governance, development and poverty reduction – both nationally and internationally	*Some of the indicators listed below are monitored separately for the least developed countries (LDCs), Africa, landlocked countries and small island developing states.* *Official development assistance* 33. Net ODA, total and to LDCs, as percentage of OECD/DAC donors' gross national income 34. Proportion of total bilateral, sector-allocable ODA of OECD/DAC donors to basic social services (basic education, primary health care, nutrition, safe water and sanitation)
Target 13: Address the special needs of the least developed countries Includes: tariff and quota-free access for least developed countries' exports; enhanced programme of debt relief for HIPC and cancellation of official	35. Proportion of bilateral ODA of OECD/DAC donors that is untied 36. ODA received in landlocked countries as proportion of their GNIs 37. ODA received in small island developing states as proportion of their GNIs

Cont'd...

...Cont'd

bilateral debt; and more generous ODA for countries committed to poverty reduction **Target 14:** Address the special needs of landlocked countries and small island developing states (through the Programme of Action for the Sustainable Development of Small Island Developing states and the outcome of the twenty-second special session of the General Assembly) **Target 15:** Deal comprehensively with the debt problems of developing countries through national and international measures in order to make debt sustainable in the long-term	*Market access* 38. Proportion of total developed country imports (by value and excluding arms) from developing countries and LDCs, admitted free of duties 39. Average tariffs imposed by developed countries on agricultural products and textiles and clothing from developing countries 40. Agricultural support estimate for OECD countries as percentage of their GDP 41. Proportion of ODA provided to help build trade capacity[e] *Debt sustainability* 42. Total number of countries that have reached their HIPC decision points and number that have reached their HIPC completion points (cumulative) 43. Debt relief committed under HIPC initiative, US$ 44. Debt service as a percentage of exports of goods and services
Target 16: In co-operation with developing countries, develop and implement strategies for decent and productive work for youth	45. Unemployment rate of 15–24 year olds, each sex and total[f]
Target 17: In co-operation with pharmaceutical companies, provide access to affordable, essential drugs in developing countries	46. Proportion of population with access to affordable, essential drugs on a sustainable basis
Target 18: In co-operation with the private sector, make available the benefits of new technologies, especially information and communications	47. Telephone lines and cellular subscribers per 100 population 48. Personal computers in use per 100 population and Internet users per 100 population

[a] For monitoring country poverty trends, indicators based on national poverty lines should be used, where available.

[b] Among contraceptive methods, only condoms are effective in preventing HIV transmission. The contraceptive prevalence rate is also useful in tracking progress in other health, gender and poverty goals. Because the condom use rate is only measured among women in union, it will be supplemented by an indicator on condom use in high-risk situations. These indicators will be augmented with an indicator of knowledge and misconceptions regarding HIV/AIDS by 15–24 year olds (UNICEF – WHO).

[c] To be measured by the ratio of proportion of orphans to non-orphans aged 10–14 who are attending school.

[d] Prevention to be measured by the per cent of under-five years sleeping under insecticide-treated bednets; treatment to be measured by per cent of under-five years who are appropriately treated.

[e] OECD and WTO are collecting data that will be available from 2001 onwards.

[f] An improved measure of the target is under development by ILO for future years.

Source: Alliance, 2015.

existing development programmes and policies across the globe. These goals have further provided the nations with a good reference point to develop programmes and policies. More than a decade later, the world has witnessed considerable progress and even some stunning successes in achieving the goals set at the turn of the century. Yet, this progress has bypassed large numbers of the world's poor. 'Inequality has become the ugly underbelly of global prosperity.'[1] Overall, progress towards the MDGs has been described as 'patchy' and 'uneven'. The broad conclusion is that few goals are entirely on track globally, and those that show substantial variation have least progress in Africa and often in South Asia. Whereas MDG 1 (eradication of extreme poverty and hunger) is on course to be achieved and 'remarkable improvements' have been made regarding aspects of MDG 6 (combating of HIV/AIDS, malaria and other diseases), insufficient progress has been made towards achievement of MDG 2 (provision of universal primary education), MDG 4 (reduction of child mortality) and MDG 5 (reduction of maternal mortality). Steps towards MDG 3 (promotion of gender equality and empowerment of women) have been labelled 'sluggish'; 'alarmingly high' rates of deforestation are hampering MDG 7 (ensuring of environmental sustainability); and Africa is 'short-changed' by the aid flows included under MDG 8 (development of a global partnership for development). Moreover, the global economic crisis has accentuated the urgency of the discussion, and progress is being jeopardized because of new financial constraints (Waage et al., 2010).

Viewing India's Social Sector from MDG Lens: The Emerging Issues and Challenges

A cursory view over the internationally agreed framework of sustainable development provided by MDGs will explore that the agenda of social development lies at the heart of Millennium Commitments. The first six goals, i.e., (1) Goal 1: eradicate extreme poverty and hunger; (2) Goal 2: achieve universal primary education; (3) Goal 3: promote gender equality and empower women; (4) Goal 4: reduce child mortality; (5) Goal 5: improve maternal health; and (6) Goal 6: combat HIV/AIDS, malaria and other diseases – fall under the broad purview of social sector which puts an intense focus and concerted efforts on tackling the issues of poverty alleviation, hunger reduction, universalization of primary education, women empowerment and health sector development to ensure a sustainable growth across the globe. So an inadequate attention on social sector may jeopardize any country's overall progress towards MDGs.

Being a signatory of the Millennium Declaration, India's planned development strategies have put intensive effort towards social development with an aim to ensure a more equitable distribution of development benefits for the deprived section of the society with a better living environment, making social welfare services more accessible for its entire poor population. The Central Government expenditure on social services and rural development (plan and non-plan), which contributes directly to human development, has gone up consistently over the years. It has increased from 13.75 per cent in 2005–2006 to 19.27 per cent in 2010–2011.[2] The central support for social welfare programmes has continued to expand in various forms, although most social sector subjects fall within the purview of the states. Major programme-specific funding is available to the states through Centrally Sponsored Schemes (CSSs). Expenditure on social services (which include education, medical and public health, family welfare, water supply and sanitation, welfare of Scheduled Castes [SCs], Scheduled Tribes [STs] and Other Backward Classes [OBCs], labour and labour welfare, social security, nutrition, and relief for natural calamities, etc.) by the government (centre and states combined) has also shown increase in recent years, reflecting the higher priority given to this sector. Expenditure on social services as a proportion of total expenditure increased from 21.1 per cent in 2005–2006 to 23.8 per cent in 2008–2009 and further to 25.2 per cent in 2010–2011 (BE). As a proportion of GDP, its share increased from 5.49 per cent in 2005–2006 to 6.63 per cent in 2010–2011 (BE). Expenditure on education as a proportion of total expenditure has increased marginally from 10 per cent in 2005–2006 to 11.3 per cent in 2010–2011 (BE). While the expenditure on health as a proportion of the GDP has increased from 1.23 per cent in 2005–2006 to

1.27 per cent in 2010–2011 (BE), its share in total expenditure has increased marginally from 4.7 per cent in 2005–2006 to 4.8 per cent in 2010–2011 (BE) (Government of India, 2011a). Recent statistics show that concerted efforts and intense focus have provided a major boost to the overall progress of India's social sector towards the achievement of MDGs, which will be very much reflective from the following table:

Table 2 *Progress of India's Social Sector towards the Millennium Development Goals: A Statistical Profile*

Goal 1: Eradicate extreme poverty and hunger	• The poverty headcount ratio declined from 55% in 1973–74 to 36% in 1993–94 and further to 27.5% in 2004–05. • The share of poorest quintile in total consumption (consumption that is accounted for by the poorest fifth of the population) in the rural areas declined from 9.6% in 1993–94 to 9.5% in 2004–05 based on URP. This decline was sharper in the urban areas where the ratio declined from 8.0% to 7.3%.
Goal 2: Achieve universal primary education	• The enrolment in primary classes (class I–V) was 97.4 million in 1990–91 which rose to 113.8 million in 2000-01 and further to 135.5 million in 2007–08. The enrolment in middle/upper primary classes (class VI–VIII) was 34.0 million in 1990-91 which increased to 42.8 million in 2000–01 and then to 57.2 million in 2007-08. • The Gross Enrolment Ratio (GER) at the primary level was 83.8 in 1990–91 and it increased to 95.7 in 2000–01 and to 113.97 in 2007–08. For the middle/upper primary level, the GER was 66.7 in 1990–91 which declined to 58.6 in 2000-01 and then gradually increased to 78.1 in 2007-08.
Goal 3: Promote gender equality and empower women	• The sex ratio (number of female per 1000 male) at birth in India was 880 (rural 882, urban 872) during 2003–05 which increased to 892 (rural 895, urban 881) during 2004–06 and further to 904 (rural 907, urban 894) during 2006–08. • The life expectance of women in India is more than that for men. It was 60.9 years in 1991–95 for women compared with 59.7 years for men and rose to 64.2 years in 2002–06 for women as against 62.6 years for men in the same year. • The Worker Participation Rate for women was 25.63 per cent in 2001. This is an improvement from 22.27 per cent in 1991 and 19.67 per cent in 1981.
Goal 4: Reduce child mortality	• The proportion of children under three years of age who are underweight decreased from 43 percent in 1998-99 to 40 percent in 2005–06. Stunting decreased by a larger margin, from 51 percent to 45 percent. Wasting increased from 20 percent to 23 percent.

Cont'd...

...Cont'd

	• The under-five mortality rate was 107 in 1992–93 which dropped to 95 in 1998-99 and further to 74 in 2005–06. • The country has observed a continuous decline in infant mortality rate (IMR). It was 80 in 1991 and decreased to 57 in 2006, 53 in 2008 and further to 50 in 2009.
Goal 5: Improve maternal health	• The MMR has come down from 398 per 100,000 live births in 1997–98 to 254 per 100,000 live births in 2004–06, a 36% decline over a span of seven years as compared to a 25% decline in the preceding eight years from 1990–97. • At the all-India level, the coverage of institutional deliveries increased rather slowly: from 26.1% in 1992–93 to 33.6% in 1998–99 and then to 41% in 2005–06 and 47% in 2007–08.
Goal 6: Combat HIV /AIDS , malaria and other diseases	• The estimated number of people living with HIV/AIDS in India was 27.3 lakh in 2002 which has gradually declined to 22.7 lakh in 2008. • Information from persons testing positive for HIV at the Integrated Counselling and Testing Centres across the country during 2009–2010 shows that 87.1 percent of HIV infections are still occurring through heterosexual routes of transmission. While parent to child transmission accounts for 5.4 percent of HIV cases detected, injecting drug use account for 1.6 percent, men who have sex with men account for 1.5 percent and contaminated blood and blood products account for 1.0 percent. • There were 3.03 million cases of malaria in 1996 which came down to 1.53 million in 2008. The annual parasite incidence was 3.48 in 1996 which declined to 1.36 in 2008. • TB mortality in the country has reduced from over 42 per lakh population in 1990 to 28 per lakh population in 2007 as per the WHO global report 2009.

Source: Based on Government of India (2011b).

But as far as progress of social sector in the context of Millennium Commitments is concerned, the mid-term appraisal of the Tenth Five-Year Plan (FYP) expresses concern that while some progress has been made in education and health indicators over time, India continues to lag far behind levels achieved by East Asian and Southeast Asian countries.[3] There have been positive trends on certain social indicators, particularly those that respond to vertical, campaign-like approaches: the near eradication of polio; a significant increase in literacy rates and the enrolment of both boys and girls in primary school. However, progress has been slow in areas requiring systemic changes, such as in the provisioning quality services through poverty alleviation programmes, primary health care services and community-based nutrition services. Limited positive changes have been perceived in the quality of life of the rural poor, status of women, residing in rural India and in health indicators such as IMR and MMR. Though the rate has reduced, but the HIV/AIDS epidemic continues to spread and still poses a significant threat. Issues related to child protection, including trafficking of women and child labour, are becoming more pronounced. Thus, the social indicators have shown disturbing gender gaps, large rural-urban differences and wide variation across country despite steady economic growth over the last decade. At the current pace of progress, India may not reach many of the MDG targets, such as maternal mortality rate, infant mortality rate and gender parity in secondary enrolment ratios, within the stipulated time.[4] Development process, therefore, needs to continuously strive for broad-based improvement in the standard of living and quality of life of the people through an inclusive development strategy that focuses on both income and non-income dimensions. On the other hand, the growing incidences of corruption have put a major threat for India in the way of its journey towards sustainable and inclusive growth; it has emerged as a real cancer which destroys the benefits of development plans, ultimately leading to human deprivations. In India, the tentacles of corruption are spread far and wide in all horizons of life and not just limited to government organizations. Moreover, corruption is not just limited to India. The 2010 Corruption Perceptions Index shows that three quarters of the 178 countries in the index have fared miserably in terms of corruption problem. Specifically, India has slipped three places in global rankings of most corrupt countries, from 84 in 2009 to 87 this year; on the ranking based on the scale from 0 (perceived to be highly corrupt) to 10 (low level of corruption), India scored 3.3 to grab 87 position in sharing with Jamaica and Liberia.[5] So for India, while moving towards its millennium commitments, the challenge of establishing good governance in every level of service delivery system needs to be tackled with utmost priority.

The Issue of Human Development

Globally, India's economic image has become quite impressive in recent years. It has achieved excellence in several key areas ranging from information technology and pharmaceuticals to automotive parts, and is now considered as one of the fastest growing economies of the world. Despite these positive developments, India is still among the countries with some of the lowest indicators of human development. Its levels of malnutrition, illiteracy and poverty are unacceptably high. The rise in income inequalities and regional disparities is also a matter of concern. Employment has grown, but the jobs created are not of high quality. Although there has been an expansion in several social services such as health, nutrition and education, the quality of most of these services remains poor in most of the rural areas. And, above all, an overwhelming majority of the population is deprived of basic social protection. Policy makers are thus faced with a paradox – the persistence of deprivations and increasing insecurities among a large section of the population amidst growing affluence and prosperity for some (Institute for Human Development, 2010).

Even after over 65 years of independence, the quality of life in India continues to be appalling with the country ranked poorly at 119 among 169 countries in the Human Development Index (HDI) 2010 released by the United Nations Development Programme (UNDP), indicating that Indian plans did not bestow that much attention to social sector development as it deserved. India ranks among the top 10 global countries on income gain, but widening disparity between the rich and the poor and gender inequality have been identified as major challenges by the Human Development Report, 2010. India ranks well below comparable emerging economies and even behind poorer neighbours such as Sri Lanka and the Maldives. Other emerging economies such as Russia (69th), Brazil (73rd) and China (89th) score well above India. In value terms, India moved to 0.519 from 0.512 last year. But its rank remains unchanged under a revised method of calculating the index.[6] The Report has tried to look deeper into the indicators to establish various inequalities. These inequalities arise due to disparity in distribution of incomes, gender inequality and multidimensional poverty. In the Gender Inequality Index, India has been ranked 122nd out of 138 countries, based on 2008 data.[7] The report says 27 per cent of adult women in India have a secondary or higher level of education, compared with 50 per cent of men. For every 1,00,000 live births, 450 women in India die from pregnancy-related causes, while the adolescent fertility rate is 68 births per 1,000 live births.[8] Female participation in the labour market in India is 36 per cent, compared with 85 per cent for men.[9] The index goes beyond a nation's gross domestic product (GDP) to measure the general well-being of people under a host of parameters, such as poverty levels, literacy and gender-related issues. It has been identified that the low-level development of social sector in India is largely due to inadequacy of education, health, drinking water, sanitation and housing facilities, etc. The report's new inequality-adjusted HDI, measuring inequality across 139 countries, shows South Asia with an average of 33 per cent loss due to inequality in health, education and income – the second largest for a development region after Sub-Saharan Africa. India loses 30 per cent overall on the inequality-adjusted HDI, including 41 per cent in education and 31 per cent in health.[10]

The Issue of 'Multidimensional Poverty'

The newly introduced Multidimensional Poverty Index (MPI) released by the Oxford Poverty and Human Development Initiative (OPHI) of University of Oxford in 2010 identifies overlapping deprivations in the sphere of health, education and living standards suffered by people at household-level across 104 developing countries.[11] Although deeply constrained by data limitations, the MPI reveals a different pattern of poverty than income poverty, as it illuminates a different set of deprivations. This new framework-cum-approach of poverty estimation attempts to go beyond income poverty to provide a broader understanding of the many types of deprivation the poor may face. It is more comprehensive than the Human Poverty Index (HPI) and is composed of 10 weighted indicators that measure education, health and standard of living: years of schooling and child enrolment (education); child mortality and nutrition (health) and electricity, flooring, drinking water, sanitation, cooking fuel and assets (standard of living). The MPI measures both the incidence of poverty and its intensity. A person is identified as poor if he or she is deprived in at least 30 per cent of the weighted indicators, as per MPI. The MPI – which identifies serious simultaneous deprivations in health, education and living standard at the household level – shows that around 55 per cent of Indians are poor, while another 16 per cent is vulnerable to it, which is much higher than the official figure.[12] Almost 20 per cent of Indians are deprived on six of the 10 indicators. Among the 104 developing countries rated by MPI 2010, India has been placed in 74th position even after Bangladesh.[13] MPI 2010 explores that in India, 55 per cent of the population already suffers multiple deprivations, while another 16 per cent in vulnerable to it. The report says Delhi's rate of multidimensional poverty is close to that of Iraq and Vietnam, while that of Bihar is similar to that of Sierra Leone and Guinea. About a third of other Indian households are multidimensionally poor, with an MPI just below that of Honduras. While India stands at 10 in the top 10 movers in HDI in terms of improvements in income, it does not figure in the top 10 movers list on health and education. N.R. Bhanumurthy, professor at the think-tank National Institute of Public Finance and Policy, said India's poor HDI rank reflected a skewed development focus. He said, 'Our policies have been concentrating more on economic growth, neglecting the social sectors. That is why the Eleventh Five-Year Plan (2007–2012) tried to bring in the concept of inclusive growth. The policies are now in place; however they have not been implemented whole-heartedly. That is why, our ranking is so poor'.[14] The world's biggest job programme, the Mahatma Gandhi National Rural Employment Guarantee Scheme (MGNREGS), got special mention for improving income in rural India. But, the report said the extent of the gains from economic liberalization for society as a whole needed careful investigation. The limited reach of public health care among the poor and teacher absenteeism in public schools were cited as major constraints.

The Threat of 'Poverty': Jeopardizing India's Growth

With a population of 1.21 billion, India is the world's largest democracy and is set to become the most populous country by around 2030. In the past decade, the country has witnessed accelerated economic growth, emerged as a global player with the world's fourth largest economy in purchasing power parity (PPP) terms and made progress on most of the MDGs, but will still miss out on the target of halving poverty by 2015.[15] India is home to over one-third of poor people in the world. Recently, the World Bank and the Asian Development Bank (ADB) released separate reports estimating global poverty based on most recent data. The World Bank report upped its benchmark of extreme poverty from $1 to $1.25 per person a day, and the ADB announced an even higher poverty benchmark of $1.35 per person a day.[16] Depending on which benchmark is used, 42 per cent to 55 per cent Indians live in extreme poverty.[17] The new PPPs raise the number of poor people in India from 336 million (30.7% of the population) to 456 million (41.6%). The poverty incidence in rural India is higher at 43.83 per cent (342.9 million people) but urban poverty too is relatively high at 36.2 per cent (112.9 million people).[18] The incidence of poverty is much higher in rural areas affecting the rural economy as well as the overall economy of the nation. India has entered the Eleventh Plan period with an impressive record of economic growth; the growth rate in the last four years of the Tenth Plan has averaged 8.7 per cent, making India one of the fastest growing economies in the world.[19] The percentage of the population below the official poverty line has come down from 36 in 1993–1994 to 27.5 in 2004–2005 but the rate of decline in poverty has not accelerated along with the growth in GDP, and the incidence of poverty among certain marginalized groups, for example the STs, has hardly declined at all.[20] Because population has also grown, the absolute number of poor people has declined only marginally from 320 million in 1993–1994 to 302 million in 2004–2005.[21] This performance is all the more disappointing since the poverty line on which the estimate of the poor is based is the same as it was in 1973–1974 when per capita incomes were much lower. On the other hand, the projected population and the rural BPL population in India for the period 2008–2015 are given in Table 3, making it evident that in 2015 there will be about 18.53 crore BPL population in rural areas constituting 22 per cent of the total rural population.[22] Thus, there is a need to make special efforts to reduce the rural BPL population in time-bound manner.

Table 3 *Projected Rural BPL Population by 2015 (in crore)*

Year	*Total Population*	*Rural Population*	*Rural BPL Population*	*Rural HH*
2008–2009	114.75	80.45	20.92	4.23
2009–2010	116.25	81.13	20.50	4.12
2010–2011	117.76	81.81	20.09	4.02
2011–2012	119.27	82.49	19.69	3.94
2012–2013	120.78	83.17	19.29	3.86
2013–2014	122.29	83.85	18.91	3.78
2014–2015	125.31	84.53	18.53	3.71

Assumptions: (1) Based on the Annual Population Growth Rate 2008–2015 (1.3%)
(2) Based on the per annum decline ratio for rural poverty 2008–2015 (2%)

Source: Department of Rural Development (2008).

Since independence the Government of India has changed the focus and approach of rural poverty alleviation programme as and when required; but mere changing the approach and focus of programmes alone is not enough. Greater efforts are needed to build the capacity of administration and improve governance at the district level. The success of targeted poverty schemes in India is dependent upon proper identification of the beneficiaries, transparency, supervision over field staff and social mobilization. Funds have more than tripled in the last ten years for poorer districts, but neither the government nor donors have studied whether there is capacity at the district and sub-district level to absorb the funds and produce quality results.

Food for All: Still a Distant Dream

The Global Hunger Index (GHI) is a multidimensional measure for tracking the state of hunger and malnutrition across the globe, developed by the International Food Policy Research Institute (IFPRI) in association with a German group Concern Worldwide and Welthungerhilfe – which ranks countries on a 100 point scale, with 0 being the best score (no hunger) and 100 is considered to be the worst. The GHI 2010, which takes into consideration a total of 122 countries excluding the highly developed nations, rated 84 of them on the basis of three leading indicators, i.e., prevalence of child malnutrition, rate of child mortality and the proportion of people who are calorie deficient. The rest of the 38 countries have a GHI of less than 5 and are not included in the rankings. The GHI 2010 shows that India has made a slow progress towards ensuring food security for its entire population. A nation which could feed its entire population in terms of the amount of food it produced and have among the highest numbers of hungry children in the world has been placed in 67th position scoring 24.1 – ranking way below neighbouring countries such as China and Pakistan.[23] For India, the high index scores are driven by high levels of underweight children resulting from the low nutritional and social status of women in the country, the report pointed out, adding that India alone accounts for a large share of the world's undernourished children. In 2005–2006, about 44 per cent of Indian children under age five were underweight and 48 per cent were stunted; because of the country's sheer size, these numbers mean that India is home to 42 per cent of the world's underweight children and 31 per cent of its stunted children.[24] In order to tackle early childhood undernutrition, the GHI 2010 recommended high-priority policy actions including targeting nutrition interventions for women and children in the window of opportunity, foster gender equity and prioritize nutrition in political and policy processes.[25] The food insecurity is so rampant across the country that India is clubbed with minor economies such as Bangladesh, Timor-Leste and Yemen, recording the highest prevalence of underweight in children under five. Current hunger situation in India has been categorized as 'alarming' by the GHI 2010; the policy makers in India, who are still fighting over the need to have an expansive National Food Security Act, should look at these alarming hunger statistics more closely.

India promises to achieve the MDGs by 2015, but the promise seems futile when one looks at the latest GHI of 2010. Indian government could reduce dependency on a Public Distribution System (PDS) that is collapsing under its own weight;

simultaneously, continued growth of agriculture is essential to meet the food and nutritional security requirements of the people and provide livelihood and income in rural areas. In order to tackle the root causes of hunger, governments should encourage increased investment in agriculture, expand safety nets and social assistance programmes, and enhance income-generating activities for the rural and urban poor. We cannot blame anyone squarely for this current scenario of food crisis across the nation. Poverty, illiteracy, corruption, etc., form a part of this huge vicious cycle. Public discourse and action at the grassroot level are the need of the hour. All these supported duly at both the state and central level will lead to the destruction of that viscous cycle. It is all about making the poor and hungry step on the economic ladder, momentarily forget about climbing it. Political will and good governance need to translate into specific reform steps.

'Food Insecurity': Still Causes Concern for Rural India

As far as the current scenario of food insecurity and hunger in rural parts of India is concerned, the report on State of Food Insecurity in Rural India, released by United Nations World Food Programme (WFP) and M.S. Swaminathan Research Foundation (MSSRF) in 2009, tries to explore the dynamics of food insecurity situation of rural India as well as the operational dynamics of different nutrition safety net programmes. It clearly indicates that the number of under-nourished people is rising, reversing gains made in the 1990s. High economic growth rates have failed to improve food security in India leaving the country facing a crisis in its rural economy. Slowing growth in food production, rising unemployment and declining purchasing power of the poor in India are combining to weaken the rural economy. In spite of a number of government programmes being implemented for ensuring food security for its entire rural population, it is still a major threat for the government to take care of starving India. The report reflects the need for a revamped public distribution system and greater public investment to address the need of rural population. While examining the effectiveness of some of the important food-based interventions such as the Public Distribution System (PDS), the Integrated Child Development Services (ICDS) and the Mid-Day Meal Scheme (MDMS) – the report recommends measures for improved performance. Professor Venkatesh Athreya, the coordinator of this research study, points out that many of the social safety net and agriculture production programmes can ensure the availability and access to food, and suggests that there is a need to create a universal PDS with uniform prices affordable to the poor and the allocation should be based on the number of consumption units in the household.[26]

From a nation dependent on food imports to feed its entire population, India today is not only self-sufficient in grain production, but also has a substantial reserve. The progress made by agriculture in the last four decades has been one of the biggest success stories of free India. Agriculture and allied activities constitute the single largest contributor to the GDP, almost 33 per cent of it. Agriculture is the means of livelihood of about two-thirds of the workforce in the country. It is true that the country now produces enough food to feed its entire population. However, this upbeat version of the food situation in India neglects the reality of widespread chronic malnutrition in the country. The country is the second largest food producer in the world, yet over 300 million people go without two square meals a day. According to the Ministry of Food Processing, India produces 90 million tonnes of milk and 485 million livestock annually, the highest in the world, besides being the second largest producer of fruits and vegetables (150 million tonnes) and the third largest producer of food grain (204 million tonnes) and fish (6.3 million tonnes). Impressive statistics have meant little because a large part of perishables are wasted as the government has failed to create a farm-to-fork supply chain (Hazra, 2009).

Food security can be achieved in a better and faster way, if a decentralized approach in implementation of programme is adopted. In a predominantly rural and agricultural country like India, agricultural progress (i.e., crop and animal husbandry, fisheries, forestry and agro-forestry and agro-processing) will be the most effective social safety net against hunger and poverty. There is an urgent need for enhancement of investment in agriculture and rural infrastructure development. As far as the Indian scenario is concerned, the challenge of ensuring food security lies in the distribution of food and in making them affordable to the poor, not in food production. So, instead of insisting on improving the production, the government needs to improve the distribution of the food grain and at the same time should empower small-scale farmers rather than multinational corporations to feed its entire population. Against the popular perception among slogans such as 'India Rising' and 'Incredible India', India's current state of progress in the context of ensuring food security is not much better than that of the dark continent, Africa or specifically Sub-Saharan Africa as far as the issue of food security is concerned.

Progress of Education in India: Some Major Tasks Still Left

India has the second largest education system in the world after China. The scale of operation involved to ensure quality of education for all in the country is unique and challenging. Soon after gaining independence in 1947, making education available to all had become a priority for the government. The Government of India, as part of its constitutional commitment, has initiated a number of programmes to achieve the goal of universalization of elementary education in a time-bound manner. Some of the major initiatives have been the Operation Blackboard (1986), Non-formal Education Scheme (1986), the Shiksha Karmi Project (1987), Mahila Samakya (1989), Lok Jumbish (1992), the District Primary Education Programme (1994), the Mid-Day Meal Scheme (1995) and the Sarva Shiksha Abhiyan (2001) and the most recently introduced the Right of Children to Free and Compulsory Education Act or the Right to Education Act (RTE), which has come into force from 1 April 2010, ensuring free education to more than 92 lakh out of school children aged 6–14 in India.

The overall school enrolment has increased from 19.2 million in 1950–1951 has rose to 135.5 million in 2007–2008 while the Gross Enrolment Ratio (GER) at the primary level has increased up to 113.97 in 2007–2008. For the middle and upper primary levels, the GER was 66.7 in 1990–1991 which declined to 58.6 in 2000–2001 and then gradually increased to 78.1 in 2007–2008. In primary education, the Gender Parity Index (GPI) has gone up from 0.76 in 1990–1991 to 0.94 in 2006–2007 and in secondary education the increase is from 0.60 in 1990–1991 to 0.82 in 2006–2007. Simultaneously, the dropout rate at the elementary level (Class I–VIII) was 59.1 per cent in 1990–1991 which came down to 43.7 per cent in 2007–2008 (Government of India, 2011b). Over the last few decades, there have been enormous improvements in the education sector but issues such as high dropout rates, low-levels of learning achievement and low participation of girls as well as various systemic issues, such as inadequate school infrastructure, high teacher absenteeism, large-scale teacher vacancies, poor quality of education, poorly functioning schools, and inadequate equipment still cause concern for overall educational progress of the country. Gendered deprivation still exists and needs to be overcome. It may be seen that it took almost five decades for male-female disparity to reduce to half of what it was in the 1960s. Following the same logic, one can argue that if the present trend continues, it will take another five decades to finally close the gender gap in terms of literacy attainment. Apart from household income/wealth, caste and gender continue to determine access to education. The poor, girls, and members of SCs and STs still face formidable barriers in acquiring basic education. It has been widely acknowledged that the socio-economic conditions in India have constrained the process of primary education, and the social inequalities of caste, class and gender have been identified as the major causes of educational deprivation among children in India.

The Challenge of Educating Rural India: Need More Intense Efforts

The scenario of educational progress in rural India began to change rapidly due to the new thrusts given by the government's new National Policy of Education (1986) and the Programme of Action (1992), which aimed at improving access, reducing dropouts and improving learning achievements for all children between 6 and 14 years of age. A host of major initiatives by the government, and the mobilization of external resources for primary education, had a deep impact on the status of primary education in India. As far as the progress in rural literacy is concerned, initiative such as provision of mid-day meals in primary school has increased enrolment, attendance and retention, especially of girls. Moreover, it helps in taking care of nutritional needs of the students. This not only affects positively the health of poor students but also improves learning outcomes by ending 'school hunger'. On the other hand, the *Sarva Shiksha Abhiyan,* initiated to universalize quality education, has brought about positive changes by increasing accountability of schools to the community through greater involvement of village education committees and parent-teacher associations.

But still issues of equity, quality and access remain areas of concern particularly in the sphere of rural education in India. Children in rural areas continue to be deprived of quality education owing to factors such as lack of competent and committed teachers, lack of textbooks or teaching-learning materials and so on. A large number of teachers refuse to teach in rural areas and those who are usually underqualified. The much publicized Mid-Day Meal Scheme meant to reduce dropout rates in schools seems to be not yielding the desired results due to misappropriation of funds meant for the scheme, mismanagement, lack of seriousness among the implementing authorities, diversion of funds, lack of awareness among the parents of poor children, etc. The food served under Mid-Day Meal Scheme in rural schools is also of inferior quality. Besides that, the recent Public Report on Basic Education (PROBE) report reflects that physical infrastructure of rural schools is far behind the satisfactory level, with 82 per cent of the schools is in need of renovation.[27] Books are often unavailable, and teacher absenteeism tends to be high.

The nature of problems affecting the education system are so diverse and often deep rooted that the solution cannot lie in the alteration of any one single factor – it is not about just shortage of money or just shortage of trained teachers or lack of political will; all these undeniably contribute to the problems affecting the country's existing education system. It will also require a constant and strong central support for policy, strategy, technical assistance, and monitoring and evaluation combined with increased decentralization within government, stronger public-private partnerships and improved accountability relationships between the service providers, policy makers and the target population.

Empowering Women and Reducing Gender Disparity: Still a Long Way to Go

Though India is developing economically and technologically by leaps and bounds but women, especially rural women, still continue to be discriminated and their current status in the society still causes concern. Across the nation, women constitute a disproportionate share of the chronically poor population. Gender discrimination starts from the foetus, in terms of selection of sex, childrearing, feeding, education, employment, control over property and resources, participation and influencing decision making in public and political spheres, etc. Research on women's status in Indian societies found that the contributions that Indian women make to their families are often overlooked; instead time and again, they are regarded as economic burdens of the family and this view is more customary in rural India.

The government has attempted to involve and encourage rural women in decision-making process by providing one-third reservation for them in Gram Panchayats, to ensure their participation at the local and district levels of governance through the 73rd amendment to the Constitution. Initiatives have also been taken for reserving seats for women in parliament. The impact of reserving one-third of seats for women in the Panchayati Raj Institutions (PRIs) has been immense and has empowered women to a great extent both politically and socially. At present, there are approximately 2,60,000 panchayat representatives in India, out of which around 75,000 are women. This is the largest number of elected women in the world.[28] Reservation of seats for women in panchayats or in parliament, however, is only the first step to ensure that a certain number of women will be involved in decision-making process of the government. The very next task and challenge will be to develop their capacity so that they can perform their role properly and can make a difference. As per as educational progress of women is concerned, though significant numbers of women have been made literate but in rural India, still it is experienced that predominant patriarchal system does not provide enough chances for women to have higher education even if they wish. Spending on education and especially for a girl child is still perceived as a waste of money and resources, especially in rural India. Economic costs, social traditions, and religious and cultural beliefs limit rural girls' educational opportunities. As a result, combating the high rate of illiteracy among rural women and girls remains an area of serious concern for the government. On the other hand, rural women in India are among the most disadvantaged section of the rural communities in terms of their health status. Access to appropriate health care information, a comprehensive, adequate and affordable health services are still to be achieved for the rural women. Women experience malnutrition, anaemia, infectious diseases and illness more than men, and they are less likely to receive timely medical treatment. High maternal mortality ratio continues to remain a matter of great concern for rural India. Rural women are especially vulnerable to pregnancy and child birth-related deaths. Poor health and nutritional status of Indian women are inextricably interwoven with social, cultural and economic factors. These factors severely constrain the ability of women and adolescent girls to acquire good health services.

The Global Gender Gap Index, introduced by the World Economic Forum (WEF) in 2006, is a framework for capturing the magnitude and scope of gender-based disparities and tracking their progress. The Global Gender Gap Index examines the gap between men and women in four fundamental categories: economic participation and opportunity, educational attainment, health and survival and political empowerment. World Economic Forum in its latest Global Gender Gap Index for the year 2010, ranked India in the bottom half among 134 countries, placing it in the 112th position in terms of gender equality. As per the report, India performed very poorly on the economic, education and health sub-indexes; the overall scores are partially bolstered by relatively good performances in the sphere of political empowerment of women. India ranked 128th in terms of economic participation and opportunity, 120th in educational attainment, 132nd in health and survival and 23rd in terms of political empowerment.[29] India figures among 25 countries in the world where the gender gap is the widest and stands sixth in economic inequality between men and women, according to the WEF.

Taking into account the current scenario and dynamics in the sphere of women empowerment, all the development programmes, plans and projects should be assessed using the 'gender lens' in order to achieve gender justice for women. Reservation of seats for women in panchayats or in parliament, however, is only the first step to ensure that a certain number of women will be involved in decision-making process of the government; the very next task and challenge will be to develop their capacity so that they can perform their role properly to make a difference. Expanded policy interventions with effective implementation; awareness building at family, institution and community levels; and better follow-up and intensified efforts for integrating gender dimensions in policy formulation are needed to reduce constraints and to facilitate the participation of women in the mainstream of every societal affairs.

Making India 'Healthy': Need of the Hour

Primary health care system is considered to be the backbone of Indian health system. As of March 2010, the network consists of 1,47,069 sub-centres (SCs), 23,673 primary health centres (PHCs) and 4,535 community health centres (CHCs) in rural India;[30] while urban India is having nearly 3,500 urban centres and 12,000 hospitals in the public sector.[31] But still quality medical care needs are met by private sector hospitals, nursing homes and private practitioners. Despite continuous improvements in health indicators, progress has been slow and has not matched the impressive gains in economic growth during the past decade. Inadequate access to effective and good quality health services for a large proportion of the population largely accounts for the slow improvement in health outcomes. Only about half of pregnant women, i.e., 50.7 per cent receive adequate antenatal coverage, i.e., at least three visits during one pregnancy.[32] This percentage remains low and stagnant. Infant and maternal mortality rates are decreasing, but slowly. The national MMR level has come down from 398 per 1,00,000 live births in 1997–1998 to 254 per 1,00,000 live births in 2004–2006, while IMR has been reduced to 50 in 2009, which were 80 in 1991.[33] Despite the largest child nutrition programme in the world, rates of childhood malnutrition have remained unchanged for nearly two decades: 45 per cent of children under the age of five are stunted (low height for age), 40 per cent are underweight (low weight for age), and 23 per cent are wasted (low weight for height).[34] Although the prevalence of HIV has recently been lowered to an estimated 0.29 per cent of the adult population, or approximately 2.2 million individuals, this still poses a very significant burden and requires continued efforts to avoid a devastating, more generalized epidemic.[35] Tuberculosis, malaria, polio and dengue fever still remain serious threats in a number of states.

Health scenario in India is full of contrasts. Majority of Indians are burdened with diseases which are easily curable, yet the threats of incurable diseases get more attention. A huge section of the society is succumbing to deaths which could be avoided to a great extent with safe drinking water, proper sanitation, or may be with some very elementary medicines. Yet, the policy makers are more interested in bringing sophisticated technologies; funds are pouring in to areas such as promotion of health tourism, subsidizing import of sophisticated equipments and development of private health care. Rural health services, which form the backbone of public health system, are lacking basic infrastructure, staffs and essential medicines. According to the figures of population based on 2001 population census, the shortfall in the rural health infrastructure comes out to be of 20,855 SCs, 4,883 PHCs and 2,525 CHCs. Instead of strengthening them, subsidies are being given to the private players that establish super specialty hospitals to attract tourist from abroad. Health system in India still remains the most privatized in the world, digging people's pocket heavily; yet strategies are being devised to bring more private investment. All these clearly mean that the interests of the certain section of the society are being taken care of whereas the vast majority remain neglected (Hazra, 2010b). Steady declines have been noted in fertility, maternal, infant and child mortalities, and the prevalence of severe manifestations of nutritional deficiencies, but the pace has been slow and falls short of national and MDG targets.[36]

India's Progress towards MDG Commitments: Need to Move Faster

A critical evaluation of different indicators of MDGs in India reveals a state of uneven development, which is a feature of underdevelopment, across the nation. This uneven development path has been further exacerbated by striking and persistent inequities by gender, caste and geography. Apart from regional imbalanced growth, disparity among the economic classes has been aggravated and this has been the feature of the states where the numbers of BPL families, SC, ST and minority population are higher. This is also associated with lower health, education and income indices of the said districts. The government has made some significant progress in gender development and also initiated gender budgeting to spot the areas where further development is required most. The achievement of MDGs is also a simultaneous process of progressive realization of human rights. From a cursory look at the performance of the government, it becomes apparent that the government has not been able to perform well to ensure the right to health, right to education, right to livelihood and life with dignity of the people in the state. On the other hand, in recent drive for industrialization, the government has also violated certain fundamental constitutional rights of the citizens and provisions of the Directive Principles of State Policy. India has breached its obligations under right to food as enshrined in International Covenant on Economic, Social and Cultural Rights and International Covenant on Civil and Political Rights as well. Simultaneously, studies and researches at grassroot level have explored that the government has failed to ensure inclusive democracy at grassroots and often bypass panchayat structure in order to impose decisions from above. This is a violation of the 73rd amendment to the Indian Constitution.

As a part of planned development, India is putting its entire efforts in the direction of achieving the MDGs by 2015 despite the size and complexities of the nation. The high economic growth, together with carefully designed and targeted pro-poor policies that are crucial for attaining the MDGs, effective decentralization, efficient delivery of services and respect for human rights, rule of law and accountability have the potential to channel the MDGs into good governance. The information technology (IT) revolution is yet another boon for India with respect to employment and economic development. Progress in computer education and IT is far enriching the economy, employment prospects and social status. India still faces challenges, such as the joblessness and increasing income inequality, and the spread of communicable diseases and high incidence of HIV/AIDS concomitant to increasing migration of labour and international trade and also alarming increase in non-communicable diseases. Thus, the next generation of reforms needs to focus on fostering a knowledge-based economy to maintain consistently high economic growth as average skill levels continues to improve. Inclusive public policies should focus on balanced development by region and investments in health, education and infrastructure for future development, especially in backward areas and communities and ethnic groups. There is also the need for bridging the gap between the country's health policy and the health care needs of the poor to achieve the MDGs set for 2015 (Elizabeth, 2008). Persistent inequalities, ineffective delivery of public services, weak accountability systems and gaps in the implementation of pro-poor policies are the major hurdles in the progress of social sector in India. It seems India will find it difficult to get on the tracks of attaining goals such as food security, health, and gender equality unless intensive national efforts are made by the government and all sections of civil society working in tandem. Though India is emerging as one of the most powerful global economies, but higher economic development will become meaningful only after the emerging challenges and issues of social sector, for example, in the sphere of poverty, health, education, etc., are given due attention and tackled with utmost priority.

Notes

1. Van de Moortele (2009).
2. Government of India (2011a).
3. Asian Development Bank (2005).
4. Ibid.
5. Transparency International (2010).
6. UNDP (2010).
7. Ibid.
8. Ibid.
9. Ibid.
10. Ibid.
11. Alkire and Santos (2010).
12. Ibid.
13. Ibid.
14. *The Hindu*, November 5, 2010.

15. Bauer et al. (2008).
16. Ibid.
17. Ibid.
18. Ibid.
19. Planning Commission (2007).
20. Ibid.
21. Ibid.
22. Department of Rural Development (2008).
23. Von Grebmer et al. (2010).
24. Ibid.
25. Ibid.
26. WFP and MSSRF (2009).
27. PROBE Team and Centre for Development Economics (1999).
28. Hazra (2010a).
29. WEF (2010).
30. MoHFW (2010).
31. Hazra (2010b).
32. IIPS and Macro International (2007).
33. Government of India (2011b).
34. Ibid.
35. Ibid.
36. Paul et al. (2011).

References

Alkire, S., and Santos, M.E. (2010). *Acute Multidimensional Poverty: A New Index for Developing Countries*, OPHI Working Paper 38. London, UK: University of Oxford.

Alliance 2015. *Millennium Development Goals (MDGs)*. Retrieved from www.alliance2015.org/fileadmin/user_upload/MDGs.pdf (accessed December 10, 2009).

Asian Development Bank. (2005). *Country Strategy and Program Update: India 2006–2008*. Philippines: ADB.

Bauer, A. et al. (2008). *The World Bank's New Poverty Data: Implications for the Asian Development Bank*, ADB Sustainable Development Working Paper Series, No. 2. Philippines: ADB.

Department of Rural Development. (2008). *Poverty Eradication in India by 2015: Rural Household Centered Strategy Paper*. New Delhi, India: Government of India.

Elizabeth, K.E. (2008). India's Progress towards Achieving the Targets Set in the Millennium Development Goals. *Journal of Tropical Pediatrics*, Vol. 54 (5).

Government of India. (2011a). *Economic Survey 2010–11*. New Delhi, India: Oxford University Press.

Government of India. (2011b). *SAARC Development Goals: India Country Report 2010*. New Delhi, India: Central Statistics Office.

Hazra, A. (2009). Food for All: Still a Distant Dream. *Kurukshetra*, Vol. 56 (6).

Hazra, A. (2010a). Women Reservation Bill: Can We Hope for Gender Equality? *Kurukshetra*, Vol. 58 (8).

Hazra, A. (2010b). State of Health in India: The Current Scenario. *Kurukshetra*, Vol. 58 (4).

International Institute for Population Sciences (IIPS) and Macro International. (2007). *National Family Health Survey (NFHS-3), 2005–06: India*. Mumbai, India: IIPS.

Ministry of Health and Family Welfare (MoHFW). (2010). *Rural Health Statistics in India 2010*. New Delhi, India: Government of India.

Paul, V.K. et al. (2011). Reproductive Health, and Child Health and Nutrition in India: Meeting the Challenge. *The Lancet*, Vol. 377 (9762).

Planning Commission. (2007). *Poverty Estimates for 2004–05*. New Delhi, India: Press Information Bureau, Government of India.

PROBE Team and Centre for Development Economics. (1999). *Public Report on Basic Education in India*. New Delhi, India: Oxford University Press.

The Hindu, November 5, 2010.

Transparency International. (2010). *Corruption Perceptions Index 2010*. Berlin, Germany: Transparency International.

United Nations Development Programme (UNDP). (2010). *Human Development Report 2010*. New York: UNDP.

United Nations World Food Programme (WFP) and MS Swaminathan Research Foundation (MSSRF). (2009). *Report on the State of Food Insecurity in Rural India*. New Delhi, India: MSSRF.

Van de Moortele, J. (2009). *Taking the MDGs beyond 2015: Hasten Slowly*. Bonn, Germany: The European Association of Development Research and Training Institutes (EADI).

Von Grebmer, K. et al. (2010). *2010 Global Hunger Index: The Challenge of Hunger: Focus on the Crisis of Child Under Nutrition*. Bonn, Washington, DC, and Dublin: Deutsche Welthungerhilfe, International Food Policy Research Institute, and Concern.

Waage, J. et al. (2010). The Millennium Development Goals: A Cross-Sectoral Analysis and Principles for Goal Setting after 2015. *Lancet*, Vol. 376 (9745).

World Economic Forum (WEF). (2010). *The Global Gender Gap Report 2010*. Geneva, Switzerland: WEF.

2 Rural Poverty

Jeopardizing India's Effort towards MDG Commitments

In the current context of sustainable social development, poverty is considered to be the biggest and most serious challenge before India. The World Bank in its latest poverty estimate based on purchasing power parity (PPP) at $1.25 a day in 2005 prices – which was released in August 2008 – shows that globally there were 1.4 billion people living in extreme poverty in 2005. Three-quarters of the world's more than one billion extremely poor people live in rural areas of developing countries.[1] Despite high rates of economic growth that exceeded expectations and led to India being placed in the category of 'lower middle income countries', up from the category of 'low income countries', the rate of reduction in the incidence of poverty has been slow. Despite India being one of the 10 fastest growing economies of the world, it is home to over a third of the world's poor people. India remains predominantly a rural nation, with more than 70 per cent of its people living in rural areas and at the same time, the incidence of poverty is much higher in rural areas affecting the rural economy as well as the overall economy of the nation. Studies aptly reveals that the rural poor in India tend to have lower levels of health and education; they are more likely to have limited access to basic services such as water and sanitation; and paradoxically, despite depending on agriculture as their main source of livelihood, they also suffer the most from hunger and food insecurity. So, rural poverty not only puts adverse effect on India's economy but also poses a global threat to its Millennium Commitments; therefore, the achievement of Millennium Development Goal (MDG) target for India is solely dependent on its success towards poverty reduction (Table 4).

Table 4 *Rural Poverty and the Millennium Development Goals*

Goal 1. Eradicate extreme poverty and hunger

Rural poverty itself is a major threat to the Millennium commitments. Poverty in its various dimensions could be a manifestation, as well as a determinant of hunger. In its most basic form – as a state of food deprivation and nutritional inadequacy – rural poverty has a direct bearing on the existing hunger situation. Starvation death in various corners of rural India is a stark example of this reality.

Goal 2. Achieve universal primary education

School enrolment in rural India and are directly and inversely related to poverty. Though there is free provision of school education in India, but rural poor families prefer to engage their children to income-generating activities than to fetch their children to school, since it directly helps the family to combat the poverty situation.

Goal 3. Promote gender equality and empower women

Economic independence or economic self-reliance of women promotes women empowerment. But rural poverty provides very limited employment opportunities for rural women – which ultimately creates barrier for women empowerment or gender equality.

Goal 4. Reduce child mortality

Rural children from poor families are still the most vulnerable with very high risk of mortality in their early lives. Despite sustained reduction in under-five mortality rates in India, the rate is slower and the rural children especially from the poor families are the most vulnerable with very high risk of mortality in their early lives. In 2005–2006, the infant mortality rates were 62 per 1,000 and 42 per 1,000 respectively in rural and urban India; the under-five mortality rates were 82 and 52 per 1,000 respectively in rural and urban India. In both the neonatal and post-neonatal periods, mortality in rural areas is about 50 per cent higher than mortality in urban areas.

Goal 5. Improve maternal health

Poor mothers from rural areas are more likely to die during childbirth. One factor that is likely correlated with a high likelihood of maternal death is poverty, which may affect health service infrastructure and women's and men's prospects for education and gainful employment, which in turn affects women's ability to obtain needed prenatal and delivery care. The six Empowered Action Group (EAG) states with the highest percentages of their population living below the national poverty line – Bihar, Chhattisgarh, Madhya Pradesh, Orissa, Uttar Pradesh and Uttarakhand – are among those having maternal mortality ratios (MMRs) that are above the national average of 301 (i.e., they range from 358 in Orissa to 517 in Uttar Pradesh and its split-off part of Uttarakhand).

Goal 6. Combat HIV/AIDS, malaria, and other diseases

Studies suggest that existing burden of poverty will make rural India incapable to combat against diseases such as HIV/AIDS, malaria, etc., since it would not be possible for the rural poor to bear the cost of treatment of such diseases.

Cont'd...

...Cont'd

Goal 7. Ensure environmental sustainability

Rural poor are highly dependent on natural resources and ecosystem services (Millennium Ecosystem Assessment 2005. Environmental degradation reduces the income of rural poor disproportionately in comparison with the general population. Perversely, as the incomes of the poor shrink, they are left with little recourse but to deplete environmental resources even further, thus precipitating a vicious cycle of ever-worsening poverty and environmental deterioration. As the rural poor, in particular, are often directly dependent on the use of natural resources to sustain their livelihoods, so the growing rural poverty may impose threat for environmental sustainability.

Goal 8. Develop a global partnership for development

More than three-quarters of the world's poor live in rural areas. So addressing the multiple barriers to eliminate rural poverty necessarily requires a global partnership for development called for in MDG 8 – which should direct more resources and more coherent policy support towards the creation of a strong platform for rural development initiatives.

Source: Hazra (2009).

Concept of Poverty

There are innumerable definitions of poverty, based on the perceptions of the social scientists academics and policy makers and influenced by the personal experiences and country-specific situations. It is a multidimensional concept that signifies lack of command over minimum amount of basic commodities that would degrade the quality of life beyond an acceptable limit. Poverty is associated with vulnerability, social and political deprivation; failure to meet the basic minimum needs of life results in core poverty which has been described by Robert S. McNamara as 'a condition of life so characterized by malnutrition, illiteracy, disease, high infant mortality and low life expectancy as to be beneath any reasonable definition of human society'.[2] So poverty is the recognition of deprivation in specific consumptions, which is not enough to keep the body and soul in healthy condition. Poverty has been described as a situation of 'pronounced deprivation in well-being' and being poor as 'to be hungry, to lack shelter and clothing, to be sick and not cared for, to be illiterate and not schooled ... Poor people are particularly vulnerable to adverse events outside their control. They are often treated badly by institutions of the state and society and excluded from voice and power in those institutions'.[3]

Estimation of Poverty in India

The official definition of poverty in India is based on per capita consumption expenditure as the measure of standard of living and the variable in terms of which absolute poverty is measured. It is the minimum per capita consumption expenditure which would satisfy the basic calorie needs of an individual for carrying out an active life. The National Sample Survey Organization (NSSO) in India, which operates under the Ministry of Statistics and Programme Implementation, Government of India, estimates the consumption standard of the people on the basis of all-India households surveys every five years. The consumption expenditure on basic and some non-basic food groups only are considered, and the estimates are made on the basis of monthly per capita expenditure with different reference periods. The poverty is estimated on head count basis and is normally measured with respect to a poverty line, a cut-off point on the line of consumption or income distribution, which divides the population as poor and non-poor. In India, the poverty line is defined as minimum per capita consumption expenditure that could satisfy the basic calorie needs of an individual for leading an active life and depending on individual needs, gender and occupation. Separate poverty lines are estimated for persons in rural and urban areas. The Task Force on Projection of Minimum Needs and Effective Consumption Demand (1979) had defined the poverty line as the per capita expenditure level at which the calorie norms were met on the basis of the all-India consumption basket for 1973–1974.[4] India's official poverty line in monthly per capita expenditure, in 1973–1974 all-India prices, is ₹ 49 in rural areas and ₹ 57 in urban areas, with people below these expenditure levels are considered poor.[5] These figures correspond to a total household expenditure estimated as sufficient to provide 2,400 calories daily in rural areas and 2,100 calories daily in urban areas, plus some basic non-food items.

Nature and Causes of Poverty

Poverty is complex and multidimensional in nature. It is reflected in multiple deprivations such as inadequate resources or assets or capital required for a minimum living or livelihood; lack of access to

Table 5 *A Model Representing Causes of Rural Poverty in India*

Resource Barriers	*Supportive Barriers*	*Social System Barriers*	*Market Barriers*
Nature of Soil	Low and erratic rainfall	Inaccessibility to credit facilities	Non-feasibility of increase in prices of agricultural products
Non-exploration and/or poor quality of minerals	Inadequate irrigation	People's illiteracy and unwillingness to deviate from established expensive social practices	Denial of periodic increase in wages of agricultural labourers
Inadequate capital for industrial investment	Poor quality of livestock	Not ensuring required resources (electricity, raw materials, etc.) to small entrepreneurs	Unapproachable roads to reach markets or non-availability of marketing facility for selling products
Lack of common property resources	Absence of industries	Failure in monitoring poverty alleviation programmes leading to reaching benefit to those who are not really poor	Non-lucrative profit margin on products of village industries
			Inadequate credit system

Source: Ahuja (2006).

skill development, education, health and other facilities or amenities. The causes of rural poverty in India are manifold including inadequate and ineffective implementation of anti-poverty programmes (Table 5). The overdependence on monsoon with non-availability of irrigational facilities often results in crop failure and low agricultural productivity, forcing farmers in the debt traps. Some of the major causes of rural poverty in India include: dependence of livelihoods on natural resources (land, forest, water) which are coming under increasing biotic and abiotic stresses, including climate change; fragmentation of land-holdings; low productivity of agriculture due to inadequate access to factors of production (land, irrigation, technology, extension, credit); unemployment and underemployment; inability of the secondary and tertiary sectors to draw away surplus agricultural labour into productive off-farm activities; lack of physical infrastructure such as roads, power, markets, communication, etc.; and weak social infrastructure such as education, health, drinking water and sanitation.

The rural communities tend to spend large percentage of annual earnings on social ceremonies such as marriage, feast, etc. Our economic development since independence has been lopsided. There has been increase in unemployment creating poverty-like situations for many. Population is growing at an alarming rate. As far as the dynamics of rural poverty is concerned, major determinants of poverty are lack of income and purchasing power attributable to lack of productive employment and considerable underemployment, inadequacy of infrastructure, affecting the quality of life and employability, etc. The other causes include dominance of caste system which forces the individual to stick to the traditional and hereditary occupations. The lack of access to productive assets and financial resources are still considered to be the major causes of poverty among India's rural people. High levels of illiteracy, inadequate health care and extremely limited access to social services are common among poor rural people. Micro-enterprise development, which could generate income and enable poor people to improve their living conditions, has only recently become a focus of the government.

Extent of Poverty in India

A recent World Bank paper, based on purchasing power parity (PPP), estimates that 45.6 crore persons (42% of total population) are living below poverty line in India if the new international poverty line of $1.25 per day is taken as the standard.[6] If $2 per day level is considered, then about 75.6 per cent population of India will fall below the poverty line.[7] The study also suggests that the proportion of the poor based on poverty line of $1.25 (PPP) per day in India decreased from 60 per cent in 1981 to 42 per cent in 2005. In absolute numbers, the poor have risen from 421 million in 1981 to 456 million in 2005. Furthermore, the study argues on the basis of its new data that poverty in India declined faster between 1981 and 1990, from 60 per cent to 51 per cent than between 1990 and 2005, when it fell to 42 per cent. Thus, 9 percentage points decrease in the first 10 years and the same 9 percentage points in the subsequent 15 years.

In India, the Planning Commission is the nodal agency of the government for estimating poverty at national and state levels. The estimates of poverty are made using the large sample survey data on household consumer expenditure conducted by the NSSO under the Ministry of Statistics and Programme Implementation. The state-specific poverty ratios are worked out from state-specific poverty lines and distribution of persons by expenditure groups obtained from the NSS data on consumer expenditure. The poverty ratio at all-India level is obtained as the weighted average of the state-wise poverty ratios. The national poverty line at 2004–2005 prices is ₹ 356.30 per capita per month (₹ 21,378 or say ₹ 22,000 per household [HH] per annum) in the rural areas and ₹ 538.60 per capita per month (or say ₹ 32,316 per HH per annum) in the urban areas.[8] As per the estimates of Planning Commission, the population living below the poverty line (BPL) in the rural areas is still unacceptably high, at over 22 crore.[9] Despite high rates of economic growth that exceeded expectations, according to the estimates of Planning Commission, India is a home to 301.7 million poor – which is the highest in the world; out of this total number, 220.92 million of them reside in rural and 80.79 million in urban areas (Table 3). Poverty measured in terms of head count ratio (HCR) declined from 54.9 per cent in 1973–1974 to 27.5 per cent in 2004–2005. The pace of poverty reduction over the last decade has been much lower than anticipated.[10] The decline in poverty was 12.4 percentage points over the decade, i.e., from 51.3 per cent in 1977–1978 to 38.9 per cent in 1987–1988 while the corresponding decline was only 8.5 percentage points over 11 years, i.e., from 36 per cent in 1993–1994 to 27.5 per cent in 2004–2005. Thus, income poverty in the country has declined over three decades by less than one million a year.[11] Because population has also grown, the absolute number of poor people has declined only marginally from 321 million in 1973–1974 to 302 million in 2004–2005[12] (Table 6). This performance is all the more disappointing since the poverty line on which the estimate of the poor is based is the same as it was in 1973–1974 when per capita incomes were much lower. The slowdown in the pace of poverty reduction may indicate relative difficulties in addressing hard core poverty, much of which is likely to be chronic in nature.

Table 6 *Trends of Poverty in India: 1973–1974 to 2004–2005*

Year	*Poverty line for India (₹ per capita per month, in current prices)*		*Total % of BPL population in India*	*% of India's poor located in*		*Population under poverty (millions) located in*		
	Rural	*Urban*		*Rural*	*Urban*	*Total*	*Rural*	*Urban*
1973–1974	49.63	56.76	54.9	81.33	18.67	321.3	261.3	60.0
1977–1978	56.84	70.33	51.3	80.36	19.64	328.9	264.3	64.6
1983	89.5	115.65	44.5	78.04	21.96	322.9	252.0	70.9
1987–1988	115.2	162.16	38.9	75.51	24.49	307.1	231.9	75.2
1993–1994	205.84	281.35	36	76.18	23.82	320.3	244.0	76.3
1999–2000*	327.56	454.11	26.1	74.3	25.7	260.2	193.2*	67.0*
2004–2005	356.30	538.60	27.5	73.2	26.8	301.7	220.9	80.8

* Estimates for 1999–2000 are based on the mixed recall period (MRP) method and are not comparable with estimates for other years, which are based on the uniform recall period (URP) method.

Source: Planning Commission (2007, 2008) and author's calculations.

India has entered the Eleventh Plan period with an impressive record of economic growth; the growth rate in the last four years of

Table 7 *A Comparison of Below Poverty Line (BPL) Population (in %) between Rural and Urban Areas of India (2004–2005)*

Indian States	*Rural Poverty*					*Urban Poverty*					*Rural and Urban Combined*
	SC	*ST*	*OBC*	*Others*	*Over all*	*SC*	*ST*	*OBC*	*Others*	*Over all*	
Andhra Pradesh	15.4	30.5	9.5	4.1	11.2	39.9	50.0	28.9	20.6	28.0	15.8
Assam	27.7	14.1	18.8	25.4	22.3	8.6	4.8	8.6	4.2	3.3	19.7
Bihar	64.0	53.3	37.8	26.6	42.1	67.2	57.2	41.4	18.3	34.6	41.4
Chhattisgarh	32.7	54.7	33.9	29.2	40.8	52.0	41.0	52.7	21.4	41.2	40.9
Delhi	0.0	0.0	0.0	10.6	6.9	35.8	9.4	18.3	6.4	15.2	14.7
Gujarat	21.8	34.7	19.1	4.8	19.1	16.0	21.4	22.9	7.0	13.0	16.8
Haryana	26.8	0.0	13.9	4.2	13.6	33.4	4.6	22.5	5.9	15.1	14.0
Himachal Pradesh	19.6	14.9	9.1	6.4	10.7	5.6	2.4	10.1	2.0	3.4	10.0
Jammu & Kashmir	5.2	8.8	10.0	3.3	4.6	13.7	0.0	4.8	7.8	7.9	5.4
Jharkhand	57.9	54.2	40.2	37.1	46.3	47.2	45.1	19.1	9.2	20.2	40.3
Karnataka	31.8	23.5	20.9	13.6	20.8	50.6	58.3	39.1	20.3	32.6	25.0
Kerala	21.6	44.3	13.7	6.6	13.2	32.5	19.2	24.3	7.8	20.2	15.0
Madhya Pradesh	42.8	58.6	29.6	13.4	36.9	67.3	44.7	55.5	20.8	42.1	38.3
Maharashtra	44.8	56.6	23.9	18.9	29.6	43.2	40.4	35.6	26.8	32.2	30.7

Cont'd...

...Cont'd

Orissa	50.2	75.6	36.9	23.4	46.8	72.6	61.8	50.2	28.9	44.3	46.4
Punjab	14.6	30.7	10.6	2.2	9.1	16.1	2.1	8.4	2.9	7.1	8.4
Rajasthan	28.7	32.6	13.1	8.2	18.7	52.1	24.1	35.6	20.7	32.9	22.1
Tamil Nadu	31.2	32.1	19.8	19.1	22.8	40.2	32.5	20.9	6.5	22.2	22.5
Uttar Pradesh	44.8	32.4	32.9	19.7	33.4	44.9	37.4	36.6	19.2	30.6	32.8
Uttarakhand	54.2	43.2	44.8	33.5	40.8	65.7	64.4	46.5	25.5	36.5	39.6
West Bengal	29.5	42.4	18.3	27.5	28.6	28.5	25.7	10.4	13.0	14.8	24.7
All India	36.8	47.2	26.7	16.1	28.3	39.9	33.3	31.4	16.0	25.7	27.5

Source: Planning Commission (2007) and author's calculation.

the Tenth Plan has averaged 8.7 per cent, making India one of the fastest growing economies in the world. As far as poverty is concerned the percentage of the population below the official poverty line has come down from 36 per cent in 1993–1994 to 27.5 per cent in 2004–2005 but the rate of decline in poverty has not accelerated along with the growth in GDP, and the incidence of poverty among certain marginalized groups, for example, the STs, has hardly declined at all[13] (Table 7). Rather, poverty is deepest among members of SCs and STs in the country's rural areas. In 2005, these groups accounted for 80 per cent of poor rural people, although their share in the total rural population is much smaller. On the map of poverty in India, the poorest areas are in parts of Rajasthan, Madhya Pradesh, Uttar Pradesh, Bihar, Jharkhand, Orissa, Chhattisgarh and West Bengal. Large numbers of India's poorest people live in the country's semi-arid tropical region. In this area, shortages of water and recurrent droughts impede the transformation of agriculture that the Green Revolution has achieved elsewhere. There is also a high incidence of poverty in flood-prone areas such as those extending from eastern Uttar Pradesh to the Assam plains, and especially in northern Bihar (IFAD, 2009).

The marginal farmers, landless labourers and casual worker households are the worst sufferers of these deprivations. Even within the category of the poor, SCs, STs, woman-headed households, the elderly and female children are the worst affected. The rural poor in India are highly concentrated in select states of the country, viz., Uttar Pradesh, Uttarakhand, Bihar, Jharkhand, Madhya Pradesh, Chhattisgarh, West Bengal, Maharashtra and Orissa. The poor from these nine states together account for nearly 76.2 per cent of the total rural poor in India in 2004–2005 as compared to 62.3 per cent in 1973–1974 (Table 8).[14] The concentration of poor has increased in these states.

Taking into consideration the current scenario, trends of Indian poverty can be characterised by some of its distinguished features, which are as follows: (i) poverty is declining but vulnerability, defined as the chance of movement into poverty, still remains strong. Although poverty incidence has gone down to 29 per cent in 2006–2007 from around 45 per cent in 2001–2002, more than 50 per cent of households are still vulnerable. So, pro-poor initiatives focusing on the mitigation of vulnerability along with poverty are necessary to sustain the downward trend.[15] (ii) Indian poverty is more rural in nature as more than three-fourths of the poor live in rural areas. (iii) Poverty is getting concentrated in the poorer states. In terms of absolute numbers, Uttar Pradesh, Bihar and Jharkhand account for around 27 per cent of the country's population but 30 per cent of India's poor lived there in 1973–1974, which has increased to over 41 per cent by 2005. (iv) There has been hardly any decline in poverty for the scheduled tribe households, almost half of them continue to be below the poverty line, which aptly indicates that they should be the target groups of social protection programmes. Poverty is still higher among Scheduled Tribes (STs), Scheduled Castes (SCs), landless and marginal farmers. (v) More than three-fourths of the rural poor depend on agriculture. Agricultural growth will therefore have greatest potential for poverty reduction.

Table 8 *Geographical Concentration of Rural Poor in Select States (in lakh)*

Name of the State	*1973–1974*	*1983–1984*	*1993–1994*	*2004–2005*
Uttar Pradesh & Uttarakhand	449.99 (17.2)	448.03 (17.7)	496.17 (20.3)	500.11 (22.6)
Bihar & Jharkhand	336.52 (12.9)	417.70 (16.5)	450.86 18.4)	439.91 (19.9)
Madhya Pradesh & Chhattisgarh	231.21 (8.8)	215.48 (8.6)	216.19 (8.8)	247.25 (11.2)
West Bengal	257.96 (9.9)	268.60 (10.6)	209.90 (8.6)	173.22 (7.8)
Maharashtra	210.84 (8.1)	193.75 (7.6)	193.33 (7.9)	171.13 (7.7)
Orissa	142.24 (5.4)	164.65 (6.5)	140.90 (5.7)	151.75 (6.7)
Sub-Total	1628.76 (62.3)	1708.21 (67.7)	1707.35 (69.9)	1683.27 (76.19)
Grand Total: All India	2612.90	2519.57	2440.31	2209.24

Source: Planning Commission (2007). Figures in parentheses denote percentages.

Whatever be the source of poverty estimates, whether the Planning Commission at 27.5 per cent and 30.2 crore or the World Bank study at 42 per cent and 45.6 crore, both figures are very high and point to the need for a time-bound Mission Mode approach to poverty eradication. The MDG of reducing the proportion of poor by half by 2015 is likely to be achieved, as the proportion of poor in the 1990 was about 36 per cent, which declined to 27.5 per cent in 2004–2005 and is likely to fall further to 18 per cent in 2015, thereby achieving the MDG. However, the absolute number of poor even with 18 per cent rural population below poverty will still be unacceptably high at 18.53 crore. Hence, there is a need for more rapid reduction of poverty (Department of Rural Development, 2008).

Initiatives towards Poverty Eradication

In India, the need for poverty alleviation has been recognized since the time the country achieved its independence 60 years back, which has aptly been reflected in almost every five-year plan (Table 9). Poverty alleviation has been one of the guiding principles of the planning process in India.

Table 9 *Pro-poor Responses of the Government as Reflected in Different Five-Year Plans*

The First Five-Year Plan (1951–1955) attempted to stimulate balanced economic development while correcting imbalances caused by World War II and partition. Agriculture, including projects that combined irrigation and power generation, received priority. It was an attempt to strike a balance between the prevailing socio-economic conditions and the building up of a model society founded on the Indian Constitutional norms relating to the protection and advancement of the people belonging to the weaker sections.
The objective of acceleration of economic growth, as perceived and applied during this period, was primarily based on higher investment in the domestic capital goods producing sector (and the associated metal-producing sectors). Since private entrepreneurial capacity in the capital goods sector was inadequate and the political scenario was more inclined towards a public sector expansion, the Second Plan (1956–1961) heralded a massive industrial development programme with an emphasis on balanced regional development of the industrial and the agricultural economy. The Industrial Policy Resolutions, too, echoed the importance of balanced regional development in order to ensure that the people in backward areas derived benefits of industrial development through increased employment and enhanced incomes.
A major development that took place during the Third Plan period (1961–1966) was the beginning of a comprehensive programme of rural works with the objective of generating additional employment opportunities and utilizing the large reserve of rural labour force for accelerating the process of economic development.

Cont'd...

...Cont'd

The Fourth Plan (1969–1974) aimed at accelerating the tempo of development of reducing fluctuations in agricultural production as well as the impact of uncertainties of foreign aid. It sought to raise the standard of living through programmes designed to promote equality and social justice. The plan laid particular emphasis on improving the conditions of the less privileged and weaker sections especially through provision of employment and education. Efforts were directed towards reduction of concentration of wealth, income and economic power to promote equity.

The Fifth Plan (1974–1979): Economic empowerment of weaker sections was accorded a very high priority and Minimum Needs Programmes was also introduced during the Fifth Five-Year Plan. The Fifth Plan was formulated against the backdrop of severe inflationary pressures. The major objectives of the plan were to achieve self-reliance and adopt measures for raising the consumption standard of people living below the poverty line.

Poverty alleviation and employment generation gained highest priority in the Sixth Five-Year Plan (1980–1985). The new Twenty Point Programme, aimed at accelerating the pace of development was introduced.

Seventh Five-Year Plan (1985–1990) was introduced with the objectives of maximization of production in key sectors of the economy with special emphasis on rural economy, progressive reduction in poverty and an increasing emphasis on employment.

The Eighth plan (1992–1997) was another important landmark in the development strategy when the limitation of an income and commodity-centric notion of poverty and human well-being was recognized. It aimed at faster growth, generation of more employment opportunities, reduction in poverty and regional disparities, provision of basic minimum facilities and enhancement in people's participation, reduction in population growth rate, completion of ongoing projects within stipulated time and diversification of agriculture to horticulture, livestock, fisheries and agro-processing, etc.

Direct poverty alleviation programmes on an expanded scale are also an important feature of The Ninth Plan (1997–2002). Priority was given to agriculture and rural development with a view to generate adequate productive employment and eradication of poverty. Schemes were introduced for generating incomes through supplementary employment, for improving the welfare of the poor in rural and urban areas and for a targeted public distribution system to ensure that the poor have access to food grains at prices they can afford.

The Tenth Plan (2002–2007) recognizes that the development objectives need to be defined not only in terms of increase in GDP but also in terms of human well-being. The plan aims at harnessing the benefits of growth to improve the quality of life of the people by setting one of its key targets of reduction in the poverty ratio from 26 per cent to 21 per cent, by 2007.

Sources: Five-Year Plan Documents.

Table 10 *A Profile of India's Major Initiatives towards Poverty Alleviation since Independence*

Initiatives	*Initiation Period*	*Aims/Objectives*	*Target Groups/Beneficiaries*
Initiatives towards Land Reforms and Agricultural Development			
In the two decades of 1950 and 1960, the primary policy focus of Government of India on poverty reduction was on land reforms. Land reforms have been an important plank of the poverty alleviation strategy. Land reforms have been viewed as an instrument to enable landless to have access to land and for attaining higher levels of agricultural production and income in the rural areas. Land is still a major source of employment and income in rural areas. Initiatives towards land reform were taken in early 1950s as it was necessary not only because of their welfare implications, but also because of their likely effect on agrarian productivity and on demand for mass consumption goods, which, in turn, would allow for improved productivity in those sectors as well. Land reforms consisted of four distinct components: (i) elimination of intermediary tenancy (abolition of zamindari), (ii) land redistribution, (iii) tenancy reforms to offer greater security of tenancy, and (iv) land consolidation to bring about efficiency in land use. As land is a state subject in the constitution, pace of these reforms varied across the country. In practice, land reforms were reasonably effective in abolition of intermediary tenancy, implying elimination of absentee landlordism. Simultaneously, taking into consideration the importance of agriculture, some major initiatives were directed towards agricultural development with the desired goals – to make credit available to farmers of different sizes and agricultural labourers, to enable them to use latest technology, to practise intensive agriculture and multiple cropping and to take up subsidiary activities such as dairying, poultry, fishing, horticulture with a major focus on improving the earning capacity of landless agricultural labourers.			
Tenancy Reforms and Consolidation of Land Holdings	Launched in early 1950s after independence	The major objectives of these initiatives were: abolition of intermediary tenures, tenancy reforms, ceiling on agricultural holdings and redistribution of surplus land, consolidation of agricultural holdings and updating and maintenance of land records. The Centrally Sponsored Schemes (CSS) of 'Strengthening of Revenue Administration and Updating of Land Records' (SRA & ULR) were designed to provide support to the ongoing programmes of tenancy reforms.	Rural poor and the tillers

Cont'd...

Cont'd...

Strengthening of Revenue Administration and Updating of Land Records (SRA & ULR)	1988–1989	The scheme places emphasis on modernization of cadastral survey procedures through protogrammetric check methods, further strengthening of training infrastructure facilities for revenue, survey and settlement staff, to enable them to handle modern survey equipments effectively, construction of Record Rooms and office cum Residence of Patwarais/Talathis in remote and tribal areas, purchase of survey equipments for offices of revenue administration particularly at grassroots level, etc.	
Computerization of Land Records (CLR)	1988–1989	Later, CLR and SRA & ULR were merged into the shape of National Land Records Modernization Programme (NLRMP). NLRMP aims at (i) providing citizen services, such as providing records of rights with maps to scale; other land-based certificates such as caste certificates; information for eligibility for development programmes; land passbooks, etc, and (ii) developing a comprehensive tool for supporting and planning developmental, regulatory, and disaster management activities.	
Programmes for Smalland Marginal Farmers	Late 1960s	Development of agriculture by preparing appropriate programmes, helping to ensure availability of inputs, services and credit. The emphasis in both the schemes was on self-employment through diversification of farm economy. In addition, there was a limited road works component of the schemes for marginal farmers and agricultural labour.	Poorest of the poor (small and marginal farmers and agricultural labourers)

Cont'd...

Cont'd...

Area Development Initiatives			
In the 1970s, although the area development programmes such as the Drought Prone Areas Development Programme (DPAP), the Desert Development Programme (DDP), the Hill Area Development Programme (HADP) and the Command Area Development Agency (CADA) had emphasized on land development but they all had a distinct objective to generate wage employment for the poor, as did other initiatives started during this period to support special groups, such as the Small Farmer Development Agency (SFDA) and the Marginal Farmer and Agricultural Labour Development Programme (MFAL).			
Drought Prone Area Programme (DPAP)	1970–1971	Mitigating adverse effects of drought on the production of crops and livestock and productivity of land water and human resources, restoration of ecological balance, improving the socio-economic conditions of the poor and disadvantaged by generating employment.	Poor and the disadvantaged section of the rural community
Desert Development Programme (DDP)	1977–1978	The main objectives of this programme are: (i) combating drought and desertification; (ii) encouraging restoration of ecological balance; (iii) mitigating the adverse effects of drought and adverse climatic conditions on crops and livestock and productivity of land, water and human resources; (iv) promoting economic development of village community; and (v) improving socio-economic conditions of the resourceless poor and disadvantaged sections of village community like the assetless and the women.	
Integrated Wasteland Development Programme (IWDP)	1978	Integrated Wastelands Development Programme (IWDP) was started with the objective of development of wastelands based on village or micro watershed plans. It aims at promoting the overall economic development and improvement of economic condition of the resource poor and disadvantaged section of inhabitants.	

Cont'd...

Cont'd...

		Self-employment Programmes	
Self-employment programmes were introduced in 1970s in rural India with Integrated Rural Development Programme (IRDP) with an aim of increasing the source of income of the rural families. The beneficiaries were provided subsidized training, need-based suitable infrastructure and credit so that they could find new sources of livelihood and earning.			
Integrated Rural Development Programme (IRDP)	1978–1979	The ultimate objective of the programme was to enable the selected families to cross the poverty line through a strategy of productive assets endowment.	BPL families with special emphasis on rural youth, rural women, deprived rural artisans, small and marginal farmers
Training of Rural Youth for Self-Employment (TRYSEM)	1979	Training programmes as a subsidiary of IRDP with focus on rural youth selected under IRDP	Rural youth
Development of Women and Children in Rural Areas (DWCRA)	1982–1983	Training programmes as a subsidiary of IRDP with focus on poor rural women	Poor rural women

Cont'd...

Cont'd...

Supply of Improved Toolkit for Rural Artisans (SITRA)	1992	Training programme as a subsidiary of IRDP for modernization and improvement of productivity and efficiency of poor rural artisans	Poor rural artisans
Ganga Kalyan Yojana (GKY)	1996–1997	Programme as a subsidiary of IRDP with focus on land-based activities particularly irrigation requirement of the small and marginal farmers	Small and marginal farmers

Wage Employment Programmes

The main purpose of the wage employment programmes is to provide a livelihood during the lean agricultural season as well as during drought and floods. Under these programmes, villagers worked to improve the village infrastructure such as deepening the village ponds, constructing village schools and improving the rural roads. Thus the programmes not only provided employment to the villagers but also improved village infrastructure and created village public assets. A positive fall out of this programme is that it created higher demand for village labour, thereby pushing up the wage of the labourer in the villages.

Rural Manpower Programme (RMP)	1960–1961 till 1968–1969 (Third Plan)	The programme aimed at providing employment for 100 days to at least 2.5 million persons by the last year of the Third Plan especially in areas exposed to pronounced seasonal unemployment.	BPL families
Crash Scheme for Rural Employment (CSRE)	1971	Provide employment to at least 1,000 persons in each of 350 districts of the country every year through labour-intensive works and creation of durable assets	BPL families
National Rural Employment Programme (NREP)	1980	The Programme was having threefold objectives of generation of additional gainful employment, creation of durable community assets and raising of nutritional standards	BPL families

Cont'd...

Cont'd...

Rural Landless Employment Guarantee Programme (RLEGP)	1983	Provide 100 days of employment to at least one member of each household in a year	Landless households
Jawahar Rozgar Yojana (JRY)	1989	The primary objective of the JRY was to generate additional gainful employment through creation of rural economic infrastructure, community and social assets and improve quality of life in the rural areas.	Unemployed and underemployed men and women
Employment Assurance Scheme (EAS)	1993	EAS was initiated with the primary objective of creating additional wage employment opportunities during the period of acute shortage of wage employment through manual work for the rural poor living below the poverty line. The secondary objective is the creation of durable community, social and economic assets for sustained employment and development. EAS is open to all the needy rural poor living below the poverty line.	Adult rural poor in need of employment during lean agricultural season.
Jawahar Gram Samridhi Yojana JGSY)	1999	JGSY was introduced with the primary objective of creating demand driven village infrastructure including durable assets at the village level and assets for enabling the rural poor to increase the opportunities for sustained employment. The secondary objective was generation of supplementary employment for the unemployed poor in the rural areas. The wage employment under the programme was exclusively designed for Below Poverty Line (BPL) families.	Unemployed villagers with preference to SCs/STs, families below poverty line and handicapped persons

Cont'd...

Cont'd...

Swarnjayanti Gram Swarozgar Yojana (SGSY)	1999	SGSY is conceived as a holistic programme of micro-enterprises covering all aspects of self-employment, viz., organization of the rural poor into self-help groups (SHGs) and their capacity building, planning of activity clusters, infrastructure build up, technology, credit and marketing. Micro-enterprises in the rural areas are sought to be established by building on the potential of the rural poor. The objective of the programme is to bring the existing poor families above the poverty line.	BPL families
Sampoorna Grameen Rozgar Yojana (SGRY)	2001	The threefold objective of this programme is generation of employment for the rural poor, creation of community assets and infrastructure, and ensuring food and nutrition security for the rural poor.	BPL families
National Food for Work Programme (NFFW)	2004–2005	To provide additional resources apart from the resources available under the Sampoorna Grameen Rozgar Yojana (SGRY) to 150 most backward districts of the country so that generation of supplementary wage employment and providing of food-security through creation of need based economic, social and community assets in these districts is further intensified.	All rural poor who are in need of wage employment and desire to do manual and unskilled work.
Mahatma Gandhi National Rural Employment Guarantee Act (MGNREGA)	2005	The Act guarantees 100 days of employment in a financial year to any rural household whose adult members are willing to do unskilled manual work. The primary objective of the act is augmenting wage employment through work such as building roads, improving water supply and works that are necessary to improve the village infrastructure. MGNREGA is one of the largest single rights-based social protection initiatives and the first ever law internationally, that guarantees wage employment at an unprecedented scale.	All rural poor who are in need of wage employment and desire to do manual and unskilled work.

Cont'd...

Cont'd...

Food Security and Social Security Initiatives			
Ensuring the very basic need of access to food was considered to be one of the major challenges to the government in the post-economic reform era. Those who are below poverty line face the problem of meeting this very basic need. Starvation and hunger have been reported in different parts of the country, even in economically advanced states such as Maharashtra. Taking into consideration these emerging needs, the government initiated food security programmes to ensure the basic minimum food for its people. Social security programmes were designed for those who are at the bottom of the BPL facing destitution and desertion.			
National Social Assistance Programme (NSAP)	1995	Article 41 of the Constitution of India directs the state to provide public assistance to its citizens in case of unemployment, old age, sickness and disablement and in other cases of undeserved want within the limit of its economic capacity and development. In accordance with the Directive Principles of State Policy, the Government of India introduced in 1995 the National Social Assistance Programme (NSAP) to lay foundation to a National Policy for Social Assistance for the poor. The NSAP aims at ensuring minimum national standard for social assistance in addition to the benefits that state are currently providing or might provide in future. At present, NSAP comprises Indira Gandhi National Old Age Pension Scheme (IGNOAPS), National Family Benefit Scheme (NFBS) and Annapurna.	BPL families

Cont'd...

Cont'd...

		Under IGNOAPS which was launched on 19 November 2007, ₹ 200 per month per beneficiary is provided by way of central assistance to all persons who are 65 years or higher and belonging to a family living below the poverty line. Earlier under National Old Age Pension Scheme (NOAPS), the pension was restricted to destitute only. The number of beneficiaries under IGNOAPS is estimated to reach 160 lakh persons as compared to 87 lakh under NOAPS. The amount of old age pension was increased from ₹ 75 to ₹ 200 per month with effect from 1 April 2006 and the states were urged to contribute at least another ₹ 200 so that an old age pension beneficiary could get at least ₹ 400 per month. At present 25 states/UTs are providing pension which is more than ₹ 200 per month. Annapurna Scheme was introduced on 1 April 2000 to provide 10 kg of food grains per month free of cost to eligible beneficiaries who could not be covered under NOAPS, Under NFBS, ₹ 10,000 is provided to a BPL family in case of natural or accidental death of a primary bread winner in the family while in the age group of 18 to 64 years.	
Targeted Public Distribution System (TPDS)	1997	In order to ensure availability of minimum quantity of food grains to the families living below the poverty line, the government launched the TPDS in June 1997. It was intended to benefit about six crore poor families in the country for whom a quantum of 72 lakh tonnes of food grains was earmarked annually at the rate of 10 kg per family per month. The allocation was increased from 10 kg to 20 kg from 1 April 2000. This was increased from 20 to 25 kg per family per month from July 2001. From 1 April 2002, this allocation was further increased from 25 to 35 kg per family per month. The Central Issue Price (CIP) for BPL families is ₹ 4.15 per kg for wheat and ₹ 5.65 per kg for rice.	BPL families

Cont'd...

Cont'd...

Antyodaya Anna Yojana (AAY)	2000	In order to make TPDS more focused and targeted towards the poorest section of population, the 'Antyodaya Anna Yojana' (AAY) was launched in December 2000, with the provision of ensuring food grains at a highly subsidized rate of ₹ 2 per kg for wheat and ₹ 3 per kg for rice to the poor families under the Targeted Public Distribution System (TPDS). The scale of issue, which was initially 25 kg per family per month, was increased to 35 kg per family per month from 1 April, 2002.	BPL families

Source: Author's articulation based on Bandyopadhyay (2007) and Publication Division (2010).

While initially it was expected that the overall economic development strategies incorporated in the government's five-year development plans would also reduce poverty among the masses, later on programmes specifically designed and addressed to the cause of poverty alleviation among the rural poor became indispensable. The entire range of planned interventions spanning over a period of five decades indicate a wide range of experiments, from macro level to micro level, from regional development to settlement development, a combination of re-distributive policy and individual income development and access to infrastructure services and community approach to minimizing the leakages in all possible manner for mainstreaming the poor. There are numerous poverty alleviation programmes all over India, which have experimented, outside the standard programmes of Government of India and State Governments, with innovative approaches (Table 10). These have been designed and implemented with different focus groups and having objectives, that are invariably related to addressing the challenges of poverty in various dimensions.

Since independence the Government of India has changed the focus and approach of rural poverty alleviation programme as and when required; but mere changing the approach and focus of programmes alone is not enough. Greater efforts are needed to build the capacity of administration and improve governance at the district level. At the same time, several of these schemes have undergone reforms, rationalization and better targeting with a greater role to local government for implementation, beneficiary selection and monitoring. The reforms laid stress on transparency, making information about the programmes public at the village level, and on the importance of physical, financial, and social audits. In the context of leakages and diversion of funds meant for poverty reduction, it needs to be recognized that state failure or governance failure can be corrected if empowered communities are willing to put in the time and effort needed to demand transparency and accountability. The success of targeted poverty schemes in India indeed is dependent upon proper identification of the beneficiaries, transparency, supervision over field staff and social mobilization. Funds have more than tripled in the last 10 years for poorer districts, but neither the government nor donors have studied whether there is any capacity at the district and sub-district level to absorb the funds and produce quality results. And more than the capacity, one needs to examine if the states have the required will to improve themselves.

There has been a discernible evolution of poverty alleviation efforts from redistributing land and changes in property relations to promotion of wage employment with the attendant food security for the poor. Such a pragmatic change is made possible with growing food self-sufficiency, empowerment with mandated elections to local bodies and enactment of the right to information act. But the realization of the potential is constrained by balanced budget rules, a self-imposed restraint under the liberal regime. Numerous initiatives on poverty reduction have been undertaken but relatively limited efforts have been done in identifying and obtaining a deep understanding of those initiatives, e.g., in terms of defining and measuring poverty, selecting approach and the target groups, and evaluating its impact. Successful implementation of poverty alleviation programmes will require appropriate policy framework, adequate funds and effective delivery mechanism (see Table 11). The success of these programmes will be ultimately depending on the capability of the delivery system to absorb and utilize the funds in a cost-effective manner. An effective and responsive district level field machinery with a high degree of commitment, motivation, professional competence and, above all, integrity has been recognized as one of the prerequisites for successful implementation of an anti-poverty strategy. An effective governance system has to ensure people's participation at various stages of formulation and implementation of the programmes, transparency in the operation of the schemes and adequate monitoring. International experience shows that greater functional and financial devolution to local governments results in higher allocation of resources for social sectors which are accompanied by efficiency gains in resource use.

Involvement of the local communities is key to the success of poverty alleviation programmes. In the absence of community involvement, the programmes are plagued with bureaucratic muddle and corruption at every level. Wage employment is an example to show how too much of administrative interference has led to underutilization of funds, high administrative cost, corruption and poor employment generation. Contrary to the wage employment programme, self-employment programmes such as microcredit is successful because of people's participation in the form of SHGs (Yesudian, 2007). So, economic growth should be participatory. It must be planned and managed locally by people whose lives it affects. Communities must participate actively to shape programmes, ensure that opportunities are expanded, and that the benefits are shared equitably. For this, structures of local self-governance must be strengthened; and people's participation has to become a norm of public life.

Table 11 *Initiatives Need to be Ensured for a Better Progress towards Poverty Alleviation*

- Strengthening community participation in management and implementation of poverty alleviation programme will promote transparency in funds utilization and will enhance community's sense of belongingness and project sustainability as well. Therefore, a shift in approach to service delivery through community participation and community contribution will be a welcome change.
- Spreading more awareness among the rural poor about the programmes and schemes which have exclusively designed and being implemented for their welfare and development, so that they can grab their every entitlements.
- Suitable measures need to be adopted in establishing good governance for controlling corruption in different stages of programme implementation process.
- Promoting decentralization of the implementation process of poverty alleviation programmes by strengthening the Panchayati Raj Institutions; shift from centralized approach to decentralized approach; shifting implementation, decision making and management responsibilities to local/regional governments by empowering them with appropriate authority.
- Promoting growth in agricultural productivity and non-farm rural activities as well as improving household incomes through diversified farming and off-farm activities
- Ensuring marketing linkage for farmers' groups for their production.
- Public investment in rural infrastructure and agricultural research. Agricultural research benefits the poor directly through an increase in farm production, greater employment opportunities and growth in the rural non-farm economy.
- Encouraging more and more spontaneous participation and involvement of rural poor in MGNREGS.
- It is often noticed that allocated funds for poverty alleviation and goods such as food grains are not fully utilized by the states; so there is a need to strengthen the financial management capacity of certain states to use the funds efficiently.
- Proper targeting of poor through suitable poverty mapping mechanism.
- Encouraging more transparency in the programme implementation process by introducing and strengthening social audit for each poverty alleviation programmes.

Cont'd...

...Cont'd

- Removing the design defects of various schemes and programmes based on earlier experiences and replication of successful experiments on mass scale.
- Developing local data base for designing programmes and building up a strong Monitoring and Evaluation (M&E) system, with active involvement of beneficiaries' group.
- Encouraging greater role of private micro-finance institutions in the provision of financial services in rural India.
- Organizing workshops, need-based training programmes and capacity building programme for the government functionaries, responsible for implementation of poverty alleviation programmes at the grassroots level.
- Provision of an enabling policy environment that will facilitate the increased participation of the NGOs and private sector in micro-finance.
- Promoting competitive, integrated and efficient banking system for the rural poor.
- Getting the priorities right for public spending. Expenditures must be utilized for improving the quality and efficacy of services, correcting imbalances in public expenditures, plugging leaks and reducing wastage as well as ensuring greater efficiency in spending.
- Promoting a viable, pro-poor and effective microfinance system that enables the poor to enhance income and reduce poverty.
- Public Distribution System (PDS) needs to be reformed and better targeted.
- Enhance the capacity of financial institutions and the private sector to operate in the poverty-stricken rural areas.
- At the macro-level, there is a need to co-ordinate a myriad of poverty alleviation programmes of the Central Government and the state governments. The transfer of central funds to the states for different programmes should be efficient.
- Introducing policies to promote human capital for expanding the capabilities of the poor.
- Self-Help Group approach to be strengthened as it is a proven method of empowerment of the poor.
- Provision of safety nets such as targeted food subsidies, nutrition programmes and health need to be enhanced.
- Targeted poverty alleviation programmes to continue as the poor of the developing world may not have the patience to wait for the trickle-down effect.
- Improving livelihood opportunities for communities in semi-arid tropical areas, where better water management and new technologies for agriculture help reduce poverty.
- The link between ignorance and poverty and ill health and poverty are well established. There are diseases of poverty such as malaria, tuberculosis, diarrhoea and malnutrition. Having fallen ill due to poverty, the poor do not have the resources to seek quality health care, for which he/she has to borrow money for treatment. Indebtedness due to hospitalization leading to poverty has been well documented. Poverty therefore is a complex phenomenon of many dimensions, not merely the economic dimension. Poverty alleviation programmes should address the issue of poverty from broader social and economic perspectives (Yesudian, 2007).

Cont'd...

...Cont'd

- Maintain a balance between economic growth and an expansion of social opportunities; high priority should be given to basic education, to preventive and promotive health care, to assuring basic economic security and livelihoods.
- The state needs to play a more proactive role in expanding social opportunities. The state has to show dynamism in reducing controls, liberalizing as well as opening up the rural economy.
- Opportunities must be created and expanded for rural women to participate more fully in economic activities; empowering women by improving their access to microfinance and to activities as micro-entrepreneurs.
- Build the capacity of civil society organizations in monitoring and follow-up of poverty alleviation programmes.
- To accumulate sufficient capital in the village to support a new investment and production.

Accelerating agriculture development with emphasis on watershed development in dry land areas and a special focus on small farmers will increase employment and help reduce poverty in rural areas. The Eleventh Plan also places emphasis on several other initiatives which will increase economic well-being and opportunities in rural areas. The National Rural Employment Guarantee Programme (NREGP) provides income support for those in need of employment while helping to create assets that will increase land productivity as well. The *Bharat Nirman* programme will provide electricity and drinking water to all habitations before the end of the plan period. *Pradhan Mantri Gram Sadak Yojana* (PMGSY) will provide all-weather connectivity to all villages with a population of over 1,000 or with a population of over 500 in hilly areas. *Sarva Shiksha Abhiyan* (SSA) will provide eight years of education to all children. The other measures taken for improving education will help give opportunities to all children to fully develop their capabilities. The Rural Health Mission is directed to reach health services to all. The total sanitation campaign (TSC) should provide clean environment in villages. An important element of the Eleventh Plan strategy is to empower PRIs through special training as well as funds, supplemented by the Backward Regions Grant Fund (BRGF), to implement and oversee these programmes. When these programmes will be effectively implemented, the benefits of growth would spread widely, especially in rural areas and backward regions of the country.

Conclusion

For the last six decades of planned development, the challenge of poverty reduction has been and still remains a key policy concern for India. The Indian poverty alleviation strategy has been based on the principle to address poverty effectively but simultaneously it should be taken into consideration that the strategy has to be responsive, inclusive and dynamic, taking into perspective the emerging new dimensions of poverty in a functionally integrated manner. A people-centric strategic framework with emphasis on social mobilization, productive and remunerative work, people's participation in choice of work and occupation, social security network to mitigate risk and financial inclusion along with dedicated, motivated professional machinery is necessary to tackle the poverty in a time-bound manner. Besides, macro-economic policies have to be pro-poor through the emphasis on labour-intensive approach to the growth process. These issues have intra-ministerial implications and thus need comprehensive integrated approach through convergence and coordination. Further, concerted efforts are required from all stakeholders, i.e., Central/State Governments, private sector, community-based organizations (CBOs), NGOs, civil society organizations (CSOs), etc., for intensifying the efforts towards this direction. Taking into consideration the dynamic nature of rural poverty, an integrated approach is required as far as the context of rural India is concerned, where the programme components are to be decided upon the local poverty scenario and the key causative factors. The strategy components should seek to address these factors and take into account the poverty dimensions. A need-based programme has to be designed rather than a fund supply based programme. The capability of implementing agency has to be accordingly strengthened with technical assistance and capacity building inputs. The participatory process has to be the operational principle for encouraging a better coordination and an effective partnership among all the local stakeholders, carrying out the mission of poverty alleviation.

Notes

1. Hazra (2009).
2. IBRD (2000).
3. Ibid.

4. Planning Commission (1979).
5. Ibid.
6. Ravallion and Chen (2008).
7. Ibid.
8. Department of Rural Development (2008).
9. Ibid.
10. Planning Commission (2007).
11. Ibid.
12. Ibid.
13. Planning Commission (2007).
14. Planning Commission (2007).
15. Akter et al. (2008).

References

Ahuja, R. (2006). *Social Problems in India.* New Delhi, India: Rawat Publication.

Akter, S. et al. (2008). *Livestock, Vulnerability, and Poverty Dynamics in India*. Discussion Paper No. 10. Addis Ababa, Ethiopia: International Livestock Research Institute.

Bandyopadhyay, K.R. (2007). *Poverty Alleviation and Pro-Poor Growth in India*. New Delhi, India: Asian Institute of Transport Development.

Department of Rural Development. (2008). *Poverty Eradication in India by 2015: Rural Household Centered Strategy Paper*. New Delhi, India: Ministry of Rural Development, Government of India.

Hazra, A. (2009). Poverty in Rural India: Jeopardizing the Future Growth. *Kurukshetra*, Vol. 58 (1).

International Bank for Reconstruction and Development (IBRD). (2000). *India Country Study on Reducing Poverty: Accelerating Development*. New Delhi, India: Oxford University Press.

International Fund for Agricultural Development (IFAD). (2009). *Enabling Poor Rural People to Overcome Poverty*. Rome, Italy: IFAD.

Planning Commission. (1979). *Report of the Task Force on Projections of Minimum Needs and Effective Consumption Demand*. New Delhi, India: Perspective Planning Division, Government of India.

Planning Commission. (2007). *Poverty Estimates for 2004–05*. New Delhi, India: Press Information Bureau, Government of India.

Planning Commission. (2008). *Eleventh Plan (2007–12)*, Vol. I, II and III. New Delhi, India: Government of India.

Planning Commission. *Five Year Plan Documents*. Government of India. Retrieved from http://www.planningcommission.nic.in (accessed November 15, 2010).

Publication Division. (2010). *India 2010: A Reference Manual*. New Delhi, India: Ministry of Information and Broad Casting, Government of India.

Ravallion, M., and Chen, S. (2008). *New Global Poverty Estimate: What It Means for India?* Washington DC: The World Bank Development Research Group, World Bank.

Yesudian, C.A.K. (2007). Poverty Alleviation Programmes in India: A Social Audit. *Indian Journal of Medical Research*, Vol. 126 (4).

3 Scarcity in the State of Surplus

Exploring the 'Starving' India

After 65 years of independence, it gives me a feeling of exasperation to write about lack of food or food insecurity as a pertinent issue – an issue which seems to have a perennial root in the wet roots of Indian development journey. We live in a world of cruel paradox. Millions go to bed without food. Food security is said to exist when all people, at all times, have physical, social and economic access to sufficient, safe and nutritious food that meets their dietary needs and food preferences for an active and healthy life,[1] but the current global food crisis, which has emerged from the recent unprecedented increase in the price of food, especially of staples, coupled with shortages and diminishing food stocks, has reduced access to food for many people, particularly for the poor in a large number of developing countries. Today food insecurity remains one of the most pressing global problems and the number of undernourished people in the world is close to one billion.

The Food and Agriculture Organization of the United Nations (FAO) estimates that a total of 925 million people are undernourished in 2010 compared with 1.023 billion in 2009.[2] It further observes that most of the world's hungry live in developing countries, where they account for 16 per cent of the population. Latest available statistics indicate that some progress has been made towards achieving MDG 1, with the prevalence of hunger declining from 20 per cent undernourished in 1990–1992 to 16 per cent in 2010, but despite the decline, the ability to achieve international targets of reducing hunger is still at risk.[3]

India promises to achieve the Millennium Development Goals (MDGs) by 2015, but the promise seems futile when one looks at the current scenario of hunger and food insecurity across the country (see Table 12). Though India has made substantial progress in terms of overcoming national food insecurity by giving priority to self-sufficiency in food grain production which is the resultant of modern agriculture system; however, chronic food insecurity exists in various part of India despite mounting buffer stock.

Hunger is defined as the discomfort, exhaustion or painful sensation caused by the lack of food. The task of combating and ending hunger is not merely an issue of making it possible to avoid this pain and discomfort. It is a call to find the means to end food deprivation and its manifold consequences, such as fatigue, malnourishment, sickness and death. There are two types of hunger: acute and chronic. Both are matters of grave concern. However, we hear more about the problem of acute hunger, that is, famine. It is more dramatic and sensational, and lends itself to political wrangling. It makes a better story and the images are more lasting and moving. This kind of hunger is a very visible tragedy. We see it in Ethiopia, Sudan, Central Africa, Bangladesh and closer home in Kalahandi in Orissa (India).

Chronic hunger, however, is less amenable to headlines. It is the 'insidious sabotage' wrought on millions of children, women and men in several places around the globe. It is silent and only the sufferer can hear the growls in her or his stomach. The hungry grow to live with it by 'shrinking their stomachs' to survive. It is the inadequacy of food in terms of both quality and quantity which results in malnutrition and related diseases. Globally, 40,000 people die from hunger-related causes every day (McHarry et al., 2002). According to an estimate made by the UNICEF, in the year 2000, about 2,420,000 children in India died before their fifth birthday. This was the highest total for any country. It was estimated that in the same year about 10,929,000 children in the world died before their fifth birthday. Thus, India accounts for more than a fifth of child mortality worldwide. About half of these deaths of children under five are estimated to be associated with malnutrition. This means that more than a million children die in

India each year from causes associated with malnutrition.[4] Many may not be dying of hunger but they live their whole lives at the edge of hunger. Their lives are short, harsh and insecure. It shows itself in malnutrition, illness and low life expectancy. This keeps hungry people in persistent and desperate poverty.

Table 12 *Food Crisis in India: Some Alarming Statistics*

- India is home to more than 230 million undernourished people – highest for any country in the world. More than 27 per cent of the entire global undernourished population lives in India
- 43 per cent of children (under-five years) in the country are underweight. The figure is among the highest in the world and is much higher than the global proportion of 25 per cent and also Sub-Saharan Africa figure of 28 per cent.
- The proportion of stunted children (under-five) at 48 per cent is again among the highest in the world. Every second child in the country is stunted.
- 30 per cent of babies in India are born underweight
- Malnutrition accounts for nearly 50 per cent of child deaths in India
- Every third adult (aged 15–49 years) in the country is reported to be thin (Body Mass Index less than 18.5).
- 70 per cent of children (under-five) suffer from anaemia. More than 80 per cent do not get vitamin supplements.
- While the general inflation declined from a 13 year high exceeding 12 per cent in July 2008 to less than 5 per cent by the end of January 2009, the inflation for food articles doubled from 5 per cent to over 11 per cent during the same period.
- More than 1.5 million children in India are at risk of becoming malnourished because of rising global food prices.

Source: WFP (2009).

Both acute and chronic hunger makes for the greatest economic and moral scandal of our time. It is the greatest human right violation, for to be human one must live, and to live one must have food and drink. It makes for a situation wherein anyone who has even two assured meals a day is to be considered a privileged person and which, in one sense, deprives many others of a basic right. The direct manifestation of chronic hunger is undernourishment or undernutrition. Undernourishment leads to several kinds of diseases and shorter life expectancy.

Extent of Hunger and Undernourishment

The latest estimate made by the FAO shows that even before the recent surge in food prices, worrisome long-term trends of increasing hunger were already apparent. The FAO estimates that 849 million people suffered from chronic hunger or undernourishment worldwide in 2003–2005[5] (Table 13). This represents an increase of 6 million over 843 million in 1990–1992, the World Food Summit baseline period, against which progress is measured. With the number of chronically hungry people in the world now higher than during the baseline period, the World Food Summit target of reducing that number of the hungry to half by the year 2015 has become more difficult to reach.

Table 13 *Global Undernourishment in 1990–1992 and 2003–2005*

Country/Region	*1990–1992*		*2003–2005*	
	People in Million	*Percentage*	*People in Million*	*Percentage*
India	207	26	231	28
China	178	21	123	14
Asia & The Pacific (excluding India & China)	198	23	189	22
Sub-Saharan Africa	169	20	212	25
Near East and North Africa	19	2	33	4
Latin America & The Caribbean	53	6	45	5
Developed Countries	19	2	16	2
Across the World	843	100	849	100

Source: FAO (2008a).

Asia and the Pacific region recorded modest progress in reducing the incidence of hunger leading to undernourishment from 20 to 16 per cent, as well as a moderate reduction in the number of hungry people from 583 to 543 million. The region is home to over half of the world's population and to nearly two-thirds of the world's hungry people. While Southeastern Asia has maintained progress in reducing the incidence of undernourishment, this gain has been offset by setbacks elsewhere in the region, primarily in India. By virtue of their size, China and India alone account for 42 per cent of the chronically hungry people in the developing world. In India, despite rapid economic growth, the number of hungry people was increased by over 20 million compared to the baseline period. This can be partly explained by the fact that life expectancy in India has increased from 59 to 63 years since 1990–1992, which has had an impact on the overall population structure with the result that in 2003–2005 the growth in minimum energy requirements had outpaced that of dietary energy supply (DES). China has continued registering a steady reduction in undernourishment, with 31 per cent drop in the number of the undernourished from 178 million in 1990–1992 to 123 million in 2003–2005 (FAO, 2008a).

Rising Food Prices and Hunger

The current global food crisis, which has emerged from the recent unprecedented increase in the price of food, especially of staples, coupled with shortage and diminishing food stock has reduced access to food of many people (particularly the poor) in a large number of developing countries. There has also been a substantial increase in the food import bills of developing countries. This has created a host of humanitarian, socio-economic, developmental, political and security-related challenges. The consequences of the crisis are most pressing in low income, net food-importing countries — particularly the least developed countries, where 50–80 per cent of personal income is spent on food[6] — but also in the larger developing economies such as India and China, as well as in some countries in Latin America. Even developed countries are not free from the negative consequences of the crisis. Rising food prices have added to inflationary or poverty tensions already being felt as a result of rising energy price and crash in financial and housing markets. The most pressing cases of immediate attention are the urgent hunger needs in over 37 developing countries, identified by the FAO, 20 of which are the least developed countries.[7] Chronic hunger and malnutrition were profound problems for the world before the food price rise of 2007–2008 began. The origin of the current crisis lies not in global lack of food – there is enough food in the world to meet the demand – but in the long-term lack of access to food in the case of many people. Poverty and inequality are at the heart of hunger. Poor people do not have the opportunities to grow food or the resources to buy food, because the resources needed to get access to food are inequitably distributed.

World food prices have roughly doubled over the past three years. They increased by 85 per cent between April 2007 and April 2008 alone. This price rise has been broad-based, led by wheat (whose price almost doubled) and maize (up by 67% since July 2007), and followed by rice (which has tripled since September 2007 and soared by 160 per cent between January and April 2008 alone). Prices for vegetable oilseeds and oils also shot up, multiplying by about 2.5 times since early 2006 (UNCTAD, 2008b). The impact of the rising food price on the prevalence of hunger is even more striking. Progress towards achievement of the MDG of eradicating poverty and hunger in the developing world has been steady from almost 20 per cent in 1990–1992 to less than 18 per cent in 1995–1997 and just above 16 per cent in 2003–2005. However, the FAO estimates for the end of 2007 show a slight reversal, with the proportion of hungry people in the developing world sliding back towards 17 per cent, about the same level as a decade ago. Meeting the internationally agreed hunger-reduction goal by 2015 is becoming an enormous challenge (FAO, 2008a).

From a nation dependent on food imports to feed its population, India today is not only self-sufficient in grain production, but also has a substantial reserve. The progress made by agriculture in the last four decades has been one of the biggest success stories of free India. Agriculture and allied activities constitute the single largest contributor to the gross domestic product, almost 33 per cent of it. Agriculture is the means of livelihood of about two-thirds of the workforce in the country. It is true that the country now produces enough food to feed its entire people. When there are rapid increases in hunger in some parts of India, it is now usually attributed to short-term natural events such as hurricanes or droughts. These are described as transitory, episodic events, temporary deviations from normal. India no longer suffers through large-scale famines as it had in the past. It means that there has been substantial reduction in acute hunger.

However, this upbeat food situation in India neglects the reality of widespread chronic hunger and malnutrition in the country. Temporary disruptions in the food system by natural calamities are disastrous for so many people only because they live so close to the edge of disaster under normal conditions. India could feed its entire people, but it does not. The chronic conditions – the conditions that are normal – for many millions of people in India are unacceptable in terms of the basic requirements of human dignity. The State of Food Insecurity in the World 2008 released by the FAO estimates that India is home to more than 230 million undernourished people, which is 21 per cent of the national population. The DES for India has been estimated to be 2,360 kcal per capita per day. With more than 200 million food-insecure people, India is home to the largest number of hungry people in the world.[8]

The cost of food items is increasing rapidly, making them unaffordable to a majority of the people. Added to these woes is the short supply of pulses and edible oils, which forces the Central Government to import them. A large section of people suffer from food and nutrition insecurity in India, the worst affected groups are landless or land poor households in rural areas and people employed in ill paid occupations and casual labourers engaged in seasonal activities in the urban areas. The food insecure people are disproportionately large in some regions of the country, such as economically backward states with high incidence of poverty, tribal and remote areas, regions more prone to natural disasters, etc. In fact, the states of Uttar Pradesh (eastern and south-eastern parts), Bihar, Jharkhand, Orissa, West Bengal, Chhattisgarh, parts of Madhya Pradesh and Maharashtra account for largest number of food insecure people in the country.

Extent of Hunger in India

An attempt has been made by the International Food Policy Research Institute (IFPRI) to develop the Global Hunger Index (GHI). The GHI is a multidimensional measure of hunger and malnutrition or undernourishment. It combines three equally-weighted indicators: (1) the proportion of the under-nourished as a percentage of the total population (reflecting the share of the population with insufficient dietary energy intake); (2) the incidence of underweight in children under the age of five years (indicating the proportion of children suffering from weight loss and/or reduced growth); and (3) the mortality rate of children under the age of five years (partially reflecting the fatal synergy between inadequate dietary intake and unhealthy environments). This multidimensional approach for calculating the GHI offers several advantages. It captures various aspects of hunger and undernutrition in one index number, thereby presenting a quick overview of a complex issue. It takes account of the nutrition situation not only of the population as a whole, but also of a physiologically vulnerable group – children – for whom lack of nutrients creates high risk of illness and death. In addition, by combining independently measured indicators, it reduces the effects of random measurement errors.

The GHI ranks countries on a 100 point scale, with 0 being the best score (no hunger) and 100 being the worst, though neither of these extremes is achieved in practice. It is composed of three equally weighted indicators: the proportion of undernourished in the population, the prevalence of those underweight in children under five and the under-five mortality rate. Values less than 4.9 reflect low hunger, values between 5 and 9.9 reflect moderate hunger, values between 10 and 19.9 indicate a serious problem, values between 20 and 29.9 are alarming, and values exceeding 30 are extremely alarming.[9] India has consistently ranked poorly on the GHI. GHI, released in 2010 by the IFPRI, Welthungerhilfe – a German NGO, and Concern Worldwide – an Irish Charity which ranks India at 67th position out of 84 countries, placing it way below its neighbouring countries such as China and Pakistan and putting it firmly in the 'alarming levels of hunger' category.[10] The Global Hunger Index 2010 examined the current scenario of hunger in 122 countries across the world and ranked 84 countries with significant levels of hunger. The rest of the 38 countries have a GHI of less than 5 and are not included in the rankings.[11] Highly developed countries have not been included in the data. The 2010 report focuses on child malnutrition, which is the biggest component of hunger worldwide. For India, the high GHI scores of 24.1 are driven by high levels of underweight children, resulting from the low nutritional and social status of women in the country, the report reflects.

Like the GHI, the India State Hunger Index (ISHI) released in 2009 was computed by averaging the three underlying components of the hunger index, viz., percentage of calorie undernourishment, proportion of underweight children below the age of five years and mortality rate of children below the age of five years. The ISHI score was estimated for 17 major states in India, covering more than 95 per cent of the population of India.[12] To make the ISHI comparable with the GHI, the IFPRI has used a calorie norm that yields a national calorie undernutrition of exactly 20 per cent – which leads to a calorie norm of 1,632 kcal per person per day.

Table 14 *The India State Hunger Index and Its Underlying Components*

State	*Percentage of calorie undernourishment*	*Proportion of Underweight children under-five years*	*Mortality rate among children under-five*	*ISHI score*	*ISHI rank*
Punjab	11.1	24.6	5.2	13.6	1
Kerala	28.6	22.7	1.6	17.6	2
Andhra Pradesh	19.6	32.7	6.3	19.5	3
Assam	14.6	36.4	8.5	19.8	4
Haryana	15.1	39.7	5.2	20.0	5
Tamil Nadu	29.1	30.0	3.5	20.9	6
Rajasthan	14.0	40.4	8.5	21.0	7
West Bengal	18.5	38.5	5.9	21.0	8
Uttar Pradesh	14.5	42.3	9.6	22.1	9
Maharashtra	27.0	36.7	4.7	22.8	10
Karnataka	28.1	37.6	5.5	23.7	11
Orissa	21.4	40.9	9.1	23.8	12
Gujarat	23.3	44.7	6.1	24.7	13
Chhattisgarh	23.3	47.6	9.0	26.6	14
Bihar	17.3	56.1	8.5	27.3	15
Jharkhand	19.6	57.1	9.3	28.7	16
Madhya Pradesh	23.4	59.8	9.4	30.9	17
India	20.0	42.5	7.4	23.7	

Source: Menon et al. (2009).

The ISHI scores for the states in India range from 13.6 for Punjab to 30.9 for Madhya Pradesh, indicating substantial variation among the states in India. Punjab is ranked 34th and Madhya Pradesh 82nd, when compared with the GHI 2008 country rankings.[13] All the 17 states have ISHI scores that are significantly worse than the 'low' and 'moderate' hunger categories. Twelve of the 17 states fall into the 'alarming' category, and one – Madhya Pradesh – falls into the 'extremely alarming' category.[14] On the other hand, the increase in severity of food insecurity in rural India can be gauged from following points:

Table 15 *Glimpses of Food Insecurity in Rural India at a Glance*

- The proportion of population consuming less than 1,890 kcal/cu/diem has in fact increased in the states of Orissa, Madhya Pradesh, Karnataka, West Bengal, Rajasthan and marginally for Punjab.
- Almost two-third of rural households in Jharkhand did not have access to safe drinking water in 2001.
- More than 90 per cent of rural households in Chhattisgarh, Jharkhand, Orissa and Madhya Pradesh did not have access to toilets within their premises.
- As many as eight states – Andhra Pradesh, Bihar, Gujarat, Haryana, Karnataka, Kerala, Madhya Pradesh and Rajasthan – have shown increase in the incidence of anaemia among women in the reproductive age group. The highest increase in anaemia levels has been observed in Andhra Pradesh (51 to 64%), followed by Haryana (48 to 57%) and Kerala (23 to 32%).
- The proportion of women with CED has drastically increased for Assam (28 to 40%) followed by Bihar (40 to 46%), Madhya Pradesh (42 to 45%) and Haryana (31 to 33%).
- 12 out of 20 states under consideration have figures higher than 80 per cent for proportion of rural anaemic children. Bihar, that already had a high figure of 81 per cent, has further increased to 89 per cent.
- The proportion of rural stunted children in Karnataka has increased from 39 to 43 per cent.

Source: WFP/MSSRF (2008).

Food insecurity in rural India is primarily a reflection of rural poverty, and thus overall economic growth and its distributional pattern cannot but be important in solving the hunger problem. It is particularly critical to pay attention to employment opportunities, other ways of acquiring economic means, and also food prices, which influence people's ability to buy food, and thus affect the food entitlement they effectively enjoy. Beside that corruption exacerbates poverty in most of rural India. The money that the central or state government earmarks for poverty eradication is cleverly pocketed by politicians, corrupt government officials and some village leaders. On the other hand, there is a lot of food stored in the Food Corporation of India (FCI) warehouses and they are not being distributed fast enough. FCI complains that a lot of food gets spoilt because they are not consumed fast enough. This means that a lot of food gets wasted before it reaches the plates of the common man (Hazra, 2011).

Hunger, Malnutrition and Poverty: Interlinkages

Hunger is the obvious manifestation of poverty. The poor spend a high proportion of their earning on food. Eradication of poverty, therefore, should go along with elimination of hunger. Without adequate nutrition, an individual will not have the energy needed for higher productive work output. Malnutrition contributes to poverty because it causes or aggravates illness, lowers cognitive function and thus educational attainment, reduces productivity and relegates the individual to reduced options for livelihoods.

Food security in terms of access to adequate and quality food is required for an active healthy life as nutritious food is necessary for physical growth, resistance to, or recovery from diseases, during the period of pregnancy and lactation, and physical work. The current crisis of food price could lead to short-term results of increase in malnutrition and malnutrition-related diseases, more micronutrient deficiencies (especially in women and children), larger number of children being born with low birth weight, and increase in infant and maternal mortality. In the long run, this crisis can result in impaired mental development, diminished learning ability, reduced work productivity and increase in the incidence of nutrition-related non-communicable diseases.

Food insecurity, in terms of lack of access to adequate nutritious food, and poverty mutually reinforce each other. Eradicating extreme hunger speeds up progress towards the development goals in other sectors. Hunger and undernutrition make it extremely difficult for poor people to improve their own livelihoods and to make any meaningful contribution towards sustainable and broad-based growth. The persistence of hunger is a direct challenge to the efforts to reduce child mortality, to improve educational attainment and to enable people to invest in their own futures.

The challenges in achieving food security are many: reducing poverty, increasing food production and accessibility without further degrading natural resources, and coping with population growth, rising prices and demands of urbanization. The challenge has to be met at two levels. The first is to achieve subsistence or basic food security which requires provision of the main dietary requirements to the people. Food security should safeguard the rights and interests of local communities, allowing each individual the basic human right to have access to food. Second, food security must contribute to sustainable agriculture, rural development and achievement of sustainable production and consumption.

Consensus is emerging among stakeholders around a common framework based on a twin-track strategy for poverty and hunger reduction. This includes carefully targeted safety nets and social programmes to protect the most vulnerable population groups from immediate threats, with measures aimed at enabling small-scale farmers to boost production in a sustainable way. This will require well-targeted investments and policy measures that increase small farmers' asset endowments, facilitate their access to inputs and markets, and improve their capacity to manage risks.

Food Security: The Recent Initiatives

For tackling this challenge to ensure food for all, currently the government has been implementing some major programmes such as the Public Distribution System (PDS), the Integrated Child Development Services (ICDS) Scheme and 100 day-employment guarantee system under the MGNREGA, Antyodaya Anna Yojana (AAY), etc. Apart from these four major programmes, the government is implementing the Mid-day Meal Scheme for ensuring food security for the school children in particular. But these programmes did not turn out as expected with allegations that the food grains sold in PDS are of sub-standard quality. With a view to enhance production of food grains to meet increasing demand on account of burgeoning population, National Food Security Mission (NFSM) was initiated, which is now operational in 467 districts of 17 states.[15]

Table 16 *The Major Food Security Initiatives in India*

Integrated Child Development Services (ICDS) Scheme

The Integrated Child Development Services (ICDS) Scheme was launched in 1975 as a Centrally Sponsored Scheme with the following objectives: (a) to improve the nutritional and health status of children below the age of six years and pregnant and lactating mothers, (b) to lay the foundation for the proper psychological, physical and social development of the child, (c) to reduce the incidents of mortality, morbidity, malnutrition and school dropouts, (d) to achieve effective coordination of policy and implementation among various departments to promote child development, (e) to enhance the capability of the mother to look after the health and nutritional needs of the child through proper health and nutrition education. The scheme provides for a package of services to children below six years and pregnant women and lactating mothers, comprising (i) Supplementary nutrition (ii) Immunization, (iii) Health check-ups, (iv) Nutrition and Health education, (v) Referrals and (vi) Pre-school, non-formal education. Launched in 1975, the programme has gradually increased from 33 projects to 7,073 projects in 2009, catering to about 87.3 million beneficiaries through a network of about 1 million Anganwadi centres.16

The Mid-Day Meal Scheme

The Mid-Day Meal Scheme was launched by the Ministry of Human Resource Development (Department of Education) with effect from 15 August 1995 for the benefit of students in primary schools under Employment Assurance Scheme (EAS)/earlier Revamped Public Distribution System (RPDS) blocks (2,368). The scheme covers students (Class I–V) in the Government Primary Schools/Primary Schools aided by the government and in the Primary Schools run by local bodies. Food grains (wheat and rice) are supplied free of cost @ 100 gram per child per school day where cooked/processed hot meal is being served with a minimum content of 300 calories and 8–12 g of protein each day of school for a minimum of 200 days and 3 kg per student per month for 9–11 months in a year, where food grains are distributed in raw form. In drought-affected areas, the mid-day meal is distributed in summer vacations also. Twelve crore children are so far covered under the Mid-day Meal Scheme, which is the largest school lunch programme in the world.

Targeted Public Distribution System (TPDS)

In order to ensure availability of minimum quantity of food grains to the families living below the poverty line, the government launched the TPDS in June 1997. It was intended to benefit about 6 crore poor families in the country for whom a quantum of 72 lakh tonnes of food grains was earmarked annually at the rate of 10 kg per family per month. The allocation was increased from 10 kg to 20 kg from 1 April 2000. This was increased from 20 to 25 kg per family per month from July 2001. From 1 April 2002, this allocation was further increased from 25 to 35 kg per family per month. The Central Issue Price (CIP) for BPL families is ₹ 4.15 per kg for wheat and ₹ 5.65 per kg for rice. The total offtake of food grains (wheat and rice) under Targeted Public Distribution System (TPDS) during April 2007 to March 2008 was about 33.5 lakh tonnes comprising 265.6 lakh tonnes of rice and 109.07 lakh tonnes of wheat.

Cont'd...

...Cont'd

Antyodaya Anna Yojana (AAY)

In order to make TPDS more focused and targeted towards the poorest section of population, the 'Antyodaya Anna Yojana' (AAY) was launched in December 2000 for one crore poor families. Initially AAY contemplated identification of one crore poorest of the poor families from among the BPL families covered under TPDS within the states and providing them food grains at a highly subsidized rate of ₹ 2 per kg for wheat and ₹ 3 per kg for rice. The states/UTs are required to bear the distribution cost, including margin to dealers and retailers as well as the transportation cost. Thus, the entire food subsidy is being passed on to the consumers under the scheme. The scale of issue that was initially 25 kg per family per month has been increased to 35 kg per family per month with effect from 1 April 2002. The AAY Scheme has been expanded in subsequent years and presently it is covering 2.5 crore households.

Annapurna Scheme

Article 41 of the Constitution of India directs the state to provide public assistance to its citizens in case of unemployment, old age, sickness and disablement and in other cases of undeserved want within the limit of its economic capacity and development. In accordance with the Directive Principles of State Policy, the Government of India introduced the National Social Assistance Programme (NSAP) in 1995 to lay foundation to a National Policy for Social Assistance for the poor. The NSAP aims at ensuring minimum national standard for social assistance in addition to the benefits that state are currently providing or might provide in future. At present NSAP comprise Indira Gandhi National Old Age Pension Scheme (IGNOAPS), National Family Benefit Scheme (NFBS) and Annapurna. Under IGNOAPS which was launched on 19 November 2007, ₹ 200 per month per beneficiary is provided by way of central assistance to all persons who are 65 years or higher and belonging to a family living below the poverty line. Earlier under National Old Age Pension Scheme (NOAPS), the pension was restricted to destitutes only. The number of beneficiaries under IGNOAPS is estimated to reach 160 lakh persons as compared to 87 lakh under NOAPS. Annapurna Scheme was introduced on 1 April 2000 to provide 10 kg of food grains per month free of cost to eligible beneficiaries who could not be covered under NOAPS.

National Food for Work Programme (NFFWP)

The scheme for National Food for Work Programme was launched with effect from 13 October 2004. This programme is being implemented in 150 most backward districts of the country so that the generation of supplementary wage employment and providing of food security through creation of need-based economic, social and community assets in these districts is further intensified. Most of the backward districts, which would benefit from the scheme are in the tribal belts. The scheme will provide 100 days of employment at minimum wages for at least one able-bodied person from each household in the country.

Cont'd...

...Cont'd

Mahatma Gandhi National Rural Employment Guarantee Act (MGNREGA)

Initiated in 2005, MGNREGA is the first ever international law that guarantees wage employment at an unprecedented scale. The primary objective of the act is augmenting wage employment. Its auxiliary objective is strengthening natural resource management through works that address causes of chronic poverty such as drought, deforestation and soil erosion and so encourage sustainable development. The process outcomes include strengthening grassroot processes of democracy and infusing transparency and accountability in governance. Implemented by the Ministry of Rural Development, Mahatma Gandhi National Rural Employment Guarantee Act (MGNREGA) is the flagship programme of the government that directly touches lives of the poor and promotes inclusive growth. The act aims at enhancing livelihood security of households in rural areas of the country by providing at least 100 days of guaranteed wage employment in a financial year to every household whose adult members volunteer to do unskilled manual work. Up to December 2009, 160 crore person days employment has been generated across the country.17

National Food Security Mission

Centrally Sponsored Scheme on National Food Security Mission has been launched in the country to enhance the production of rice, wheat and pulses by 10, 8 and 2 million tonnes respectively by the end of the Eleventh Plan. The mission covers 312 districts in 17 states and has become operational from Rabi 2007–2008. The focused and target-oriented technological intervention under NFSM has made a significant impact since inception which is reflected by the fact as per the third advance estimate of 2008–2009, the production of rice has raised to a level of 99.37 million tonnes, thus depicting increase of 2.68 million tones when compared to 2007–2008 and 6.02 million tonnes against 2006–2007. Similarly, the situation is also promising in case of wheat, wherein the production of wheat showing an increase of 2.76 million tonnes over the last year. Consequently, as per the third advance estimate of 2008–2009, the production of wheat is estimated to the level of 77.63 million tonnes which is 1.82 million tonnes more than 2006–2007. With regard to pulses, the production was recorded at 14.20 million tonnes during 2006–2007 Accordingly, as per the third advance estimate of 2008–2009 the production of pulses is estimated at 14.18 million tonnes, which is almost stagnated production trend when compared to 2006–2007.

Source: Based on Hazra (2012).

At the same time, an ambitious and revolutionary 'Food Security Bill' is being drafted by the newly set up National Advisory Council (NAC). In its recent meeting in the month of October in 2010, it has suggested that legal entitlements to subsidized food grains be extended to at least 75 per cent of the population — 90 per cent in rural areas and 50 per cent in urban areas. Further, the 'priority households' (46 per cent in rural areas and 28 per cent in urban areas) should be entitled to 35 kg (equivalent to 7 kg per person) every month at a subsidized price of Re 1 per kg for millets, ₹ 2 for wheat and ₹ 3 for rice, with rural coverage adjusted state-wise based on the Planning Commission's 2004–2005 poverty estimates. In its recent meeting held in the month of October, the NAC has also suggested that the 'general households' comprising of 44 per cent in rural areas and 22 per cent in urban areas should be entitled to get 20 kg (equivalent to 4 kg per person) every month at a price not exceeding 50 per cent of the existing Minimum Support Price (MSP) for millets, wheat and rice (Hazra, 2011).

Tackling the Threat of Food Crisis and Hunger

The immediate need in the current situation of food crisis is to prevent hunger and ensure that people have access to safe and nutritious food. It requires multi-sector actions that involve the health sector to address the health challenges associated with adequacy, quality and safety of food access. Cooperation and collaboration with other sectors should facilitate actions to address non-health issues associated with food crisis. Renewed attention to food and nutrition should prompt action for designing and implementing sound food and nutrition policies.

The desired goal of food security can be achieved only if a decentralized approach to implementation of the policies and programmes is adopted. Elected local bodies, together with the concerned departments of the government (health, education, women and child welfare, rural and tribal development, etc.), should prepare micro level action plans. They should form a local level 'alliance for a healthy and productive life for all'. The one million elected women members of local bodies can be empowered to spearhead the movement of freedom from hunger, since they are more aware of the problems of nutrition and drinking water. Decentralization will enhance accountability, reduce transaction costs and remove corruption in delivery systems.

There is an urgent need for enhancement of investment in agriculture and rural infrastructure development. It is also necessary to empower the small-scale food producers through cooperatives, self-help groups and other socially viable methods of group endeavour both at the production and post-harvest phases of farming.

A sustainable approach to food security in both the net food-importing and exporting developing countries is necessary in building endogenous agricultural food production capacity in order to meet the current and future food needs for domestic consumption and export. In pursuit of this development strategy, it is important to have an enlightened approach that includes short-term emergency relief to the immediate hunger situation and longer-term structural measure for building food security.

The neglect of agriculture has to be stopped and greater attention should be paid to financing agriculture for food security. A two-pronged channel can be considered — a rapid and comprehensive elimination of all trade-distorting subsidies and support measures in advanced countries on the one side, and aid for low-income net food importing countries on the other side. Increase in assistance for agriculture development in developing countries is urgently needed to support the development and implementation of agricultural policies, supporting institutions including agricultural development banks that provide rural financing for food production, undertaking programmes of agricultural research and development especially through support to local agricultural institutions in enhancing their research and disseminating them, promoting availability of real-time information on food supplies including commodities, and building infrastructure, especially transport and logistics networks for transporting food. Agricultural aid would also help poor and developing countries cope with the short and medium-term adjustment costs associated with the increase in their food import bill. This type of aid must come in the form of grants, easy subsidized loans that are really targeted at generating a future stream of income from agriculture.

At the international level, preparing a coordinated global response to global speculation in food prices is another urgent task. This should include measures to allow concerted government intervention in food markets if there is a strong indication that speculation is driving prices. Similarly, international coordination could help minimize the potentially dangerous implications of food hoarding and restrictions or bans on food exports. Producer-consumer cooperation plans and schemes, which promote integrated agricultural production for food and fuel, should also be looked anew.

Combating the food crisis will require more food aid for poor people; much more investments in agriculture, especially the small farm sector; more investment in social security schemes in social sectors such as education and health; reforms to create a fair world trading system; changes to bio-fuel policies; measures to calm global food markets; better data collection and improved monitoring of the food and nutrition situation; and more support for non-government organizations that work on behalf of poor people in developing countries.

Mass media, particularly those in the public sector, such as Doordarshan and All India Radio in India, can play a very important role in making the hunger-free India movement a success. Community radio stations, giving location-specific information, should be encouraged to assist other mass media in spreading messages of hope. It will be useful to set up media resource centres for hunger-free India. Priority could be given to employment of women in the most food-insecure districts. Identification of projects could be left to the gram panchayats. Monitoring of community work could be carried out by school teachers or anganwadi workers.

For ensuring nutrition security at the level of each individual, a life-cycle approach is necessary so that the nutrition needs of an individual can be met from birth to death. Special programmes for adolescent girls, pregnant women, nursing mothers, infants (0–2 years), and old and infirm persons should continue. What is needed is the horizontal integration of numerous vertically structured programmes. Such a functional integration will help synchronization at the level of each village/town/city to ensure that all links in the food availability-access-absorption chain function efficiently and effectively. In keeping with the basic approach, of food provision with human dignity, the scheme of Food for Work (FFW) seems to be the best existing vehicle of food delivery for the poor.

Effectiveness of the FFW programme could be ensured through two approaches. One is that of fine tuning, i.e., ensuring that FFW is made available during the peak hunger season, which varies across agro-climatic regions. The other major change required is to broaden the scope of the programme in order to ensure wider coverage, suitability to pregnant and lactating women, to help the old and weak and to help embark on achieving the stated nutrition targets in a mission mode.

The recent food crisis can be seen as a wake-up call which can be turned into an opportunity by developing countries to respond to, and for the international community to do more to rectify the systemic imbalances in global agricultural production and trade that have contributed over the years to today's problem. The crisis has highlighted inherent tensions that exist because the food sector is seen as being unlike any other.

Concluding Remarks

It is quite evident that the challenge of ensuring food security lies in the distribution of food and in making them affordable to the poor, not in food production. What makes the task of distribution more daunting is the fact that India has the responsibility of feeding 1.2 billion people. So, instead of insisting on improving the production, the government needs to improve the distribution of the food grain and at the same time should empower small-scale farmers rather than multinational corporations, to feed the population – as local food production drives food security. It will also reduce migration to urban slums by encouraging the development of community-based economies. By protecting farmers' land rights, incentivizing them to stay in business and encouraging consumers to source directly from the villages, the Indian government could reduce dependency on a public distribution system that is collapsing under its own weight; simultaneously, continued growth of agriculture is essential to meet the food and nutritional security requirements of the people and provide livelihood and income in rural areas. In order to tackle the root causes of hunger, governments should encourage increased investment in agriculture, expand safety nets and social assistance programmes and enhance income-generating activities for the rural and urban poor.

There is not a single day when we do not read or hear about the different dimensions of the food crisis, which India is witnessing for last few years. India promises to achieve the MDGs by 2015, but the promise seems futile when one looks at the latest Global Hunger Index (GHI) of 2010. Persistent inequalities, ineffective delivery of public services, weak accountability systems and gaps in the implementation of pro-poor policies are the major hurdles in the progress. It seems India will find it difficult to get on the tracks of attaining goals such as health, gender equality and environmental sustainability unless intensive national efforts are made by the government and all sections of civil-society working in tandem. The national media is also, by and large ignorant of the fact and cover articles only on food festivals and restaurants, ignoring the state of hunger. India may be the second fastest growing economy in the world, happens to be the world's largest producer of milk and edible oils and the second largest producer of wheat and sugar – but it fares far worse than lesser economies when it comes to taking care of its malnourished children. It is very interesting to note that most of the world's rich people hail from India and at the same time, most of the malnourished group of the world also belong to India. Food price inflation is one of the most critical economic problems in the country today, and the ability to control prices of food articles quickly and effectively is one of the main bases on which people will judge the performance of this government which is on the verge of giving its people the realization that eating is not a privilege but a basic human right, through the enactment of revolutionary and path-breaking 'Right to Food Act'.

We cannot blame anyone squarely for this current scenario of food crisis across the nation. Poverty, hunger, corruption, societal ills, etc., are all ills and form a part of one huge viscous cycle. Public discourse and action at the grass root level are the need of the hour. All these supported duly at both the state and central level will lead to the destruction of that viscous cycle. It is all about making the poor and hungry step on the economic ladder, momentarily forget about climbing it. Political will and good governance need to translate into specific reform steps. We must come forward and work together to help the impoverished people in our country because against the popular perception among slogans such as 'India Rising' and 'Incredible India', India's condition is not much better than that of the dark continent, Africa or specifically Sub-Saharan Africa as far as the scenario of hunger and food insecurity is concerned.

Keeping in view the country's current food stock and the rate of food grain production during the last few years, I would like to conclude that sustaining the current rate of food production if the government puts minute attention towards proper storage and distribution of available food grains and at the same time if it can ensure proper implementation of the existing food security initiatives in maintaining good governance in every sphere of service delivery system, then the government might not have to go for an exorbitant initiative like 'The Right to Food Act' for ensuring food for all.

Notes

1. FAO (2009).
2. FAO (2010).
3. Ibid.
4. UNICEF (2002).
5. FAO (2008a).
6. UNCTAD (2008a).
7. Ibid.
8. FAO (2008b).
9. Von Grebmer et al. (2010).
10. Ibid.
11. Ibid.
12. Menon et al. (2009).
13. Ibid.
14. Ibid.
15. Hazra (2011).
16. Ministry of Women and Child Development.
17. Government of India (2011).

References

FAO. (2008a). *Assessment of the World Food Security and Nutrition Situation*. Rome, Italy: FAO.

FAO. (2008b). *The State of Food Insecurity in the World*. Rome, Italy: FAO.

FAO. (2009). *The State of Food Insecurity in the World*. Rome: Food and Agriculture Organisation of the United Nations.

FAO. (2010). *The State of Food Insecurity in the World: Addressing Food Security in Protracted Crises*. Rome: Food and Agriculture Organisation of the United Nations.

Government of India. (2011). *SAARC Development Goals: India Country Report 2010*. Central Statistics Office. New Delhi: India

Hazra, A. (2011). Exploring the Starving India. *Kurukshetra*, Vol. 59 (5).

Hazra, A. (2012). Food Security in Rural India: Poverty in the Land of Plenty. *Kurukshetra,* Vol. 60 (5).

McHarry, J. et al. (2002). *Towards Global Food Security: Fighting against Hunger*. New York: UNEP (United Nations Environment Programme).

Menon, P. et al. (2009). *India State Hunger Index Report 2008*. Bonn, Washington, DC, and Riverside: International Food Policy Research Institute.

Ministry of Women and Child Development. Integrated Child Development Services. *Monthly Progress Report*. Retrieved from http://wcd.nic.in/icdsimg/sanoprAWCs300909.pdf and http://wcd.nic.in/icdsimg/mpr2009.pdf (accessed November 27, 2009).

UNCTAD (United Nations Conference on Trade and Development). (2008a). *Addressing the Global Food Crisis: Key Trade, Investment and Commodity Policies in Ensuring Sustainable Food Security and Alleviating Poverty*. Rome, Italy: United Nations.

UNCTAD. (2008b). *Tackling the Global Food Crisis*. Rome, Italy: United Nations.

UNICEF (United Nations Children's Fund). (2002). *The State of the World's Children*. New York; UNICEF.

Von Grebmer, K. et al. (2010). *2010 Global Hunger Index: The Challenge of Hunger: Focus on the Crisis of Child Under Nutrition*. Bonn,

Washington, DC, and Dublin: Deutsche Welthungerhilfe, International Food Policy Research Institute, and Concern.

WFP (World Food Programme). (2009). *WFP India Fact Sheet*. Rome, Italy: WFP.

WFP/MSSRF. (2008). *Report on the State of Food Insecurity in Rural India*. New Delhi, India: World Food Program/M S Swaminathan Research Foundation.

4 The Challenge of Educating India

The Task Ahead

As a basic right, education is an intrinsic good in itself, leading to broadened individual capacities and freedoms. The importance of education can hardly be over emphasized since a large gamut of social issues and reforms are linked with it. Education in its broadest sense of development is the most critical input for empowering people with skills and knowledge. It plays a major role in improving economic opportunities for people and enhancing their quality of life by building capabilities, enhancing skill levels and providing more productive employment. So, it is also associated with a host of positive development outcomes – interacting in this way with other factors to contribute to the achievement of Millennium Development Goals (MDGs) (Table 17). The importance of education can hardly be over emphasized since a large gamut of social issues and reforms are linked with it. Evidences show that the reduction of fertility, morbidity and mortality rates, the empowerment of women, the improvement in the quality of the working population and the promotion of genuine democracy are largely assisted by progress in education.

Table 17 *Education and the Millennium Development Goals*

Goal 1: Eradicate extreme poverty and hunger	Education equips people with the knowledge and skills they need to increase income and expand employment opportunities. Greater equity in education can help fuel a virtuous cycle of increased growth and accelerated poverty reduction, with benefits for the poor and for society as a whole. When education is broadly shared and reaches the poor, women and marginalized groups, it holds out the prospect that economic growth will be broadly shared. On the other hand, poverty pushes children out of school and into work because parents cannot afford to educate their children.

Cont'd...

...Cont'd

Goal 2: Achieve universal primary education	Universal primary education involves entering school at an appropriate age, progressing through the system and completing a full cycle. Many governments are neglecting the 'education poor' – those on the fringes of society, ranging from indigenous populations to street children, from the disabled to linguistic and cultural minorities. New approaches must be tailor-made for such groups – simply increasing opportunities for standard schooling is not enough. Unless we reach the children who are being left behind, the goal of education for all children will not be reached.
Goal 3: Promote gender equality and empower women	No other policy intervention is likely to have a more positive multiplier effect on progress across all the MDGs than the education of women and girls. Evidence shows a strong correlation between educating women and girls and an increase in women's earnings, improved child and family health and nutrition, an increase in school enrolment, protection against HIV infection, higher maternal and child life expectancy, reduced fertility rates and delayed marriage.
Goal 4: Reduce child mortality	Educating a girl greatly reduces the chance that her child will die before the age of five. In many countries, having a mother with secondary or higher education more than halves the risk of child mortality compared to having a mother with no education. Having a mother with primary education reduces child death rates by almost half in the Philippines and around one third in Bolivia. Having a mother who had completed primary education reduces the risk of stunting by 22 per cent in Bangladesh and 26 per cent in Indonesia.
Goal 5: Improve maternal health	Maternal education is one of the strongest antidotes to childbearing-related risks. Educating girls and women empowers them to make better health-related decisions. Complications in pregnancy and childbirth are a leading cause of death and disability among women of childbearing age, claiming over 500,000 lives a year. Girls who are educated are more likely to seek antenatal care.
Goal 6: Combat HIV and AIDS, malaria and other diseases	Education can impart knowledge and skills and encourage positive attitudes and behaviour that will reduce a person's chance of getting HIV. Educational institutions take a central role in HIV prevention efforts because they are the best way to reach large numbers of young people. Similarly, school health, awareness and hygiene programmes help to combat malaria and other diseases. Education has been recognized by United Nations Programme on HIV/AIDS (UNAIDS) to be a key element of effective HIV prevention. Even in the absence of HIV-specific interventions, education offers an important measure of protection against HIV. The Global Campaign for Education has estimated that universal primary education would prevent 700,000 new HIV infections each

Cont'd...

...Cont'd

	year. Education reduces the vulnerability of girls, and each year of schooling offers greater protective benefits.
Goal 7: Ensure environmental sustainability	Education helps individuals to make decisions that meet the needs of the present without compromising those of future generations. Education for Sustainable Development (ESD) addresses key issues such as poverty reduction, sustainable livelihoods, climate change, gender equality, corporate social responsibility and protection of indigenous cultures. ESD can help us to live sustainably. It aims to change the way we think, behave, look at the world, interact with nature and address social, economic and environmental problems. Governments are realizing this: according to a recent survey, 79 countries now have a national ESD coordination body.
Goal 8: Develop a global partnership for development	Aid for basic education in the world's poorest countries came to only US$2.7 billion in 2007, a far cry from the $US16 billion needed annually to reach education-related development goals. Developing countries can also do more – by making education a priority. If low-income countries spent 0.7 per cent of their GDP on education, it could make about US$7 billion available per year for basic education.

Source: Author's articulation based on UNESCO (2010).

Education in its broadest sense of development is the most critical input for empowering people with skills and knowledge. It plays a major role in improving economic opportunities for people and enhancing their quality of life by building capabilities, enhancing skill levels and providing more productive employment. The India school system follows the British structure. Primary school consists of grades I–V (age group 6–11 years) and middle school consists of grades VI–VIII (age group 11–14 years). A policy of automatic promotion has been introduced at the elementary stages to encourage children to continue their education to at least grade VIII, while minimizing repetition and dropout. The scenario of educational progress in India has began to change towards positive direction due to the new thrusts given by the government's new National Policy of Education (1986) and the Programme of Action (1992), which aimed at improving access, reducing dropouts and improving learning achievements for all children between 6 and 14 years of age (Table 18).

Table 18 *State of Education in India: The Current Scenario*

- The enrolment in primary classes (I–V) was 97.4 million in 1990–1991, which rose to 113.8 million in 2000–2001 and further to 135.5 million in 2007–2008. The enrolment in middle/upper primary classes (Class VI–VIII) was 34.0 million in 1990–1991, which increased to 42.8 million in 2000–2001 and then to 57.2 million in 2007–2008.
- The Gross Enrolment Ratio (GER) at the primary level was 83.8 in 1990–1991 and it increased to 95.7 in 2000–2001 and to 113.97 in 2007–2008. For the middle/upper primary level, the GER was 66.7 in 1990–1991 which declined to 58.6 in 2000–2001 and then gradually increased to 78.1 in 2007–2008.
- The Net Enrolment Rate (NER) for primary grade, which is the proportion of students of official school age of 6–10 years enrolled in Grades I–V to the population of children of age group 6–10 years, is the indicator for primary enrolment. NER figures are available from District Information System for Education (DISE). As per DISE 2009–2010, there has been a 13.75 per cent increase in national NER between 2005–2006 and 2009–2010: from 84.53 per cent in 2005–2006 to 98.28 per cent in 2009–2010.
- Gender Parity Index (GPI) in enrolment at primary and secondary levels is the ratio of the number of female students enrolled at primary and secondary levels in public and private schools to the number of male students. A GPI of 1 indicates parity between the sexes or no gender disparity. A GPI that varies between 0 and 1 typically means a disparity in favour of males, whereas a GPI greater than 1 indicates a disparity in favour of females. The female-male ratio in education has been steadily improving over the years. In primary education, the GPI has gone up from 0.76 in 1990–1991 to 0.94 in 2006–2007 and in secondary education the increase is from 0.60 in 1990–1991 to 0.82 in 2006–2007.
- About 14 per cent of population in the age-group 5–29 years had not entered the education system at all, while another 34 per cent were found to have been enrolled at some time but currently not attending any educational institution. In rural areas, the proportion of never enrolled was 15.8 per cent, while in urban areas it was much lower – 8 per cent. Again, about 18 per cent of females and 10 per cent of males of age 5–29 years were never enrolled.
- The three most frequently given reasons for non-enrolment were (a) parents not interested in education of their children (33.2%), (b) financial constraints (21%) and (c) education not considered necessary (21.8%). For urban males, 'financial constraints' was most commonly given as the reason for non-enrolment (37.7%), while for both urban females and rural males, 'financial constraints' was the second most commonly reported reason. Among rural females, only 16.2 per cent reported that they did not enrol for financial reasons. For all population categories except urban males, 'parents not interested' was the most common reason.
- More than 90 per cent of rural and urban households had a school with primary classes within 1 km in 2007–2008. However, only 61.6 per cent of rural households, compared to 82.5 per cent of urban households, had a school within a kilometre providing middle-level classes.

Cont'd...

...Cont'd

- The net enrolment rate at primary level was 84.53 per cent in 2005–2006 which increased to 98.28 per cent in 2009–2010.
- The dropout rate at the elementary level (Class I–VIII) was 59.1 per cent in 1990–1991 which came down to 43.7 per cent in 2007–2008.
- The survival rate at primary level up to Grade V was 67 per cent in 2004–2005 which has gradually increased to 70 per cent in 2005–2006, 73 per cent in 2006–2007, 76 per cent in 2008–2009 and 76 per cent in 2009–2010. It was 72 per cent in 2007–2008.
- The adult (age 15 and above) literacy rate in India was 48.2 per cent in 1991 which increased to 61 per cent in 2001 and further to 66 per cent in 2007–2008.
- The number of teachers in primary schools was 16.16 lakh (11.43 lakh men and 4.73 lakh women) in 1990–1991 which rose to 21.84 lakh (13.26 lakh men and 8.58 lakh women) in 2005–2006 and further to 23.15 lakh (12.88 lakh men and 10.27 lakh women) in 2007–2008.
- The percentage of trained teachers in primary schools was 86 in 2005–2006 and it increased to 90 in 2007–2008. It was 87 per cent for upper primary schools in 2005–2006 and rose to 91 per cent in 2007–2008. The percentage of trained teachers in high schools was 89 in 2005–2006 and it remained 89 in 2007–2008. For senior secondary schools, the percentage of trained teachers was 90 in 2005–2006 and it rose by 3 percentage points to 93 in 2007–2008.
- The pupil (student) teacher ratio was 43 for primary schools, 37 for upper primary schools and 31 for secondary/senior secondary schools in 1990–1991. This ratio stood at 46, 34 and 33 in 2005–2006 and 47, 35 and 35 in 2007–2008 for primary schools, upper primary schools and secondary/senior secondary schools respectively.
- The percentage of schools (all schools) having girls' toilet was 50.55 per cent in 2007–2008, 53.60 per cent in 2008–2009 and 58.82 per cent in 2009–2010. The schools with functional girls' toilet were 74.64 per cent in 2009–2010.

Source: Government of India (2011).

In Indian context, education is the joint responsibility of the central and state governments. India's commitment to the spread of knowledge and freedom of thought among its citizens is reflected in its Constitution. In 1950, India made a constitutional commitment to provide free and compulsory education to all children up to the age of 14 and the constitutional amendment of 2002 made free and compulsory education a fundamental right for children aged 6–14. Article 29 (i) provides that any citizen having a distinct language, script, special care of the economic and educational interests of the underprivileged sections, particularly, the SCs and STs is laid down as an obligation of the state under

Article 46. The Directive Principles contained in Article 45 enjoin 'the State shall endeavour to provide within a period of ten years from the commencement of this Constitution, for free and compulsory education for all children until they complete the age of fourteen years'. The role of education in facilitating social and economic progress is well accepted. Access to education is critical for benefiting from emerging opportunities that are accompanied by economic growth. Keeping in view of this accepted fact there has been a major thrust on education since independence (Table 19). India viewed education as the best way of bringing social change. Soon after gaining independence in 1947, making education available to all had become a priority for the government.

Table 19 *A Glimpse of Major Initiatives towards Educating India since Independence*

1948	The First Education Commission was constituted chaired by Dr S. Radhakrishnan and also known as the Radhakrishnan Commission. This commission stressed on autonomous status of universities and pointed out 'democracy depends for its very life on high standard of general, vocational and professional education'.
1956	As an outcome of the recommendations of Radhakrishnan Commission, the University Grants Commission was established in 1956.
1960	Sergeant Commission recommended night schools for primary education, technical education at certificate level in every district, stressing that teachers should be local, and the distance of the school should be minimal.
1964	Second Education Commission known as the Kothari Commission was appointed in July 1964 to establish well-designed, balanced, integrated and adequate system of national education capable of making the powerful contribution to national life. The commission emphasized on expansion of higher education, enhancing quality of higher education and research and use of dynamic techniques for management and organization.
1968	Based on the recommendations of the Kothari Commission, the National Policy on Education (NPE) was adopted, which led to the considerable expansion of education facilities all over the country. In rural habitations, schooling facilities were developed within a radius of 1 km but these did not get translated into detailed structure of implementation.
1975	Integrated Child Development Services (ICDS) Scheme was launched to provide for holistic development of children up to the age of 6 by making provision for their free pre-school training and education.
1976	42nd Constitutional Amendment to change education from being a state subject to concurrent.

Cont'd...

...Cont'd

1986	The National Policy on Education was adopted again in response to the non-implementation of 1968 educational policy, which emphasized on elimination of disparities, equal access to every Indian of requisite merit, enhancement in support to research and inter-disciplinary research promotion.
1987	Operation Blackboard was launched and aimed at improving the school environment and enhancing retention and learning achievement of children by providing minimum essential facilities such as large rooms that are usable in all weather conditions, necessary toys and games material, blackboards, maps, charts and other learning material in all primary schools.
1988	The National Literacy Mission, set up in May 1988, aims to attain a sustainable threshold level of 75 per cent literacy by 2007 by imparting functional literacy to non-literates in the age group of 15–35 years, which is the productive and reproductive age group and constitutes a major segment of the work force. Apart from predetermined levels of reading, writing and numeracy with comprehension, functional literacy includes imbibing values of national integration, conservation of environment, women's equality, observance of small family norms, etc.
1990	The Ramamurthy Committee was appointed to review the National Policy on Education, which laid emphasis on the quality of higher as well as technical education and its relevance to the needs of society and industry.
1992	Revised NPE and Programme of Action (POA) were adopted based on recommendation of Acharya Ramamurti Commission and aimed at improving access to education, reducing dropouts and improving learning achievements for all children between 6 and 14 years of age. It provided major emphasis on inclusive education, especially education of tribal children. Accordingly Lok Jumbish project was launched in Rajasthan with an aim of spreading inclusive education and encouraging participation of village communities to ensure quality education for each child.
1993	73rd and 74th Constitutional Amendments laid down responsibility on local self-government bodies or panchayats for the overall development of local area, incorporating the issue education.
1994	The Government of India launched the District Primary Education Programme (DPEP), a centrally sponsored scheme funded by the World Bank and other foreign agencies, which emphasized on Universalization of Elementary Education through developmental management, a participatory process, and capacity building at all levels with the objectives: • To provide all children with access to primary education either in the formal system or through non-formal education (NFE) programme. • To reduce differences in enrolment, dropout rates and learning achievement among gender and social groups to less than 5 per cent. • To reduce overall dropout rates for all students at primary school to less than 10 per cent

Cont'd...

...Cont'd

	• To raise average achievement levels by at least 25 per cent over measured base line levels and ensuring achievements of basic literacy and numeric competencies and a minimum of 40 per cent achievement levels in other competencies by all primary school children.
1995	National Programme for Nutritional Support to Primary Education (1995), presently well-known as Mid-Day Meal scheme, was initiated with central assistance with an aim to provide boost to the universalization of primary education by increasing enrolment, retention and attendance and simultaneously giving an impetus to the nutritional status of students in primary classes, making provision of cooked meal daily for children of Class I–V of all government, government-aided and local body schools. In some cases, grain was distributed on a monthly basis, subject to a minimum attendance.
1997	Saikia Commission recommended that a primary school should be established within a distance of 1 to 1.5 km from every catchment of 250 households and an upper primary school within 3 km of every catchment of 500 households. It also recommended that the school timing should fit with work, and there should be hostels in districts to support those children who would not otherwise reach the schools.
2000	Revised National Curriculum Framework formulated laying new direction to educational issues.
2001	Sarva Siksha Abhiyan (SSA) launched – aims to provide effective and quality elementary education to all children in the age group 6 –14 by 2010 with a special priority on girls, SC/ST children and children with special needs.
2002	Right to Education was incorporated in the constitution under Article 21A, which was included in the 86th Amendment (of 2002), making 'provision for free and compulsory education to all children of the age 6–14 years, which is a fundamental right.
2005	National Plan of Action for Children was formulated.
2006	National Commission for Protection of Child Rights was set up under the Commission for Protection of Child Rights Act, 2005. Sachar Committee Report tabled, highlighting low levels of education among Muslims in India.
2008	SSA II, i.e., Rashtriya Madhyamik Shiksha Abhiyan launched – extension to secondary education. The Rights of Children for free and compulsory Education Bill (2008) tabled in Parliament, as a step towards eventual notification of the Constitutional Amendment.
2009	The Right of Children for Free and Compulsory Education Act or The Right to Education Act (RTE) has been enacted to ensure free education to more than 92 lakh out of school children aged 6–14 in India.

Source: Based on Hazra (2012).

The National Policy on Education, which was introduced in 1986, envisages that the basic learning needs of every person, child, youth and adult should be met through a variety of delivery systems, there is no trade-off between quantity and quality, achievement of minimum levels of learning are as important as participation, the traditional forms of primary education do not actually deliver, supply of services should be matched by generation of demand, and only by returning education to the community and by partnership between the government, civil society and stakeholders can basic education needs be met satisfactorily. The policy paved the way for enhanced support to the state governments for school improvement, in service teacher training and non-formal education. It took a serious note of the conditions related to basic facilities and other support systems in the country. It emphasized on elimination of disparities in the education system and on improvement in the quality of publicly funded schools so that irrespective of the socio-economic background every child has access to basic education of a comparable quality. This policy also focused on the need for improvements to school environments including building conditions, availability of tap water and toilet facilities, instructional material and teacher training.

For educating its entire population since independence, India has adopted a comprehensive approach which includes opening of a primary school/alternate schooling facility within 1 km of every habitation, provision of free textbooks to all SCs/STs children and girls at the primary and upper primary school, management and repair of school buildings through school management committees, provision of opportunities for non-formal and alternative education for out of school children in the most backward areas and for unreached segments of the population in response to local needs and demands articulated at the grassroot level. Steps would have to be initiated to fill up all the existing vacancies of the teachers through a time-bound manner, with defined responsibility to local bodies and communities, and to remove legal impediments in the recruitment of para-teachers. India, being one of the very promising developing country which has near a quarter of the world's population, did not wait for the MDGs to improve its education attainments, especially its primary education. Indeed, since the new National Policy of Education, set in 1986 by the government, one can observe a constant and increasing mobilization of resources and a regular flow of initiatives both aiming at improving the features of (primary) education within the country; one could cite, among the most important initiatives, the

Non-formal Education Scheme (1986), the Shiksha Karmi Project (1987), the District Primary Education Programme (1994), the Mid-Day Meal Scheme (2001) and the Sarva Shiksha Abhiyan (2001) which aimed at completion of eight years of schooling by all children between 6 and 14 years old, by 2010 (Table 20). Furthermore, one can note that elementary education has been made a fundamental right by the 83rd Constitutional Amendment.

Table 20 *Major Schemes and Programmes Promoting Education in India*

Sarva Shiksha Abhiyan (SSA)

As a national flagship programme, Sarva Shiksha Abhiyan (SSA) was launched in 2001 and currently under operation in all districts of the country with an aim to provide useful and relevant elementary education for all children in the age group of 6–14 by 2010. The goals of SSA include: (i) All 6–14 age children in school/EGS (Education Guarantee Scheme) centre/Bridge Course by 2005. (ii) Bridge all gender and social category gaps at primary stage by 2007 and at elementary education level by 2010. (iii) Universal retention by 2010. (iv) Focus on elementary education of satisfactory quality with emphasis on education for life. SSA, which has been a major flagship programme of the present UPA government, addresses the needs of 195 million children in the age group of 6–14 years. Another recent development is the proposal to tag on early childhood education to the SSA programme (The Economic Times, 3 September, 2007).

Education Guarantee Scheme (EGS) and Alternative and Innovative Education (AIE)

As one of the core component of Sarva Shiksha Abhiyan (SSA), Education Guarantee Scheme and Alternative and Innovative Education (EGS and AIE) was initiated to bring out-of-school children in the fold of Elementary Education. The scheme ensures that child-wise planning is undertaken for each out-of-school children and targets the inaccessible habitation where there is no formal school within the radius of 1 km and at least 15–25 children of 6–14 years age group who are not going to school are available. Alternative Education interventions has been designed for the most deprived children, e.g., child labour, street children, migrating children, working children, children living in difficult circumstances. Special focus has also been given to cover adolescent girls under EGS and AIE centres.

Mid-Day Meal Scheme

With the aim of enhancing enrolment, retention and attendance and simultaneously improving nutritional levels among children, the National Programme of Nutritional Support to Primary Education (NP-NSPE), now familiar as 'Mid-Day Meal' was launched as a Centrally Sponsored Scheme on 15 August 1995, initially in 2408 blocks, which is now covering all the blocks of the country, catering to the nutritional needs of children at primary level of government, government aided and local body schools, as well as of the children studying in EGS and AIE centres. Central Assistance under the scheme consisted of free supply of food grains @ 100 grams per child per school day, and subsidy for transportation of food grains up to a maximum of ₹ 50 per quintal. The objectives of the mid-day meal scheme are:

Cont'd...

...Cont'd

(i) Improving the nutritional status of children in Classes I–V in government, local body and government-aided schools, and EGS and AIE centres. (ii) Encouraging poor children, belonging to disadvantaged sections, to attend school more regularly and help them concentrate on classroom activities. (iii) Providing nutritional support to children of primary stage in drought affected areas during summer vacation. About 12 crore children studying at the primary stage in over 9.50 lakh government and government-aided schools including EGS and AIE Centres are being covered under the Mid-Day Meal Programme. The norms under the scheme have been revised in September 2006 to upgrade the nutrition norms. In the year 2007–2008, provision has been made in the Union Budget to extend the scheme to the upper primary level in educationally backward blocks in the country (Department of Elementary Education and Literacy). In addition to the recurring assistance, funds for construction of 94,500 kitchen sheds and kitchen devices for 2.60 lakh schools have been sanctioned in 2006–2007. It is proposed to extend the programme to upper primary stage in 3247 Educationally Backward Blocks (EBB) from 2007–2008.

Jan Shikshan Sansthan

The objective of the Jan Shikshan Sansthan (JSS) is educational, vocational and occupational development of the socio-economically backward and educationally disadvantaged groups of urban/rural population particularly neo-literates, semi-literates, SCs, STs, women and girls, slum dwellers, migrant workers, etc. At present, there are 172 JSSs in the country. Jan Shikshan Sansthans run a number of vocational programmes with varying duration of different skills. More than 250 types of courses and activities are offered by these institutions.

District Primary Education Programme

District Primary Education Programme (DPEP) was launched in 1994 as a Centrally Sponsored Scheme. The ultimate aim was to revitalise the primary education system and to achieve the objective of universalization of primary education. Presently DPEP is in operation in nine states covering 123 districts. DPEP at its peak was operational in 273 districts in 18 states. However, with the progressive closure of the programme, it now exists only in 123 districts.

Mahila Samakhya Scheme

With an aim to translate the goals enshrined in the NPE into a concrete programme for the education and empowerment of women in rural areas particularly those from socially and economically marginalized groups, the Mahila Samakhya Scheme was introduced in 1989, acknowledging the core essence of education in empowering women as well as in establishing gender equality. The Mahila Sanghas through various programmes and awareness campaigns have brought about a change in the outlook of rural women and the effects can now be seen in various facets of life at home within the family, the community and at the block and panchayat levels. The programme has also focused on awareness of the need to educate the children, especially girls, to give the equal status and opportunities which has resulted in a direct impact on enrolment and retention of girls in schools. The Mahila Samakhya Scheme is currently being implemented in nine states, viz., Andhra Pradesh, Assam, Bihar, Jharkhand, Karnataka, Kerala, Gujarat, Uttar Pradesh and Uttarakhand, spread over 83 districts and covering more than 21,000 villages.

Cont'd...

...Cont'd

Prarambhik Shiksha Kosh (PSK)

A two per cent Education Cess was levied on all major Central taxes through the Finance (No. 2) Act, 2004, to help finance government's commitment to quality basic education. In order to receive the proceeds of this Education Cess, the creation of a dedicated, non-lapsable fund called Prarambhik Shiksha Kosh (PSK) in the Public Account was approved by government in October 2005. The fund available in the PSK is being utilized exclusively for Sarva Shiksha Abhiyan (SSA) and National Programme for Nutritional Support of Primary Education (MDM Scheme). The levy of education cess is a concrete step towards providing assured funding for elementary education.

National Programme for Education of Girls at Elementary Level (NPEGEL)

As one of the integral part of Sarva Shiksha Abhiyan (SSA), NPEGEL provides additional components for education of girls from less privileged section of the society at the elementary level. The scheme is being implemented in Educationally Backward Blocks (EBBs) where the level of rural female literacy is less than the national average and the gender gap exists above the national average, as well as in blocks of districts that have at least 5 per cent SC/ST population and where SC/ST female literacy is below 10 per cent based on 1991 census.

Kasturba Gandhi Balika Vidyalaya

Under the scheme of Kasturba Gandhi Balika Vidyalaya, 750 residential schools are being set up in difficult areas with boarding facilities at elementary level for girls belonging predominantly to the SCs, STs, OBCs and minorities.

This scheme has been exclusively designed for those identified Educationally Backward Blocks (EBBs) where the rural female literacy is below the national average and gender gap in literacy is more than the national average, as per census data 2001.

Source: Based on Publication Division (2010) and Department of Elementary Education and Literacy (2007).

A host of major initiatives taken by the government, and the mobilization of external resources for primary education, had a deep impact on the status of primary education in India. The Government of India, as part of its constitutional commitment, has initiated a number of programmes to achieve the goal of universalization of elementary education in a time-bound manner. Some of the major initiatives have been the Operation Blackboard (1986), Non-formal Education Scheme (1986), the Shiksha Karmi Project (1987), Mahila Samakya (1989), Lok Jumbish (1992), the District Primary Education Programme (1994), the Mid-Day Meal Scheme (1995) and the Sarva Shiksha Abhiyan (2001) and the most recently introduced the Right of Children to Free and Compulsory

Education Act or the Right to Education Act (RTE), which has come into force from 1 April 2010 ensuring free education to more than 92 lakh out of school children aged 6–14 in India.[1] Village education committees, parent-teacher and mother-teacher associations have become active across the country. Legislative moves to bring elementary education under Panchayati Raj Institutions (PRIs or local self-governments) have given further impetus to community mobilization at the grassroots level. Besides these, with an aim to expand educational access, several Acts have been enacted by different states of India, which is reflective form the following table (Table 21):

Table 21 *Major Education Acts Initiated by Different States of India*

States	*Title of Act and Year Enacted*
Andhra Pradesh	The Andhra Pradesh Education Act, 1982
Assam	The Assam Elementary Education Act, 1974
Delhi	Delhi Primary Education Act, 1960
Himachal Pradesh	The Himachal Pradesh Compulsory Primary Education Act, 1997
Jammu & Kashmir	The Jammu and Kashmir School Education Act, 2002
Karnataka	The Karnataka Education Act, 1983
Kerala	Kerala Education Act, 1958
Madhya Pradesh	Madhya Pradesh Jan Shiksha Adhiniyam, 2002
Maharashtra	Bombay Primary Education Act, 1947
Meghalaya	Meghalaya School Education Act, 1981
Puducherry	Pondicherry School Education Act, 1987
Punjab	Punjab Primary Education Act, 1960
Rajasthan	The Rajasthan Primary Education Act, 1964
Sikkim	Sikkim Primary Education Act, 2000
Tamil Nadu	The Tamil Nadu Compulsory Primary Education Act, 1994
West Bengal	The West Bengal Primary Education Act, 1973

The District Primary Education Programme (1994) brought additional resources to the sector through the involvement of bilateral and multilateral donors. The Alternative, Innovative and Education Guarantee Scheme (EGS/AIE) provides education in smaller, isolated habitations in rural areas and/or urban slums that do not qualify as regular formal schools; and schooling to difficult-to-reach groups such as working and migrating children. The National Programme for Education of Girls at Elementary Level (NPEGEL) and Kasturba Gandhi Balika Vidyalaya (KGBV) target girls often from SCs, STs and minorities in difficult areas. Through these programmes, scholarships, free uniforms and textbooks are being given to recipients. The Mid-Day Meal Scheme offers free lunch to all children attending primary schools and EGS/AS throughout India. Anganwadis provide nutritional support and pre-school education to children aged 0–6 years and early childhood care and education (ECCE) centres are operational in some selected areas. These initiatives have had considerable impact on children's access to education resulting into rapid increase in the overall enrolment at the primary, upper primary, secondary and senior secondary levels since the time of independence, which is very much reflective from Table 22.

Table 22 *Enrolment by Stages from 1950–1951 to 2005–2006 (in millions)*

Year	*Primary (I–V)*			*Middle/Upper Primary (VI–VIII)*			*High/Hr. Sec/Inter/ Pre-Degree (IX–XII)*		
	Boys	*Girls*	*Total*	*Boys*	*Girls*	*Total*	*Boys*	*Girls*	*Total*
1950–1951	13.8	5.4	19.2	2.6	0.5	3.1	1.3	0.2	1.5
1955–1956	17.1	7.5	24.6	3.8	1.0	4.8	2.2	0.4	2.6
1960–1961	23.6	11.4	35.0	5.1	1.6	6.7	2.7	0.7	3.4
1965–1966	32.2	18.3	50.5	7.7	2.8	10.5	4.4	1.3	5.7
1970–1971	35.7	21.3	57.0	9.4	3.9	13.3	5.7	1.9	7.6
1975–1976	40.6	25.0	65.6	11.0	5.0	16.0	6.5	2.4	8.9
1980–1981	45.3	28.5	73.8	13.9	6.8	20.7	7.6	3.4	11.0
1985–1986	52.2	35.2	87.4	17.7	9.6	27.1	11.5	5.0	16.5
1990–1991	57.0	40.4	97.4	21.5	12.53	4.0	12.8	6.3	19.1
1991–1992	58.6	42.3	100.9	22.0	13.63	5.6	13.5	6.9	20.4
1992–1993	57.9	41.7	99.6	21.2	12.93	4.1	13.6	6.9	20.5
1993–1994	55.1	41.9	97.0	20.6	13.53	4.1	13.2	7.5	20.7
1994–1995	60.0	45.1	105.1	22.1	14.33	6.4	14.2	7.9	22.1
1995–1996	60.9	46.2	107.1	22.7	14.83	7.5	14.6	8.3	22.9

Cont'd...

...Cont'd

1996–1997	61.4	46.8	108.2	22.9	15.23	8.1	15.3	8.7	24.0
1997–1998	62.3	48.0	110.3	23.6	15.93	9.5	16.1	9.3	25.4
1998–1999	62.7	48.2	110.9	24.0	16.34	0.3	17.3	10.5	27.8
1999–2000	64.1	49.5	113.6	25.1	17.04	2.1	17.2	11.0	28.2
2000–2001	64.0	49.8	113.8	25.3	17.54	2.8	16.9	10.7	27.6
2001–2002	63.6	50.3	113.9	26.1	18.74	4.8	18.4	12.1	30.5
2005–2006	70.4	61.5	132	28.8	23.35	2.1	22.2	16	38.3

Source: Department of Education (2008).

There has also been considerable increase in the spread of educational institutions since India gained its independence in 1947. For instance, during the period 1950–1951 and 2001–2002, the number of primary schools grew threefold, while the number middle (upper primary) schools increased 16 times. Today India has more than six hundred thousand primary schools serving 115 million students with an average teacher to student ratio of 1: 43 and more than 2 million upper primary schools serving 45 million students with an average teacher to student ratio of 1:38. Another recent trend is the growth of private schools that receive no government aid and rely on student fees (Cheney et al., 2006). Rapid growth is quite evident in the context of physical access to education with new schools being constructed on scale as 103,106 primary schools, 68,170 upper primary schools and 63,696 secondary schools were built during 1990–2001.[2] This is partly due to the pledge of the Saikia Commission (1997). Another factor for access improvement is the scaling up of the Mid-Day Meal Scheme (1995) with a provision of 300 calories and 8–12 grams of protein to all children studying in classes 1–5 in government and aided schools, EGS/AIE centres.[3] In addition to the grains, the subsidy is given for transportation of food grains and assistance for cooking. Further, there is provision for MDM during summer vacations in drought affected areas.

State of Education in Rural India: A Threat to India's Millennium Commitments

The issue of educating rural India is still in need of attention as it imposes a major threat for India in achieving its Millennium

Commitments. In 1951, only 12.1 per cent of rural population and 4.87 per cent of females in India were literate. In 2001, rural literacy rate increased to 59.4 per cent (71.4% for males and 46.7% for females). During 1991–2001, the increase in female literacy rate (16.1 percentage points) in rural area was relatively more compared to that of the male (13.5 percentage points). In 1991, the gaps in the male-female literacy rate in rural and urban areas were 27.3 and 17.1 percentage points respectively, which came down to 24.7 and 13.5 percentage points in 2001. In 1991, rural-urban gap in literacy rate was 28.4 percentage points, which decreased to 20.9 percentage points in 2001. But still more than two-fifth of the rural population was illiterate in 2001. As per the recent report of the National Sample Survey Organization (NSSO), literacy in India is increasing at a sluggish rate of 1.5 per cent per year. But the positive trend is that 'as compared to 2004–2005, the literacy rate increased by 2 per cent for the rural populace and 1 per cent in urban areas during 2005–2006', says the report. It says there were 656 literate men out of 1,000 in India's villages in 2005–2006, compared to 636 in 2004–2005. During that year, the number of literate village women went up from 450 to 467 per 1,000. Educating all the rural people is a huge challenge, and much is still to be done considering the number of out-of-school children living in rural areas (Hazra, 2010).

Table 23 *Progress of Rural Education in India at a Glance*

- 96.5 per cent of children in the 6 to 14 age group in rural India are enrolled in school
- 71.1 per cent of these children are enrolled in government schools, 24.3 per cent are enrolled in private schools.
- The proportion of girls (age 11–14) who are still out of school has declined from 6.8 per cent in 2009 to 5.9 per cent in 2010; in states such as Rajasthan (12.1%) and Uttar Pradesh (9.7%), this percentage remains high and shows little change since 2009.
- Enrolment in private schools in rural India increased from 21.8 per cent in 2009 to 24.3 per cent in 2010.
- Nationally, the percentage of 5 year olds enrolled in schools increased from 54.6 per cent in 2009 to 62.8 per cent in 2010. The biggest increase was visible in Karnataka where the proportion of 5 year olds enrolled in school increased from 17.1 per cent in 2009 to 67.6 per cent in 2010.

Cont'd...

...Cont'd

- Nationally there is not much change in reading levels as compared to last year. Only 53.4 per cent children in Standard V can read a Standard II level text. This suggests that even after five years in school, close to half of all children are not even at the level expected of them after two years in school.
- On average, there has been a decrease in children's ability to do simple mathematics. The proportion of Standard I children who could recognize numbers from 1–9 declined from 69.3 per cent in 2009 to 65.8 per cent in 2010. Similarly, the proportion of children in Standard III who could solve two digit subtraction problems decreased from 39 per cent to 36.5 per cent in the same period. Children in Standard V who could do simple division problems also dropped from 38 per cent in 2009 to 35.9 per cent in 2010.
- Annual Status of Education Report (ASER) 2010 found that over 60 per cent of the 13,000 schools surveyed satisfied the infrastructure norms specified by the RTE. However, more than half of these schools will need more teachers. A third will need more classrooms.
- For rural India as a whole, children's attendance shows no change over the period 2007– 2010. Attendance remained at around 73 per cent during this period.

Source: Pratham (2011).

Of the biggest victims of the country's educational system are those living in rural areas. Though for encouraging the growth of rural education, from making policies to introducing laws – our government has lined up the education system up to the mark but implementing the process into an effective way has been the lacunae of the entire system. Still issues of equity, quality and access remain areas of concern particularly in the sphere of rural education in India. Children in rural areas continue to be deprived of quality education owing to factors such as lack of competent and committed teachers, lack of textbooks or teaching-learning materials, and so on. A large number of teachers refuse to teach in rural areas and those who are usually underqualified. The much publicized mid-day meal scheme meant to reduce dropout rates in schools seems to be not yielding the desired results due to misappropriation of funds meant for the scheme, mismanagement, lack of seriousness among the implementing authorities, diversion of funds, lack of awareness among the parents of poor children, etc. The food served under the Mid-Day Meal Scheme in rural schools is also of inferior quality. Besides that, the Public Report on Basic Education reflects that physical infrastructure of rural schools is far behind the satisfactory level, with 82 per cent of the schools is in need of renovation. Books are often unavailable, and teacher absenteeism tends to be high.[4]

But these emerging issues which are jeopardizing the progress of rural education are being addressed and there are positive signs that the emphasis on major government programmes such as the *Sarva Shiksha Abhiyan* (SSA) is shifting its focus from universal enrolment to universal retention and quality. There is also increasing attention being given to the governance of schools with the formation and functioning of village education committees (VEC) and more transparent processes for managing school resources. In recent years, it has also been noticed that the Panchayati Raj or village council has been playing an increasingly significant role in the progress of education in rural areas across the country. On the other hand, in the last few years, the number of qualified teachers in rural schools has increased because of the augmented efforts by the government and private groups towards improving the country's overall educational status as well as towards upgrading and ensuring professional training of school teachers. The next most pressing challenge is to boost the access in rural areas to secondary education, particularly for girls, SCs, STs and minorities as well as to ensure availability of technical and vocational education and skills. At this level of the education system, the private sector is growing rapidly and playing an imperative role of service provider.

Over the last decade there have been enormous improvements in the education sector but as far as ensuring quality education in rural India is concerned, it has always been one of the biggest challenges for the government. Issues such as high dropout rates, low levels of learning achievement and low participation of girls as well as factors such as inadequate school infrastructure, high teacher absenteeism, large-scale teacher vacancies, poor quality of education, poorly functioning schools and inadequate equipment still remain the matter of concern in rural literacy scenario. Apart from household income/wealth, caste and gender continue to determine access to education. The poor, girls, and members of SCs and STs still face formidable barriers in acquiring basic education. It has been widely acknowledge that the socio-economic conditions in rural India have constrained the process of primary education and the social inequalities of caste, class and gender have been identified as the major causes of educational deprivation among children in India. To quote Jean Dreze, 'educational disparities, which contribute a great deal to the persistence of massive inequalities in Indian society, also largely derive from more fundamental inequalities such as those of class, caste and gender'.[5]

A large proportion of children from the economically poor and socially disadvantaged groups and girls, especially in rural areas, are either denied access or failing to complete even five years of basic education. However, in recent years, the situation has improved for female schooling, especially in the younger age groups, but the discrepancies between rural and urban areas continue to be large and the educational situation of SCs and STs lags considerably behind the rest of the population. Weak teacher motivations and their apathy towards teaching and high teacher truancy plague the educational system. Teacher availability in rural areas continues to be low. Teachers posted to rural and remote areas usually apply for transfers and in general their willingness to be posted in such areas is rather low. This leads to severe imbalances in the distribution of school resources between rural and urban areas and adds to the low teacher-pupil ratios which is generally observed within the school system.

Table 24 *Primary Education in Rural India: Some Major Issues of Concern*

- The quality of education provided by rural primary schools
- High-dropout rates especially among girls
- Despite efforts to incorporate all sections of the population into the Indian education system, through mechanisms such as positive discrimination and non-formal education, large numbers of young people are still without schooling.
- Frequent absenteeism and irregularity of school teachers since several of them do not stay in the same village as the school.
- Parents' apathy and indifference towards education do not provide enough motivation for their children to attend school.
- Inadequate school infrastructure. Basic infrastructural components like school building and child friendly classroom, blackboard, teaching learning materials, toilet especially for girls and water facilities, etc., are not available.
- Insufficient and inadequate number of classrooms per school to accommodate all the standards in different rooms and hence system of having multiple standards in the same room at the same time.

Cont'd...

...Cont'd

- Prevalence of several single teacher schools.
- Generally teachers refuse to teach in rural areas and those who are usually under-qualified.
- Innumerable non-teaching activities thrust on school teachers that divert their attention.
- Lack of punctuality and regularity in teaching the students.
- Lack of proper sanitation facilities in schools discouraging, especially, adolescent girls from attending schools.

All these issues adversely affect the quality of education provided by rural primary schools and severely discourage pupils from attending. As far as the progress in rural literacy is concerned, initiative such as provision of mid-day meals in primary school has increased enrolment, attendance and retention, especially of girls. Moreover, it helps in taking care of nutritional needs of the students. This not only affects positively the health of poor students but also improves learning outcomes by ending 'school hunger'. On the other hand, the SSA, initiated to universalize quality education, has brought about positive changes by increasing accountability of schools to the community through greater involvement of village education committees and parent-teacher associations. An important step in this regard is the estimation of the required scaling up effort in the rural areas of the country to increase provisioning of physical infrastructural facilities and ensuring adequate manpower supply and thereby improving the effective access of the poor to the primary education services ultimately leading to achievement of the MDGs.

Education for Every Child: An Integrated Approach is Needed

The goal of universal primary education remains a challenge to achieve even after six decades of independence. Universalization of elementary education, thus, poses a formidable challenge to India: the numbers of children dropping out, not attending school regularly and never enrolled are immense. Quality of education is poor, and teachers are inadequately trained and have lack of motivation. The priority concerns for the country remain particularly with improving the quality of education and making education effective, enjoyable and relevant to the children. Also, a major concern is to improve the skills and motivation of teachers, promoting the participation of communities in the running of schools and enrolling/retaining girls/working children of urban poor and children with special needs in schools. Also, in India, a large universe of working children exists such as the street children, neglected and destitute children, children of sex workers and children practising as sex workers. Many of these have been targeted through non-formal initiatives but never mainstreamed. Also, along with access and retention, the quality of education provided to them is questionable. Quality is what makes education valuable. The latest ASER report made it clear that substantial improvements are needed to address critical inadequacies in learning – a vital aspect of educational quality.[6] Yet quality is also key to retention, as poor levels of learning are well known to push children out of school.[7]

As far as social access to education is concerned, there is often discrimination against Dalits and occasionally against Indigenous people and Muslims in schools that push them out. Children (13.4 million) in the age group 6–14 still remain out of school and most of them are from the marginalized communities.[8] Factors outside the school – such as low levels of parental education, malnutrition and gender stereotyping – put many children at a disadvantage even before they step into the classroom. The most disadvantaged children are often concentrated in government schools, especially in more remote rural areas and in urban slums. These inequalities must be consciously tackled through a commitment to quality education for all. A concern for quality in education should therefore be matched by a commitment to its equitable, and free, distribution. Schools must develop the most disadvantaged children's ability to learn and achieve it in spite of the obstacles that they face.

With spectacular growth in higher education, India is becoming a genuine knowledge society and knowledge economy and aiming to be global superpower. But, as far as the issue of educational progress at primary level is concerned, there are serious gaps between different classes or groups of the society, different regions of the country, which is quite alarming. The issues which still remain the cause of concerns and need attention are dropout rate in rural primary schools (up to 10th standard), gender disparity in educational progress, low levels of learning and achievement, urban-rural divide in educational growth, inadequate school infrastructure, poorly functioning schools, high teacher absenteeism, the large number of teacher vacancies, poor quality of education regional imbalance, poor-rich divide, inadequate fund allocation to rural primary schools and social divide. Apart from these educational obstacles, the groups of children 'at risk', such as orphans, child labourers, street children and victims of riots and natural disasters, do not necessarily have access to schools.

India has been successful in launching SSA, combined with mid-day meal, which is an excellent decision by the national government. The observation is that the school attendance is definitely improved, but in many of the places, the attendance is between 12 noon and 1 pm, which is mid-day meal time. Rest of the time, the students disappear from the scene or teachers are not available, which effectively produces chronological growth of the students, but not academic. As per teaching-learning process is concerned, there is a gross deficit. It is observed when these students complete their fourth standard and go to middle school, they hardly have capacity to read or write, which is a serious lapse. This needs evaluation and remedial measures particularly in tribal, rural and urban poor zones (Dongaonkar, 2006). The impacts of massive interventions such as SSA, Mid-Day Meal Scheme and the para-teacher (or of their sub-components) on children's school attendance and learning outcomes have not been rigorously evaluated. This is necessary if decision-makers are to hone future education policy making in light of knowledge about the cost-effectiveness of alternative interventions. Moreover, radical measures to improve teacher and school incentives have not been considered in India, perhaps because they stand to upset powerful vested interest. While the existence of fiscally demanding education initiatives and the introduction of the 2 per cent education cess to fund them testifies the Indian government's increased commitment to school education and gives grounds for optimism about the future, serious challenges remain (Kingdon, 2007).

All the strategies, adopted by India for educating its entire population, can be put into place if it is boosted by a strong political will of the country and the linkages of the education system with the community, the functioning of the institutions and other stake-holders is strengthened. With the policy largely taking into account the needs of the disadvantaged groups and the girls, India seems to be pretty strong on the political will. Considering the community readiness for education, its participation/mobilization is not a problem. With the powers now being transferred to the PRIs, their participation will be attained in a much stronger way. Mere establishment of schools and hiring of teachers will not lead to an improvement in education if teachers remain absent as happens in many parts of the country, especially in rural areas. The participation of the local bodies (panchayats/local bodies), will therefore, help to monitor schools in a much better way.

Ensuring that every child has access to quality and convenient learning environments throughout his or her childhood necessitates action far beyond the ministries of education. The right to education can only be realized in a political and economic environment that acknowledges the importance of transparent, participatory and accountable processes, as well as broad-based collaboration both across government and in the wider society. It needs a long-term strategic commitment to the provision of adequate resources, development of cross departmental structures, engagement with the energies and capacities of parents and local communities, and partnership with non-governmental organizations. Education should promote the child's all-round development. Within the Indian context, community ownership of education is also an essential component and quality education must be realized in a way that is consistent with the Right to Education Act, 2009.

The education policy should shift its focus from enrolment to improvement in the functioning of schools as well as towards raising the quality of education outcomes. Special strategies are needed to improve the outreach of the school system to the disadvantaged and marginalized groups in the country. A more systematic school mapping exercise should be undertaken to provide these groups access to both lower and upper primary classes, for removing social barriers to education. Shared public space should be created in education to allow private schools to co-exist with government schools in the delivery of education. Further, there is a need for standardization of schools, with the mechanical provisioning of core inputs and a well-developed pedagogy. Long-term goals are required to bridge the gender gap, which constitutes a key hurdle in achieving literacy in the country, along with measures to ensure universalization of elementary education among girls. Allocation to the education sector should be raised from the existing figure of about 4 per cent to the targeted figure of 6 per cent of the GNP. Simultaneously, there must be an improvement in the targeting of the investment to address state-level disparities and social inequities. There is a need to plug the gaps in teaching inputs. For this, a well-designed programme of recruitment, retention and deployment of teachers needs to be put into place in each state to ensure a high level of teaching quality and also to clear the backlog of vacancies at all levels. The issue of child labour, which is estimated at a whopping figure of 12 million children, should be tackled at the earliest, as without it, there can be no improvement in child participation in schools. The implementation and monitoring of this strategy should be done at the state level, for which respective governments should create additional supervisory structures and mobilize financial and human resources (Institute for Human Development, 2010).

A rights-based approach to education places the primary responsibility for ensuring good quality education on the state, so consideration needs to be given to whether it has the capacity – in terms of managerial, human and financial resources – to analyse, organize and provide all the inputs necessary to make meaningful education a reality for those who are left out of the system. Education requires substantive, not just symbolic action. Merely passing laws, without sustained political attention that plugs yawning financial and administrative gaps in the school sector, is going to fail. Schools must make provision for the inclusion of socially disadvantaged groups, especially in contexts where casteism and other forms of discrimination are rife. The wider community needs to be encouraged to include these groups within the education process. Differently abled children should be allowed to flourish in mainstream schools through flexibility in curriculum and pedagogy, awareness-raising and myth-busting where necessary. Right to Education Act, 2009 is a key tool for inclusion and needs to be used accordingly. The education system must be flexible and inclusive to accommodate the urgent needs of the most 'at risk' children such as orphans, child labourers, street children and victims of natural disasters. Additional learning support must be provided to students forced to miss school due to environmental, social and political conditions. Though the state has the primary obligation to provide education for all children but non-governmental organizations and other civil society partners make a vital contribution to education in many countries by mobilizing public demand and expanding participation. So, the government needs to build effective partnerships with all key organizations and institutions that have an impact on the children's education. Collaboration, for example, is needed with non-governmental organizations, Gram Panchayats, teachers' union, the private sector, traditional leaders and religious groups to enlist their support and expertise in building capacity to ensure the right of education for all children in India.

Conclusion

India has the second largest education system in the world after China. The scale of operation involved to ensure quality of Education for All in the country is unique and challenging. At the same time, the nature of problems affecting the education system are so diverse and often deep rooted that the solution cannot lie in the alteration of any one single factor – it is not just about shortage of money or just shortage of trained teachers or lack of political will; all these undeniably contribute to the problems, affecting the country's existing education system. However, there is a need to look at the entire set of problems and deal with the issue holistically taking into consideration the specific context of different sections of the society. It will also require a constant and strong central support for policy, strategy, technical assistance, and monitoring and evaluation combined with increased decentralization within government, stronger public–private partnerships, and improved accountability relationships between the service providers, policy makers and the target population. To conclude, it can be said that in the context of globalization, education assumes greater meaning. Greatness of a nation should not be measured by its ranking in global economic order, but by its ability to provide quality education.

Notes

1. Hazra (2010).
2. ActionAid (2007).
3. Ibid.
4. PROBE Team and Centre for Development Economics (1999).
5. Dreze (2003).
6. Pratham (2011).
7. PROBE Team and Centre for Development Economics (1999).
8. Action Aid (2007).

References

ActionAid. (2007). *Education Strategic Plan 2008–2010*. New Delhi, India: ActionAid.

Cheney, G. et al. (2006). *A Profile of the Indian Education System*. Washington, DC: National Centre on Education and the Economy.

Department of Education. (2008). *Selected Educational Statistics 2005–2006*. New Delhi, India: Ministry of Human Resource Development, Government of India.

Department of Elementary Education and Literacy. (2007). *Annual Report 2005–06*. New Delhi, India: Ministry of Human Resource Development, Government of India.

Dongaonkar, D. (2006). *Missing Links in Education System in India*. New Delhi, India: Association of Indian Universities.

Dreze, J. (2003). "Pattern of Literacy and their Social Context" in Das V. et al. (eds.). *The Oxford India Companion of Sociology and Social Anthropology*, Vol. II. New Delhi, India: Oxford University Press.

Government of India. (2011). *SAARC Development Goals: India Country Report 2010*. New Delhi, India: Central Statistics Office.

Hazra, A. (2010). Rural Literacy in India: The Changing Scenario. Kurukshetra, Vol. 58 (11).

Hazra, A. (2012). The Challenge of Promoting Education in Rural India: Realities and Constraints. Social Welfare, Vol. 59 (6).

Institute for Human Development. (2010). *Human Development in India: Emerging Issues and Policy Perspectives – A Consultation Report*. New Delhi, India: Institute for Human Development.

Kingdon, G.G. (2007). *The Progress of School Education in India*. UK: Economic and Social Research Council.

Pratham. (2011). *Annual Status of Education Report 2010*. Mumbai, India: Pratham.

PROBE Team and Centre for Development Economics. (1999). *Public Report on Basic Education in India*. New Delhi, India: Oxford University Press.

Publication Division. (2010). *India 2010: A Reference Manual*. New Delhi, India: Ministry of Information and Broad Casting, Government of India.

The Economic Times, September 3, 2007.

UNESCO. (2010). *EFA (Education for All) Global Monitoring Report 2010*. Reaching the Marginalized. Paris, France: UNESCO.

5 Empowering Women in India

An Unfinished Agenda

Current framework of international development recognizes women empowerment as an immense effective stratagem for the all round development of the society. Development is one of the highest relevance in the world where the achievement of sustained and equitable development remains the greatest challenge that faces mankind today. The empowerment of women is a contemporary issue regardless of the country in which a social planner tries to bring a sustainable development. Though women empowerment is not a sufficient condition but it is being regarded as a necessary condition in order to stabilize and in turn to have sustainability of the development process. In the current context development, empowerment is now increasingly being regarded as a process by which the one's without power gain greater control over their lives. This means control over material assets, intellectual resources and ideology. It involves power to, power with and power within. Some define empowerment as a process of awareness and conscientization of capacity building leading to greater participation, effective decision-making power and control leading to transformative action.

The World Bank's *Empowerment and Poverty Reduction: A Sourcebook* defines empowerment in its broadest sense as the 'expansion of freedom of choice and action'. Although this applies to women as well as to other disadvantaged or socially marginally groups, it is necessary to understand that women's empowerment includes some additional elements. The concept of women empowerment signifies that women are not just one group among various disempowered subsets of society such as the poor, ethnic minorities and so on; they are a cross-cutting category of individuals that overlaps with all these other groups. Second, household and interfamilial relationships form the basis of women's disempowerment in a way that is not true for other disadvantaged groups. This means that efforts at empowering women must take note of the household-level implications for broader policy action. Third, it can be argued that while empowerment in general requires institutional transformation, women's empowerment requires systemic transformation not just of any institutions, but specifically of those supporting patriarchal structures (Narayan, 2002). Kabeer[1] defines empowerment as 'the expansion in people's ability to make strategic life choices in a context where this ability was previously denied to them'. For her, empowerment is inescapably bound with the condition of disempowerment and refers to the processes by which those who have been denied the ability to make choices acquire such ability. In other words, empowerment entails a process of change and women themselves must become agents of that change if empowerment has to take place. So, empowering women implies enhancing women's ability to do, their capability to accomplish tasks, their command over events and their ability to exercise influence. In essence, it is power that stems from new knowledge and skills acquired, action taken and inner strength gained from educational experiences.

The Concept of 'Women Empowerment'

The concept of women's empowerment emerged from debates generated by the women's movement during the 1980s when feminists, particularly from Third World countries, evinced dissatisfaction with the prevailing development discourse that was largely apolitical and econometric in its orientation. Ultimately, the concept of women empowerment was introduced at the International Women's Conference at Nairobi in 1985, which incorporated five components: (1) women's sense of self-worth; (2) their right to have and to determine choices; (3) their right to have access to opportunities and resources; (4) their right to have the power to control their own lives, both within and outside the home; and (5) their ability to influence the direction of social change to create a more just social and economic order, nationally and internationally.[2] During the same period, popular women's movements in Latin America and the Caribbean as well as feminist movements have seen

Table 25 *A Model Exploring the Dynamics of Women Empowerment from Multidimensional Perspectives*

Dimension	*In a Family*	*In a Society/Community*	*In a State/Nation level*
Economic	Women's control over income; relative contribution to family support; access to and control of family resources	Women's access to employment; ownership of assets and land; access to credit; involvement and/or representation in local trade associations; access to markets	Women's representation in high paying jobs; women CEOs; representation of women's economic interests in macro-economic policies, state and federal budgets
Socio-cultural	Women's freedom of movement; lack of discrimination against daughters; commitment to educating daughters	Women's visibility in and access to social spaces; access to modern transportation; participation in extra-familial groups and social networks; shift in patriarchal norms (such as son preference); symbolic representation of the female in myth and ritual	Women's literacy and access to a broad range of educational options; positive media images of women, their roles and contributions
Familial/inter-personal	Participation in domestic decision making; control over sexual relations; ability to make childbearing decisions, use of contraception, access to abortion; control over spouse selection and marriage timing; freedom from domestic violence	Shifts in marriage and kinship systems indicating greater value and autonomy for women (e.g., later marriages, self-selection of spouses, reduction in the practice of dowry; acceptability of divorce); local campaigns against domestic violence	Regional/national trends in timing of marriage, options for divorce; political, legal, religious support for (or lack of active opposition to) such shifts; systems providing easy access to contraception, safe abortion, reproductive health services

Cont'd...

...Cont'd

Legal	Knowledge of legal rights; domestic support for exercising rights	Community mobilization for rights; campaigns for rights awareness; effective local enforcement of legal rights	Laws supporting women's rights, access to resources and options; advocacy for rights and legislation; use of judicial system to redress rights violations
Political	Knowledge of political system and means of access to it; domestic support for political engagement; exercising the right to vote	Women's involvement or mobilization in the local political system/campaigns; support for specific candidates or legislation; representation in local bodies of government	Women's representation in regional and national bodies of government; strength as a voting bloc; representation of women's interests in effective lobbies and interest groups
Psychological	Self-esteem; self-efficacy; psychological well-being	Collective awareness of injustice, potential of mobilization	Women's sense of inclusion and entitlement; systemic acceptance of women's entitlement and inclusion

Source: Hazra (2011).

the notion of empowerment as being tied, on the one hand, to the seizing of power, by emphasising mainly the improvement of self-esteem and self-confidence as well as the ability to chose what direction one's life should take; and on the other to the collective power to change gender relations in the economic, political, legal and socio-cultural spheres. Feminists, particularly those from Latin American and South Asian countries, evolved their own approach, emphasizing the importance of consciousness raising, leading to organizing and building a movement for women's equality. According to this thinking, empowerment was a socio-political process that required shifts in political, social and economic power between and across both individuals and social groups. So the mid-1980s saw the emergence and spread of 'women's empowerment' as a more political and transformatory concept that challenged not only patriarchy but also the mediating structures of class, race, ethnicity and, in the case of India, caste and religion. Later it was noticed that by the beginning of 1990s, the term 'empowerment' had entered the development discourse and was widely used by the development experts as well as by the development agencies – multilateral as well as bilateral – to replace the earlier terminology of 'women welfare' and 'women's development'.

Women Empowerment: A Key to the Millennium Commitments

Since the early 1990s, women have been identified as key agents of sustainable development, and women's equality and empowerment are seen as central to a more holistic approach towards establishing new patterns and processes of development that are sustainable. The Fourth World Conference on Women in Beijing (1995) and the Beijing Platform for Action have provided new impetus for governments and civil society organizations to address women empowerment and gender inequalities in society at all levels. It recognized that without the active participation of women and the incorporation of women's perspectives at all levels of decision-making process, the goals of equality, development and peace for women and men cannot be achieved. The World Bank has suggested that empowerment of women should be a key aspect of all social development programmes. Societies that discriminate on the basis of gender have greater poverty, slower economic growth, weaker governance and a lower standard of living. Women's empowerment, lies at the heart of development and the achievement of the Millennium Development Goals (MDGs).[3]

Table 26 *Women Empowerment and the Millennium Development Goals*

Goal 1. Eradicate extreme poverty and hunger	Need-based capacity building and a better access to livelihood opportunities for women will provide a major boost to family income, accelerating country's economic growth and ensuring a stronger platform for poverty eradication for the nation.
	Equal investment in women's health and nutritional status reduces chronic hunger and malnourishment, which increases productivity and well-being.
Goal 2. Achieve universal primary education	Educated girls and women have greater control over their fertility and participate more in public life.
	A mother's education is a strong and consistent determinant of her children's school enrolment and attainment and their health and nutrition outcomes.
Goal 3. Promote gender equality and empower women	Women's empowerment which ultimately leads to gender equality lies at the heart of sustainable development and the achievement of the Millennium Development Goals. Though women empowerment is not a sufficient condition but it is still a necessary condition in order to stabilize and in turn to have sustainability of the development process.
Goal 4. Reduce child mortality	Research-based evidences proved that a mother's education, income and empowerment have a significant impact on lowering child mortality.
Goal 5. Improve maternal health	Studies revealed that a mother's education, income and empowerment have a significant impact on lowering maternal mortality.
Goal 6. Combat HIV/AIDS, malaria and other diseases	Greater economic independence for women, increased ability to negotiate safe sex, greater awareness of the need to alter traditional norms around sexual relations, better access to treatment and support for the care function that women perform are essential for halting and reversing the spread of HIV/AIDS and other epidemics.
Goal 7. Ensure environmental sustainability	Women are often regarded as primary users of environmental resources and if they are educated and empowered enough, then they can manage the environmental resources in a more sustainable manner in comparison to men
Goal 8. Develop a global partnership for development	Greater space in the political sphere for women may lead to higher investments in development cooperation.

Source: Author's articulation based on Grown et al. (2005).

Current Status of Indian Women: A Reality Check

Despite numerous global commitments affirming women's rights, women are still much more likely than men to be poor, malnourished and illiterate. They usually have less access than men to medical care, property ownership, credit, training and employment. They are far less likely than men to be politically active and far more likely to be victims of domestic violence. As far as the global scenario is concerned, only around 16 per cent of the world's parliamentarians are women, two-thirds of all children who are denied schooling are girls and, both in times of armed conflict and behind closed doors at home, women are still systematically subjected to violence. Around 70 per cent of the world's poorest people, living on less than one dollar a day, are women. Under such circumstances, projects aimed at improving the living conditions of the poor cannot, therefore, be effective unless women participate in their formulation and implementation, as contributors as well as beneficiaries. The poorest women in developing countries are among those most affected by climate change due to its impact on agriculture, food security and water management which are traditionally women's tasks. Diseases associated with dirty water kill between 5 and 12 million people a year, mostly women and children.

Table 27 *Progress of Women Empowerment in India at a Glance*

- The sex ratio (number of female per 1000 male) at birth in India was 880 (rural 882, urban 872) during 2003–2005 which increased to 892 (rural 895, urban 881) during 2004–2006 and further to 904 (rural 907, urban 894) during 2006–2008.
- The life expectance of women in India is more than that for men. It was 60.9 years in 1991–1995 for women compared with 59.7 years for men and rose to 64.2 years in 2002–2006 for women as against 62.6 years for men in the same year.
- Gender Parity Index (GPI) in enrolment at primary and secondary levels is the ratio of the number of female students enrolled at primary and secondary levels in public and private schools to the number of male students. A GPI of 1 indicates parity between the sexes or no gender disparity. A GPI that varies between 0 and 1 typically means a disparity in favour of males, whereas a GPI greater than 1 indicates a disparity in favour of females. The female-male ratio in education has been steadily improving over the years. In primary education, the GPI has gone up from 0.76 in 1990–1991 to 0.94 in 2006–2007 and in secondary education the increase is from 0.60 in 1990–1991 to 0.82 in 2006–2007.
- The Worker Participation Rate for women was 25.63 per cent in 2001. This is an improvement from 22.27 per cent in 1991 and 19.67 per cent in 1981.

Cont'd...

...Cont'd

- Women workers constituted 19.5 per cent of the total organized sector employment in the country in March 2007 which shows an increase by 0.5 per cent as compared to the preceding year.
- The mean age at marriage for women was 19.5 years in 1992 which marginally increased to 19.9 years in 2001 and to 20.7 years in 2008.
- The percentage of women parliamentarians was 9.7 in 1991 and it is 10.3 per cent in 2009.
- Of the 28 lakh elected panchayat representatives, around 10 lakh are estimated to be women. The average of women representation in panchayats across the country is 36.94 per cent.
- The proportion of women in the total Central Government employment shows an increasing trend. It was 10.28 per cent in 2006 against 9.68 per cent in 2004 and 7.53 per cent in 2001.
- Allocations for women as reflected in the Gender Budget Statement shows gradual increase in the number of Central Government Ministries coming out separately with such statement as also the increasing trend in the allocations for women.
- The Age-Specific Fertility Rates (ASFR) in India show a declining trend across all age groups. The ASFR for the women in the age-group 15–19 years was 51.1 in 2000 which has come down to 41.6 in 2008. Similarly, ASFR for the women in the age-group 20–24 years was 218.7 in 2000 which has come down to 200.1 in 2008.
- The MMR has come down from 398 per 1,00,000 live births in 1997–1998 to 254 per 1,00,000 live births in 2004–2006, a 36 per cent decline over a span of seven years as compared to a 25 per cent decline in the preceding eight years from 1990–1997.
- At the all-India level, the coverage of institutional deliveries increased rather slowly: from 26.1 per cent in 1992–1993 to 33.6 per cent in 1998–1999 and then to 41 per cent in 2005–2006 and 47 per cent in 2007–2008.
- The proportion of births attended by skilled personnel has increased from 33 per cent in 1992–1993 to 47 per cent in 2005–2006 and to 52 per cent in 2007–2008.

Source: Government of India (2011).

The Global Gender Gap Index (GGGI), introduced by the World Economic Forum (WEF) in 2006, is a framework for capturing the magnitude and scope of gender-based disparities and tracking their progress. GGGI examines the gap between men and women in four fundamental categories: economic participation and opportunity, educational attainment, health and survival and political empowerment. World Economic Forum in its latest GGGI for the year 2010 ranked India in the bottom half among 134 countries, placing it in the 112th position in terms of gender equality.[4] As per the report, India performed very poorly on the economic, education and health sub-indexes; the overall scores are partially bolstered by relatively good performances in the sphere of political empowerment of women. India ranked 128th in terms of economic participation and opportunity, 120th in educational attainment, 132nd in health and survival and 23rd in terms of political empowerment.[5] India figures among 25 countries in the world where the gender gap is the widest and stands sixth in economic inequality between men and women, according to the WEF.[6]

Contemporary Indian society has been exposed to the broad processes of social transformation, agricultural modernization and economic development, urbanization and globalization. However, these processes have generated regional imbalances, sharpened class inequalities and augmented the gender disparities. Hence, women have become critical symbols of these growing imbalances. All these have affected adversely the various aspects of women's empowerment in the contemporary Indian society. In India, women are nearly 50 per cent of the total population but their representation in public life is very low. Woman continues to bear the major load of the household work. Her primary role is often viewed by the society as housewife. The plight of women in India ranges from domestic disparity to societal oppression. In most of the areas in India, a strong cultural bias favours sons over daughters. Female children frequently suffer neglect in terms of health care and education. Studies reveal that boys received health care more often than girls, and the average amount spent on treatment was also significantly higher for boys. India likewise has the largest population of non-school-going working girls. In recent years, there has been an alarming rise in atrocities against women in India. A woman is raped every 34 minutes and in every 93 minutes, a woman is burnt to death over dowry.[7] It is found that 35 per cent of the total number of girls and women trafficked to India were abducted under the pretext of false marriage or good jobs. West Bengal, Uttar Pradesh, Uttaranchal and Bihar are the main transit states of India, as they share their border with Bangladesh or Nepal. India is both a destination and transit area for trafficking of women and children.[8] A woman in India dies delivering a baby every five minutes, a maternal mortality rate of 534 per 1,00,000 deaths. This translates to more than 1,00,000 Indian women who die each year from pregnancy-related causes. Studies found that 37 per cent of all pregnant women in India received no prenatal care during their pregnancies.[9] The gender gap in educational involvement though reduced over the years, but in India it is still a matter of great concern as reflected in one of the recent Human Development Report of South Asia which has stated that one of the discrimination that girls and women are facing in India is the fact that they are not able to enjoy the right to education. More than half of the adult illiterates 63 per cent are women and nearly two-fifth girls enrolled in primary schools are dropouts before grade 5.[10] Subordination of women in society acts a structural constraint to their participation in political activities. This constraint operates more or less for all classes and communities of women. Prevalent culture which is very complicated and often decisions are taken behind the scene may be regarded as another constraint in this regard. Recognizing women's rights and believing their ability are essential for women's empowerment and development. Females should realize their own capabilities and potentials which will strengthen their self-image and foster them with confidence to take action in life. Political empowerment does not imply just a right to role silently but to discuss, share and empower politics by knowing its pros and cons and thereby to influence policies and decision making.

Welfare Measures for Women in India

Over the past three decades, women's empowerment has been increasingly recognized as a crucial factor for any country's holistic and sustainable development. Several programmes and projects across the world have been launched and are currently in progress to bring social, economic and political equity and broader access to basic livelihood needs. To bring women into the mainstream and to encourage their participation in the process of national development has, therefore, been a major concern of the government. Since independence, the Government of India has always attached great importance to the protection and promotion of the human rights of women and has been committed towards achieving it. Within the framework of a democratic polity, India's laws, development policies, plan and programmes have aimed at women's advancement in difference spheres. The Constitution of India is firmly grounded in the principles of liberty, fraternity, equality and justice. It contains a number of provisions for the empowerment of women (Table 28). Women's right to equality and non-discrimination are defined as justiciable fundamental rights. The Constitution explicitly clarifies that affirmative action programmes for women are not incompatible with the principle of non-discrimination on the grounds of sex. Drawing the strength from the constitutional commitments, the Government of India has been engaged in the continuous endeavour of concretely translating all the rights, commitments and safe guards incorporated in the Indian Constitution for women.

Table 28 *Constitutional Safeguards for Women in India*

Article 14	Equal rights and opportunities on men and women in political, economic and social spheres.
Article 15(1)	Prohibits discrimination against any citizen on the grounds of religion, race, caste, sex, etc.
Article 15(3)	Empowers the state to make affirmative discrimination in favour of women.
Article 16	Provides equality of opportunity for all citizens in matters relating to employment or appointment to any office under the state
Article 39(a)	The state shall direct its policy towards securing all citizens men and women, equally, the right to means of livelihood.
Article 39(d)	Equal pay for equal work for both men and women.
Article 42	Directs the state to ensure provisions for just and humane condition of work and maternity relief.
Article 46	The state to promote with special care for the educational and economic interests of the weaker sections of the people and to protect them from social injustice and all forms of exploitation
Article 47	The state to raise the level of nutrition and the standard of living of its people and the improvement of public health.
Article 51 (A) (e)	Mandates every citizen to renounce practices derogatory to the dignity of women.
Article 243 D(3)	Not less than one-third (including the number of seats reserved for women belonging to the SCs and the STs) of the total number of seats to be filled by direct election in every panchayat to be reserved for women and such seats to be allotted by rotation to different constituencies in a panchayat.
Article 243 D(4)	Not less than one-third of the total number of offices of Chairpersons in the panchayats at each level to be reserved for women.

The approach on women development changed from viewing women as beneficiaries of social services to contributors of social and economic development process in nation building. Development approach has attempted to address not only women's immediate needs but also their strategic gender interests addressing inequalities in employment, political participation and cultural and legal status. In the last few decades, a significant shift has been apparent in the in the planning process of country. Approach towards empowering women, which was started with 'welfare' in the fifties, shifted to 'development' in the seventies and has been successfully continuing with the approach of 'empowerment' from the nineties onwards under different five-year plans, which is evident from Table 29.

Table 29 *How the issue of 'women empowerment' has been addressed in different Five-Year Plans?*

The First Five-Year Plan (1951–1956)	... Central Social Welfare Board was set up in 1953 to promote activities leading to women welfare through funding to voluntary organizations, charitable trusts and philanthropic agencies, etc.
The Second Five-Year Plan (1956–1961)	... recognized special needs of women at workplace such as ensuring maternity benefits, crèche facilities for the children of working women and provision of equal pay for equal work, etc.
The Third Five-Year Plan (1961–1966)	... a major focus was given on women's education, pre-natal and child health services, supplementary feeding for children, nursing and expectant mothers.
The Interim Plans (1966–1969) and the Fourth Five-Year Plan (1969–1974)	... continued with its emphasis on gender mainstreaming. The basic approach was to promote women's welfare within the family as the basic unit of operation. The outlay on family planning was stepped up.
The Fifth Five-Year Plan (1974–1979)	... identified areas of health, family planning, nutrition, education, employment, legislation and social welfare for formulating and implementing action programmes for women and called for planned intervention towards women empowerment. This plan marked a major shift in the approach towards women, from welfare towards development.
The Sixth Five-Year Plan (1980–1985)	... accepted women's development as a separate economic agenda. An integrated approach with three-pronged thrust on health, education and employment was adopted. The sixth Five-Year Plan onwards, the plan document has been including a separate chapter on women and children.
The Seventh Five-Year Plan (1985–1990)	... declared as its objective to bring women into the mainstream of national development. During this period, the Department of Women and Child (DWCD) was established within the Ministry of Human Resource Development of Government of India. This plan introduced the concept of monitoring of 27 beneficiary-oriented schemes for women by DWCD. The exercise continues and number of schemes covered is being expanded.

Cont'd...

...Cont'd

The Eighth Five-Year Plan (1992–1997)	... highlighted for the first time a gender perspective and the need to ensure a definite flow of funds from the general developmental sectors to women. The Plan document states that '... the benefits to development from different sectors should not by pass women and special programmes on women should be complement to the general development programmes. The latter, in turn, should reflect greater gender sensitivity'. This plan projected paradigm shift, from development to empowerment and promised to ensure flow of benefits to women in the core sectors of education, health and employment.
The Ninth Five-Year Plan (1997–2002)	... adopted 'Women Component Plan' (WPC) as one of the major strategies and directed both the Central and State Governments to ensure not less than 30 per cent of the funds or benefits are earmarked in all the women-related sectors. Special vigil was advocated on the flow of the earmarked funds or benefits through an effective mechanism to ensure that the proposed strategy brings forth a holistic approach towards empowering women. The National Policy for Empowerment of Women 2001 of GOI adopted during this period envisaged introduction of a gender perspective in the budgeting process as an operational strategy.
The Tenth Five-Year Plan (2002–2007)	... suggested specific strategies, policies and programmes for empowerment of women. They are as follows: measurement of development has to go beyond achievement of gross domestic product (GDP) growth to indicators of distributive justice and their monitoring; women-headed households have to be specifically targeted, identifying added disadvantages in the rural and urban locations with reference to different parameters of deprivation; formulation of Gender Development Indicators (GDI) to measure Human Development and their use as a tool for monitoring development needs to be hastened. It appreciated efforts at ensuring gender-just and gender-sensitive budget and promised to continue the process of dissecting the government budget to establish its gender-differential impact and to translate gender commitment to budgetary commitments. It made provision of outlay of ₹ 13,780 crores. It accepted that women component plan and gender budget play complimentary role for effective convergence, proper utilization and monitoring of fund from various developmental sectors. The Ministry of Women and Child Development was established during this plan period.
The Eleventh Five-Year Plan (2007–2012)	The Approach Paper of this plan mentions '... gender equity requires adequate provisions to be made in policies and schemes across Ministries and Departments'. It also entails 'strict adherence to Gender Budgeting across the board'. It promises special focussed efforts for creation of 'an enabling environment for women to become economically, politically and socially empowered'.

Source: Planning Commission.

A review of five-year plans will reflect that by framing different approaches and strategies, the government has tried to create an enabling environment with various affirmative developmental policies and programmes for women empowerment, besides providing them easy and equal access to all the basic minimum services so as to enable them to realize their full potentials. From the Fifth Five-Year Plan (1974–79) onwards, there has been a marked shift in the approach to women's issues from welfare to development. As a consequence in the Sixth Five-Year Plan (1980–1985), the issue of women welfare secured a special niche and space in the national plans, primarily with thrusts on health, education and employment of women. Empowerment of women was recognized and accepted as a distinct strategy in the Eighth Plan (1992–1997). A further impetus for sectoral contribution to women's programmes was received with the introduction of the concept of Women's Component Plan during the Ninth Plan (1997–2002) whereby identified ministries were required to indicate the flow of funds to the women's programmes and schemes. This was the first plan which involved women's groups from around the country in a consultative process. The plan aimed to create an enabling environment with requisite policies and programmes, legislative support, exclusive institutional mechanisms at various levels and adequate financial and human resources to achieve the objective. The plan also called for the expeditious adoption of the National Policy for Empowering Women along with a well-defined 'Gender Development Index' to monitor progress made towards improving women's status in the society. However, the Ninth Plan refrained from making any commitment for achieving any specific goal or target. This was overcome to some extent in the Tenth Plan (2002–2007) where for the first time, monitorable targets were set for a few key indicators of human development. The targets include, among other things, reduction in gender gaps in literacy and wage rates and reduction in Maternal Mortality Rate (MMR). The Tenth Five-Year Plan called for the three-pronged strategy of social empowerment, economic empowerment and providing gender justice to create an enabling environment of positive economic and social policies for women and eliminating all forms of discrimination against them and thus advance gender equality goals. The Eleventh Plan (2007–2012) has also laid great emphasis on removing gender disparities. It has put a major focus on reducing disparities across the regions and communities by ensuring access to basic physical infrastructure as well as health and education services to all. It has recognized gender as a crosscutting theme across all sectors and commit to respect and promote the rights of the common person.

The Government of India has shown increasing concern for women's issues through a variety of legislation and is also promoting the socio-economic status of women (Table 30). Among the major legislations, the Hindu Succession Act was enacted to give daughters equal rights as sons in ancestral property. The Immoral Traffic Prevention Act has been amended to strengthen its provisions, enforce more stringent punishment for traffickers and prevent re-victimization of victims. States are being requested to set up anti-human trafficking units. In recent times, the Mahatma Gandhi National Rural Employment Guarantee Act (MGNREGA) seeks to provide for the enhancement of livelihood security of the households in rural areas of the country by providing at least 100 days of guaranteed wage employment in a financial year to every household whose adult members volunteer to do unskilled manual work. Under MGNREGA, priority has been given to women by reserving at least one-third of the jobs for women who have registered and requested for work under this act. Some of the major legislations have been discussed in Table 30.

Table 30 *Major Legislations Protecting Women's Rights in India*

The Factories Act, 1948 Plantation Labour Act, 1951 The Mines Act, 1952 The Contract Labour Act, 1978	All these legislations aim at ensuring a better working condition, higher wages, crèches facilities and regulated working hours for employed women
Equal Remuneration Act of 1976 prohibits discrimination in payment on the ground of sex by ensuring equal pay for men and women for equal work.	
Child Marriage Restrained Act, 1976 raises the age of marriage from 15 to 18 for girls	
Hindu Marriage Act of 1955 (amended in 1976) provides the right for girls to repudiate a child marriage before attaining maturity whether the marriage has been consummated or not.	

Cont'd...

...Cont'd

The Immoral Traffic (Prevention) Act of 1956 as amended and renamed in 1986 makes the sexual exploitation of male or female, a cognizable offence. Now it is under process for further amendment to decriminalize the prostitutes and make the laws more stringent against traffickers.

The Marriage (Amendment) Act, 2001 amended the Hindu Marriage Act, Special Marriage Act, Parsi Marriage and Divorce Act and the Code of Criminal Procedure for providing a speedy disposal of applications for maintenance; the ceiling limit for claiming maintenance has been deleted and a wide discretion has been given to the Magistrate to award appropriate maintenance.

An amendment brought in 1984 to the Dowry Prohibition Act of 1961 made women's subjection to cruelty a cognizable offence. The second amendment brought in 1986 makes the husband or in-laws punishable, if a woman commits suicide within seven years of her marriage and it has been proved that she has been subjected to cruelty. Also a new criminal offence of 'Dowry Death' has been incorporated in the Indian Penal Code.

Medical Termination Pregnancy Act of 1971 legalizes abortion by qualified professional on humanitarian or medical grounds. The maximum punishment may go up to life imprisonment. The act has further been amended specifying the place and persons authorized to perform abortion and provide for penal actions against the unauthorized persons performing abortions.

Indecent Representation of Women (Prohibition) Act of 1986 and the Commission of Sati (Prevention) Act 1987 have been enacted to protect the dignity of women and prevent violence against them as well as their exploitation.

The 73rd Amendment Act, 1992 created space for political participation of women by ensuring 33 per cent seat reservation in Panchayati Raj Institutions.

The Pre-Natal Diagnostic Technique (Regulation & prevention of misuse) Act, 199`4 makes provision for punishment for detection of the sex of unborn child with pre-natal diagnostic technique.

The Protection of Women from Domestic Violence Act, 2005 provides for more effective protection of the rights of women guaranteed under the Constitution who are victims of violence of any kind occurring within the family and for matters connected therewith or incidental thereto. It provides for immediate and emergent relief to women in situations of violence of any kind in the home.

The Mahatma Gandhi National Rural Employment Guarantee Act, 2006 has given priority to women by reserving at least one-third of the jobs for women who have registered and requested for work under this act, aiming at financial independence of women.

Source: Hazra (2012).

Besides these legislative measures, India has ratified various international conventions and human rights instruments committing to secure equal rights of women. At the same time, the Ministry of Women and Child Development has been implementing a number of schemes, which strive towards both economic and social empowerment of women. The ministry has set up support systems such as working women hostels and crèches to help employed women in their struggle towards economic empowerment. *Swadhar* and short-stay homes have been set up to provide shelter and care services for women in distress. Considering the increasing need of shelter homes, it is proposed to set up one *Swadhar* home per district. The scheme for construction of working women's hostel has also been revamped. The ministry also implements laws and legislations for women including Sati Prevention Act, Dowry Prohibition Act, The Protection of Women from Domestic Violence Act, etc. The Protection of Women from Domestic Violence Act, 2005 is first of its kind in the country to get into the private sphere of a household. For the first time, the term 'domestic violence' has been widened in meaning and scope from the culture-specific restriction of 'dowry deaths' and penal provisions to positive civil rights of protection and injunction. A Scheme for Relief and Rehabilitation of Victims of Rape has also been formulated to assist the rape victims in restoring their dignity and self-confidence.

For economic empowerment, *Rashtriya Mahila Kosh* (RMK) was established in 1993 under Department of Women and Child Development to ensure micro-credit facilities through micro-credit organizations such as NGOs and voluntary organizations, women development corporations, women co-operative societies, suitable government or local bodies, etc. Flagship schemes such as *Swayamsiddha* and *Swa-Shakti* were introduced and taking into consideration the success of the programmes, the ministry proposes to take up the second phase of *Swayamsiddha* during the Eleventh Plan. The lessons learnt in *Swayamsiddha*, Phase I, and *Swa-Shakti* have been proposed to be incorporated in the next phase, giving an integrated set of training inputs relating to social and economic empowerment, including skill development and training in traditional and non-traditional sectors.

Women's Education in India

Despite reported progress, there is still a persistent gap between women and men's access to education. Combating the high rate of illiteracy among women and girls remains an area of serious concern for India. Universal basic education of good quality without discrimination, unquestionably, has been a key in reducing both the structural causes of poverty and its effects as well as to ensure sustained and equitable development. It is entrusted that the goals of growth and sustainable development can only be achieved by bringing equality through proper and sufficient education between women and men. There are considerable evidences that women's empowerment appears to have a strong influence in reducing the much observed gender bias against girl child as far as their survival is concerned. On the other hand, based on empirical evidence, it has been estimated that countries that fail to provide basic education to women are likely to face considerable costs in terms of foregone economic growth (0.1–0.3% lower per capita growth) as well as reduced rates of reduction in fertility (0.1–0.4 more children per woman); child mortality (an average of 14/1000 higher rates of under-five mortality) and undernutrition (2.4 percentage points higher prevalence of underweight children under age five).[11] Ensuring education to every woman is thus crucial for the achieving sustainable developments which will be very much apparent from Table 31.

Table 31 *Significance of Women's Education: Some Global Evidences*

- An extra year of education for girls can reduce infant mortality by 5–10 per cent, with the link especially strong in low-income countries.
- In Africa, children of mothers who have five years of primary education are 40 per cent more likely to live beyond age 5.
- A 65 country analysis finds that doubling the proportion of women with a secondary education would reduce average fertility rates from 5.3 to 3.9 per woman.
- Providing girls with one extra year of education beyond the average boosts eventual wages by 10–20 per cent.
- A 63 country study finds that more productive farming due to increased female education accounts for 43 per cent of the decline in malnutrition achieved between 1970 and 1995.
- A recent cross-country study finds that women's education generally has more impact than men's education on children's schooling.
- In Brazil, women's resources have 20 times the impact on children's health compared with men's resources.
- Young rural Ugandans with secondary education are three times less likely to be HIV positive than those with no education.
- Research in India finds that women with some formal schooling are more likely to resist violence than women with no schooling.
- Educated Bangladeshi women are three times as likely to participate in political meetings as illiterate women.
- Educated girls have better opportunities to earn higher wages, participate in community life and decision making and are better informed about health risks such as HIV and AIDS that may be relevant to both themselves and their families.

Cont'd...

...Cont'd

- Providing girls with one extra year of schooling beyond the average can boost their eventual wages by 10 to 20 per cent.
- In Africa, children of mothers who receive five years of primary education are 40 per cent more likely to live beyond age five.

Source: Herz and Sperling (2004).

Evidences show that increased education is associated with the empowerment of women with multiplier effects that spread to society at large. Clear and compelling evidence links education – particularly maternal education – with lower child mortality, better child health and nutrition, higher life expectancy and lowered fertility. Education is also a key means of empowering girls against HIV/AIDS, giving them the knowledge and self-confidence needed to protect themselves. Recent research demonstrates the importance of girls' education in preventing the transmission of HIV/AIDS and delaying early marriage and sexual activity. Educated women are also more likely to value education and send their own children to school, enhancing further the positive spiral of development. For girls and women in particular, education can be a pivotal catalyst out of gendered patterns of discrimination, a springboard by which they may claim their rightful place in society and development. So ultimately women's education will boost the effort of India's efforts towards achieving the MDGs (Table 32).

Table 32 *Women's Education and Its Impact on the Millennium Commitments*

Millennium Development Goals	*Impact of Women's Education*
Eradicate extreme poverty and hunger	An educated women participates in income-generating activities, promotes family-income and thus helps the family to get rid of poverty
Achieve universal primary education	Since women are still deprived of basic educational facilities, education to every woman broadens the scope of universalization of primary education. Beside that an educated mother will always educate her daughter but an illiterate mother may not.

Cont'd...

...Cont'd

Promote gender inequality and empower women	For girls and women in particular, education can be a pivotal catalyst out of gendered patterns of discrimination, a springboard by which they may claim their rightful place in society and development. Education would actually accord women certain advantages in areas where they have traditionally lacked access or differential rights. Thus, education promotes women empowerment, which ultimately leads to gender equality.
To reduce child mortality	An educated mother has a better understanding of child-rearing than that of an illiterate mother, which helps in the reduction of child mortality and promotion of better child health and nutrition as well as higher life expectancy
Improve maternal health	Studies suggest that an educated mother is more capable of keeping herself healthy, which enhances their life expectancy and reduces incidences of maternal mortality
Combat HIV/AIDS, malaria and other diseases	Education is also a key means of empowering girls against HIV/AIDS and other diseases, giving them the knowledge and self-confidence needed to protect themselves through proper precaution
Ensure environmental sustainability	Evidence shows that education among women usually builds environmental consciousness in them. It enriches them with the basic knowledge about the adverse impact of environmental degradation
Develop a global partnership for development	Addressing the multiple barriers faced by girls in their efforts to access quality education and to persist in school necessarily leads to integrated, multi-sectoral approaches that involve numerous partners. This goes to the heart of the integrated efforts that are required to achieve the MDGs as a whole

Source: Hazra (2009a).

The Indian government has expressed a strong commitment towards education for all; one of the Directive Principles of State Policy contained in Article 45 of our Constitution relates to education – according to which the state should strive to provide free and compulsory education to all children. The National Policy on Education (NPE) of 1986 envisages that education would be used as a strategy for achieving a basic change in the status of women. It declared that the national educational system would play (1) a positive and interventionist role in the empowerment of women; (2) contribute towards development of new values through redesigned curriculum and textbooks; and (3) that women's studies will be promoted as part of various courses.

Since independence, girls' education has been a prime agenda for national development. However, when India attained independence 65 years ago, it was a formidable challenge that the new government had to face. The national Female Literacy Rate was alarmingly low at 8.9 per cent; Gross Enrolment Ratio (GER) for girls was 24.8 per cent at primary level and 4.6 per cent at the upper primary level (in the 11–14 years age group). Social and cultural barriers to education of women and lack of access to organized schooling were the issues to be addressed immediately after independence. Significant progress has been made in the field of female literacy, which has been increasing at a faster rate as compared to male literacy from 1981 onwards. Consequently, the male-female literacy differential at 26.62 percentage points in 1981 was reduced to 24.84 percentage points in 1991, which has further been reduced to 21.6 in 2001, when growth in female literacy was higher at 14.41 percentage points as compared to corresponding figure for males at 11.17. All states have registered an increase in literacy rates and 60 per cent male literacy has been achieved without exception.[12]

Table 33 *Female Literacy in India: Achievements So Far*

Female literacy has gone up from 39.2 per cent in 1991 to 53.67 per cent in 2001.
The growth rate in female literacy at 14.39 per cent has been higher than for male at 11.13 per cent.
Gender gap in literacy has declined from 24.85 per cent in 1991 to 21.59 per cent in 2001.
GER as shown above exhibits the extent of improvement.
At the middle school level, there is a significant jump in enrolment from 52.09 per cent in 2002–2002 to nearly 65.1 per cent in 2004–2005.This shows that more girls are continuing their education in the elementary stage.
The decline in dropout rate (discussed above) is sharper for girls as compared to boys.
Gender parity (ratio of girls GER to boys GER) at primary level is 0.95 for India (based on selected educational statistics 2004–2005). Eight states, i.e., Andhra Pradesh, Haryana, Kerala, Maharashtra, Meghalaya, Punjab, Uttarakhand and Delhi have achieved gender parity and majority of the states are closed behind.

Cont'd...

...Cont'd

Gross enrolment of girls to total enrolment has increased by 17.8 percentage points at the primary level from 86.9 per cent in 2001–2002 to 104.7 per cent by 2004–2005.
There are 64 female teachers per 100 male teachers at primary level, 60 female teachers per 100 male teachers in upper primary level and 62 female teachers per 100 male teachers in high/post-basic schools in 2004–2005.

Source: Hazra (2009b).

The Government of India has, in accordance with its constitutional mandate, taken several initiatives in the form of enabling policies, legislations and interventions to spread literacy, promote educational development and bridge gender disparities. The Constitution of India guarantees equal rights for men and women. In order to achieve improvement in eliminating gender disparity in education, schooling has been made completely free for girls in most of the states up to the higher secondary stage in government and government-aided schools. Various Centrally Sponsored Schemes (CSSs) strengthen school education and a large number of girls have been benefited from these schemes. In the higher education sector, the UGC has been implementing various schemes for promoting women's education in universities and colleges. Some of these are: (i) scheme of grants to women universities for technical courses, (ii) scheme for construction of women hostels, and (iii) setting up of women study centres in 72 universities.[13] Access to higher education for girls has been expanding as also their enrolment in various courses. Their numbers in colleges, universities and professional institutions such as engineering, medicine, etc., has increased from 3.81 million in 2002–2003 to 4.04 million in 2004–2005.[14]

Gendered Deprivation in Education Still Exists

Despite rapid growth in literacy in post-independence India, gendered deprivation still exists and needs to be overcome. The gender gap in educational involvement though reduced over the years, but in India it is still a matter of great concern. In India, the participation of girls at all stages of education has been increasing steadily through the years. Since 1950–1951, girls' participation has increased manifold in primary, middle, secondary, higher secondary stages and higher education levels but still social and economic systems supported by patriarchal values continue to influence women's education right from the beginning. At the national level, the number of girls enrolled in all levels, i.e., primary, secondary and higher education is less than their counterparts (Table 34). However, the female-male ratio in education has been steadily improving over the years.

Table 34 *Male-Female Literacy Gap in India (in %)*

Census Year	*Persons*	*Males*	*Females*	*Male-Female Literacy Gap*
1951	18.33	27.16	8.86	18.30
1961	28.30	40.40	15.35	25.05
1971	34.45	45.96	21.97	23.98
1981	43.57	56.38	29.76	26.62
1991	52.21	64.13	39.29	24.84
2001	65.38	75.85	54.16	21.70

Source: Census of India (2001).

Slightly more than half of the female population was literate as against three-fourth of males (75.85%). It may be seen that it took almost five decades for male-female disparity to reduce to half of what it was in the 1960s. Following the same logic, one can argue that if the present trend continues, it will take another five decades to finally close the gender gap in terms of literacy attainment.

Educating Adolescent Girls: Still A Major Challenge

The 1998–1999 National Family Health Survey-2 (NFHS-2) reported that among young female adolescents (ages 10–14 years), 67 per cent attended school. The corresponding figure for male adolescents was 80.2 per cent. There was a sharp decline in the proportion of female adolescents (ages 15–17) attending the school. Only 40.3 per cent attended school compared to 57.7 per cent of their male counterparts. Location had a significant influence on the schooling of females. In rural areas, only 32.7 per cent of female adolescents (ages 15–17) attended school compared with 60.5 per cent of female adolescents in urban areas (IIPS and ORC

Macro, 2000). Studies reveal that lack of education for more than one-quarter of girls was ascribed to their responsibilities for caring for siblings at home and other household responsibilities. Another quarter was ascribed to the cost of education. Studies suggested that factors such as lack of female teachers, distance of schools from their homes, parental fear for their daughter's safety, and failure on exams were responsible for dropout and non-enrolment of adolescent girls in elementary education. Table 35 shows the relative importance of various factors for adolescent girls for non-enrolment in school education.

Table 35 *Reasons for Never Attending School for Adolescent Girls: 1998–1999*

Reasons	*Percentage*
Costs too much	25
Not interested in studies	16
Required for household work	15
Education not considered necessary	13
School far away	4
Required for care of siblings	3
Required for on farm/family business	3
Required for outside work for payment in cash/kind	3
No proper school facilities for girls	2
Do not know	2
Transfer not available	1
Others	13

Source: Tilak (2002).

Still in many parts of rural India, the adolescent girls are made to perform household and agricultural chores. This is one of the many factors limiting girls' education. Cleaning the house, preparing the food, looking after their siblings, the elderly and the sick, grazing the cattle and collecting firewood are some of the key tasks they have to perform. Households are therefore reluctant to spare them for schooling. Physical safety of the girls, especially when they have to travel a long distance to school and fear of sexual harassment are other reasons that impede girls' education. Taking into consideration the current scenario, it is of utmost importance to strengthen efforts and formulate innovative strategies to channelize adolescents' energies in a constructive direction. Adolescence Education Programme (AEP) is one such effort, keeping pace with the challenges of the new generation. AEP is a joint initiative by Ministry of Human Resource Development (MHRD) and National AIDS Control Organization (NACO), Government of India, to equip every adolescent (child between 10 and 19 years) with scientific information, knowledge and life skills to protect themselves from HIV infection and manage their concerns pertaining to reproductive and sexual health. AEP is an umbrella programme to cover all the secondary and senior secondary schools of the country.

Low Literacy among Muslim Girls

As far as the ensuring educational access to Muslim girls are concerned, an analysis of the trends between the 1991 Census and that of 2001 reveals the following issues of concerns: (i) the Muslim girl child is among the most vulnerable group for future education policy planners; (ii) the enrolment rates of Muslim girls have steeply fallen relative to the all-India average, especially during and after the decades of the 1990s; and (iii) the difference in literacy rates among Muslim men and women and their non-Muslim counterparts was greater in urban areas. Also, while literacy levels were more even among Muslim and Hindu women in the 1950s, 1960s, 1970s and even the 1980s, the differences have widened substantially among the younger age women around the year 2001. As per 2001 Census, 55 per cent Muslim men are literate compared to 64.5 per cent non-Muslim men, and 41 per cent Muslim women are literate compared to 46 per cent non-Muslim women (Shariff and Razzack, 2006). A Government of India commissioned study, conducted by the Social and Research Institute, says the estimate of out-of-school children is highest among Muslims (9.97%). The states and union territories that are worse than the national average are Bihar (28.34%), Daman & Diu (28%), Uttar Pradesh (14.37%), and West Bengal (11.33%). The estimate of out-of-school Muslim children in rural areas (12.03%) was the highest among all social groups.[15] Different studies conducted in India explore that negative parental attitudes towards educating daughters is a barrier to a Muslim girl's education. Many Muslim parents view educating sons as an investment because the sons will be responsible for caring for aging parents. On the contrary, they perceive the education of daughters as a waste of money because daughters will eventually live with their husbands' families, and the parents will not benefit directly from their education.

Higher Incidences of Dropouts among Girls

A major reason for lack of education among women in India is the high dropout rate among girls at the early stages of schooling as compared to boys. Evidences show that among various other causes, poverty is the prime reasons for lack of education and higher dropout rates among girls (Table 36). Economics plays a key role when it comes to coping with directs costs such as tuition fees, cost of textbooks, uniforms, transportation and other expenses. Wherever, especially in families with many children, these costs exceed the income of the family, girls are the first to be denied schooling. Often a choice is made between sending the boy or the girl to the school and the family would rather spend scarce resources educating a boy, as it is considered as a long-term and sure investment. Spending on education and especially for a girl child is still perceived as a waste of money and resources, especially in rural India. Girls' lack of access to education is not always related to scarcity of places in schools. It also emerges from expectations, attitudes and biases in communities and families. Economic costs, social traditions, and religious and cultural beliefs limit girls' educational opportunities. Whatever the underlying reasons, having large number of girls outside the formal schooling system brings developmental challenges to both current and future generations. Individuals, families, communities and nations are affected. Inability to read, write and calculate complicates a girl's efforts to engage in both market-focused production and household activities as effectively and efficiently possible. This affects her family's welfare and diminishes her potential contribution to the development of the household, local and national economy.

Table 36 *Dropout Rate at Different Stages of School Education (in %)*

Year	Primary			Elementary			Secondary		
	Boys	Girls	Total	Boys	Girls	Total	Boys	Girls	Total
1960–1961	61.7	70.9	64.9	75.0	85.0	78.3	NA	NA	NA
1970–1971	64.5	70.9	67.0	74.6	83.4	77.9	NA	NA	NA
1980–1981	56.2	62.5	58.7	68.0	79.4	72.7	79.8	86.6	82.5
1990–1991	40.1	46.0	42.6	59.1	65.1	60.9	67.5	76.9	71.3
1992–1993	43.8	46.7	45.0	58.2	65.2	61.1	70.0	77.3	72.9
1999–2000*	38.7	42.3	40.3	52.0	58.0	54.5	66.6	70.6	68.3
2000–2001*	39.7	41.9	40.7	50.3	57.7	53.7	66.4	71.5	68.5
2001–2002*	38.4	39.9	39.0	52.9	56.9	54.6	64.2	68.6	66.0
2002–2003*	35.8	33.7	34.8	52.2	53.4	52.8	60.7	64.9	62.5
2003–2004*	33.7	28.5	31.4	51.8	52.9	52.3	60.9	64.9	62.6
2004–2005*	31.8	25.4	29.0	50.5	51.3	50.8	60.4	63.9	61.9

* Provisional.

Source: Government of India (2007).

Efforts have made in this direction for tackling the high dropout rate among girls through formulation of *Kasturba Gandhi Balika Vidyalaya* (KGBV) scheme. This scheme is being implemented in educationally backward blocks where rural female literacy is below the national average as per 2001 census and gender gap in literacy is more than the national average. The KGBV scheme envisages setting up to 750 residential schools with boarding facilities at elementary level for girls belonging predominantly to the SCs, STs, OBCs and minorities in difficult areas. The scheme is being coordinated with existing schemes such as Sarva Shiksha Abhiyan (SSA), National Programme for Education of Girls at Elementary Level (NPEGEL) and Mahila Samakhya (MS). But still the dropout rates among girls at different levels of school education has been an issue of concern, which has been recorded 29 per cent at primary level, 50.8 per cent at middle level and 61.9 per cent at secondary level.[16]

Barriers to Women's Education: Tackling the Challenges Ahead

Although schooling is free but the costs of books, uniforms and transportation to school are still putting financial burden for the poor families, especially of rural India. If a family has to choose between educating a son or a daughter because of financial restrictions, typically the son will be chosen. Engaging girls in household chores is one of the major barriers to the progress of women's education. Engagement in working for their own household is more common for a girl child. Studies reveal that, in the Indian context, girl children begin to work in the household from a very early age. Girl children are mainly engaged in domestic or household activities such as cooking, cleaning, fetching water and fuel wood, looking after old and sick family members and more importantly taking care of younger siblings which ultimately keep them away from school education. Another barrier to education in India is the lack of adequate school facilities. Many states simply do not have enough classrooms to accommodate all of the school-age children. Furthermore, the classrooms that are available often lack basic necessities such as basic sanitary facilities, drinking water, etc. In Uttar Pradesh, a survey found that 54 per cent of schools did not have a water supply and 80 per cent did not have latrines.[17] Lack of latrines can be particularly detrimental to girls' school attendance. Lack of female teachers is another potential barrier to girls' education. Studies show that girls are more likely to attend school and have higher academic achievement if they have female teachers. This is particularly true in highly gender-segregated societies, which are existing in India.

Education is milestone of women empowerment because it enables them to responds to the challenges, to confront their traditional role and change their life; so that we cannot neglect the importance of education in reference to women empowerment. Our predominant patriarchal system does not provide enough chances for women to have higher education even if they wish. Girls should be motivated to take up higher education. Universal education for all below 14 years should be strictly implemented. There is an urgent necessity of framing gender sensitive curriculum at all stages of primary education to address sex-stereotyping menace. There needs to be renewed efforts to address the gender-specific causes for the high dropout rates and low learning outcomes for girls. These include violence or fear of violence; pregnancy and care giving responsibilities; and curriculum and teaching styles which reinforce gender stereotypes. In particular, female teachers have a key role in encouraging attendance, improving the education experience for girls and acting as positive role models. Education is a basic human right that increases the economic, social and political opportunities available to women. It empowers women to take control of their lives and create opportunities and choices to improve their lives as well as their families. Besides providing knowledge and skills and income-earning opportunities, education of women can reduce child and maternal mortality and fertility, improve family health and increase children's education, particularly of girls. Thus, in turn, it will ensure an improved status of women in the society. Educated women are also more likely to value education and send their own children to school, enhancing further the positive spiral of development.

Political Empowerment

In India, the position of women in grassroots politics remains weak, though at top level there were and are remarkable exceptions. Political empowerment refers to the equitable representation of women in decision-making structures, both formal and informal, as well as creating space for the women to raise their voices in the formulation of policies affecting the entire society. Evidences show that when women do get to play an important role in decision making, the whole society tends to benefit from the results. Women bring in different experiences and ideas and, most importantly, have insight into the concerns of other women. The absence of women from structures of governance inevitably means that national, regional and local priorities, i.e., how resources are allocated, are typically defined without meaningful input from women, whose life experience gives them a different awareness of the community's needs, concerns and interests from that of men. In order for spending and development priorities to change, there must be at least a critical mass of women represented, who are learning the rules, using the rules and changing the rules of the 'decision-making game', and thus having an impact on discourse and decisions at all levels, from the family, to the nation and to the international community. By including more women in the decision-making process, we can ensure that women's experience, knowledge, interests and talents are fully recognized and taken into account.

The government has attempted to empower women politically by providing for one-third reservation for women in local bodies, to ensure their participation at the local and district levels of governance through the 73rd and 74th amendments to the Constitution. Through such initiatives, democracy has been strengthened compulsorily with more presence of women through reservation; as in the local government, the impact of reserving one-third of seats for women in the Panchayati Raj Institutions (PRIs) has been immense and has empowered women both politically and socially. At present, there are approximately 2,60,000 panchayat representatives in India, out of which around 75,000 are women; this is the largest number of elected women in the world.[18] Reservation has at least succeeded in bringing the women folk of rural India into the political forum, and elected women could now imagine standing against a man in future. Representation of women in the formal structures of governance at the local level has recorded a steady increase.

Women's presence at the decision-making levels will not only enhance the status of women but also strengthen democratic traditions and make democracy more meaningful in fighting injustice and oppression while at the same time help to bring a different, explicitly female perspective to the political arena. Unless women are brought into the decision-making levels directly, important issues with regard to women will never be tackled with the seriousness they require. Women members of *panchayats* are gradually learning to adjust to the new political conditions. The political knowledge of women is increasing, and gradually a sense of confidence is getting instilled in them, as they are now aware of the problems being faced by their locality. By all accounts, as each election round passes, it is clear that up to certain extent women have made their presence felt in the power struggles once dominated by men. These affirmative actions adopted by the Government of India providing for reservation of not less than one-third seats in local self-governing bodies have facilitated more number of women to participate in the decision-making arena equally with men in these institutions. Further, these women are now in a position to access resources and utilize the powers vested in them as elected members. These are significant steps towards achieving the constitutional goal of gender equality. However, much more are needed to be done to provide an enabling and conducive environment in the political institutions to enable women to participate effectively as the political domain continues to be perceived as best suited for men and therefore remains very male dominated.

These initiatives have created political space for women but it is observed that they have not been able to guarantee a non-discriminative or conducive environment for women to participate in decision-making processes. Besides that illiteracy, dominance of patriarchal values in the society, lack of access and control over income and other resources, restrictions to public spaces and insensitive legal systems continue to impair their effective political participation. This is compounded by the absence or inadequate availability of infrastructural facilities and support services to facilitate their participation. Both nationally and at the state as well as local levels, women in elected bodies have been very few and even those who have been elected present a complex picture when observed from closer quarters. The money and muscle associated with the electoral process inhibits a large number of women from joining politics. Constraints such as restriction on mobility, lack of control over resources and low literacy rates remain the major obstacles and operate more or less for all classes and communities of women.

India has a history of strong female politicians, from former Prime Minister Indira Gandhi to her daughter-in-law, Sonia Gandhi, the current head of the Congress party but still the percentage of women in legislatures and decision-making positions always remained low. While women make up half of the population they are still poorly represented in the decision-making process. The lack of representation of women in decision-making positions results in women's agenda not getting reflected and addressed in policies and programmes. Even in the family as well as in the society the decision-making power of women is denied. Mostly males make the important decision in the family and in the society. This makes women voiceless and destroys their confidence. True empowerment will only be reached when women take part actively in the decision-making process of our country. So, to end gender discrimination women must empower with decision-making power. In cardinal goals of democracy 'of the people, by the people and for the people' cannot be optimally accomplished if the female population remains out of political empowerment. Subordination of women in society acts a structural constraint to their participation in political activities.

Representation is not only a mean of ensuring individual participation but also the responsibility of the representatives to act on behalf of the constituents, including women, who elected them and reflect their ideas and aspirations. The limited nature of female participation and representation in national decision-making institutions has important consequences for women and for the legitimacy of the institutions. Women's disproportionate absence from the political process would mean that the concerns of half the population cannot be sufficiently attended to or acted upon as it denies their viewpoints of sufficient opportunity to be integrated in the political system. Where women constitute half the population in a political system which supports equality and where both women and men are legally eligible for political office, women's participation should be equal to that of men. If this is not the case, it signifies deep flaws within the political system. Whether women work together to protest gender-based injustices or whether they participate in non-gender-specific associations and struggles, the most important group benefit from political participation is that it should have an influence on decision making to make public policies sensitive to the needs of the group in question.

Recently, the Women Reservation Bill has been passed in India's upper house of parliament on 9 March 2010 as politicians overwhelmingly voted to amend the Constitution to reserve one-third of all seats in national and state legislatures for women. This bill was proposed more than a decade ago, but has faced strong opposition from male-dominated political parties who are worried about losing their seats. But finally the idea of 33 per cent reservation for women in parliament has actively been endorsed by most of the major political parties and this has raised expectation that many more women would be nominated to contest the elections. The election manifestoes and the public pronouncements of parties as well as the print and electronic media have highlighted the idea of women's representation by reservation or by nomination of more women for elections signifying a more conscious political stand on women's representation. But record shows that these stances do not translate actually into more nomination of women candidates during elections. Many parties end up allotting some seats to women candidates only as a token and to symbolize their pro-women egalitarian policy.

Mere presence of women in parliament even if greater in numbers will not mean much unless they are truly representative of women's concerns covering all categories. In the ongoing debate about reservation of seats for women in the parliament, it has been pointed out that an undifferentiated reservation for women will reinforce the existing inequalities in women's access to positions of power because from such reservation it is expected that women from elite and politicized families as well as widows of prominent political figures will find a smooth entry in mainstream politics; but how far the women playing supportive roles to males in the family will get an entry into the politics is still a big question. On the whole, as trends show the important factors for women's active presence in politics in India are: family background, political influence, family financial position, existing involvement in politics, literacy, local conditions, campaign strategy, influence within the party and personality traits, etc., rather than only competence, capability and merit.

Besides that reservation of seats for women in panchayats or in parliament, however, is only the first step to ensure that a certain number of women will be involved in decision-making process of the government; the very next task and challenge will be to develop their capacity so that they can perform their role properly and can make a difference. Today, the political environment is deeply entrenched with corruption and criminalization. This situation needs to be changed as women have the potential to defuse and transform the mainstream political culture, by making it more transparent, accountable and participative. They can also positively contribute to the process of de-criminalizing politics, which in turn would provide a conducive environment for their entry and effective participation in politics, thus facilitating the achievement of substantive equality for women. A holistic approach based on human rights of women and welfare of the public at large can therefore remove the existing inequalities and bring about gender equality in the political arena. Women should make their voices heard and act locally, at the national, regional and global level to change the content of policies. Recognizing women's rights and believing their ability are essential for women's empowerment and development. Women should realize their own capabilities and potentials which will strengthen their self-image and foster them with confidence to take action in life. Political empowerment does not imply just a right to play a role silently but to discuss, share and empower politics by knowing its pros and cons and thereby to influence policies and decision making; but it is expected that a proper implementation of women's reservation policies for representation in the political sphere, right from village level to national level, will ensure and enhance the chances to women for a better participation in the development process to pay attention to women's needs and priorities.

State of Women's Health in India

There has been a perceptible change in recent years regarding the focus of development policies and priorities. In India, and globally, development goals are no longer defined in terms of economic growth exclusively. The vital link between health and development is increasingly recognized and an attempt has been made to reformulate health policies and programmes. Since women constitute nearly half of the total population, the emphasis on women health in developmental policies and programmes has become pertinent.

The health of Indian women is intrinsically linked to their status in society, especially for those living in a rural India. Research on women's status in Indian societies has found that the contributions that Indian women make to their families are often overlooked; instead time and again they are regarded as economic burdens and this view is more customary in rural India. There is a strong preference for sons in India because they are expected to earn for families and to take care for ageing parents. This son preference and high dowry costs for daughters result in the mistreatment of daughters. Indeed, Indian women have low levels of both education and formal labour force participation. They typically have little autonomy, living first under the control of their fathers, then their husbands, and finally their sons. These factors have a negative impact on the health of Indian women. Poor health has repercussions not only for women, but also for their families. Women in poor health are more likely to give birth to low-weight infants. They are less likely to be able to provide food and adequate care for their children. As far as Indian scenario is concerned, women from infant stage to their old age get an unfair deal regarding health care. Women are discriminated when it comes to the treatment of diseases and medical problems. If a man and a woman have the same problem requiring expensive treatment, it is invariably the man who gets the first attention and often the only one to get the attention. It is not just the poor who for want of resources and with the inherent preference for a boy are guilty of bias, even in well-to-do families parents tend to spend more on the health of the boys than the girls. It is the attitude which is responsible for ignoring the health of the women in India.

The concept of women's health today has become a major concern in India because of high prevalence of infant, child, and maternal mortality and deteriorating quality of life. Available evidences in India show that women have been suffering from many health problems and deprived of health facilities (Table 37). Though India has made considerable progress in social, economic, cultural, demographic and political arenas in recent decades, it lagged behind in the improvement of women's health. India is one of the few countries where males significantly outnumber females (933 females for 1,000 males) and its maternal mortality rate in rural areas is among the world's highest. Women experience malnutrition, anaemia, infectious diseases and illness more than men, and they are less likely to receive timely medical treatment.

Table 37 *State of Women's Health in India: A Statistical Profile*

- Maternal mortality remains unacceptably high in India, even though this hard-to-measure indicator has likely recently started to decline. For 2005–2006, mortality ratios range from the Indian government's estimate of 301 maternal deaths per 100,000 live births, to the World Health Organization's estimate of 450.
- India has the highest number of maternal deaths in the world with 117,000 women dying due to complications of pregnancy and childbirth each year, i.e., one woman dying every seven minutes.
- The major causes of maternal deaths in India are: haemorrhage (38%), illnesses or medical conditions that are aggravated by pregnancy or delivery such as tuberculosis, viral hepatitis, malaria or anaemia (34%), puerperal sepsis, i.e., infections after delivery (11%), complications of abortion (8%), obstructed labour (5%) and hypertensive disorders associated with pregnancy (5%).
- The lifetime risk of a woman in India dying during pregnancy, delivery and through the first 6 weeks after delivery is 1 in 70. The risk to women in India is two times greater than that faced by women in the Asia region, 60 times that of women in developed countries, and over 600 times greater than for women living in Sweden.

Cont'd...

...Cont'd

- Maternal death ratios are highest in the eight EAG (Empowered Action Group) states of Rajasthan, Jharkhand, Uttar Pradesh, Bihar, Uttarakhand, Chhattisgarh, Madhya Pradesh and Orissa.
- A recent decline in fertility (from 3.4 children per woman in 1993 to 2.7 children in 2006) has greatly helped to lower the number of Indian women dying from these causes and their lifetime risk of maternal death.
- Women's receipt of any professional prenatal and delivery care has increased dramatically – by one-half and one-third, respectively, from 50 per cent in 1993 to 73 per cent in 2006.
- The institutional deliveries among mothers belonging to lowest quintile of wealth index remain dismally low at 14 per cent and of scheduled tribes (STs) at 20 per cent compared to 85 per cent of mothers of wealthiest households.
- Only 36 per cent of mothers reported receiving postnatal care from health personnel within 2 days of delivery of their last birth. This was as low as 13 per cent for the lowest quintile and 22 per cent for ST women in the country.
- Most maternal deaths occur between the last three months of pregnancy and the first week following delivery. The highest number of deaths occurs on the first day after delivery.
- Maternal care practices continue to be a cause for concern in India. Lack of required services, poor quality of services and reluctance to use services are major barriers in availing maternity care service.
- Different studies and reports reveal that maternal deaths occur due to a number of delays: delays in seeking care; delays in reaching appropriate care, usually requiring a series of referrals to reach a facility capable of managing emergencies; and delays in receiving emergency obstetric care at the facility due to non-availability of skilled health personnel, equipment and supplies required for managing emergencies.
- Many women reach health facilities too late, and in such serious condition medical interventions are not effective.
- Fewer than half of deliveries (41%) are conducted in a health facility.
- Nonetheless, just over half (52%) of all Indian women deliver without assistance of any trained medical attendants. Nearly three-fourths of women still give birth with no medical professional in attendance in Uttar Pradesh and Bihar, the country's first and third most populated states, respectively. Skilled assistance by medical personnel during delivery remains low at 48 per cent. These rates are startlingly low when compared to the Asia region as a whole and developed countries where 95 per cent and 98 per cent of deliveries are by skilled attendants. Progress in use of skilled attendance between 1999 and 2005 has been slow.
- Estimation suggests that if India is to achieve its goal of 100 maternal deaths per 100,000 live births, government at all levels must redouble efforts to improve access to information and services to protect women's health during pregnancy and delivery, and to prevent unintended pregnancy and unsafe abortion.

Source: Hazra (2010b).

High maternal mortality ratio (MMR) continues to remain a matter of great concern for India (see Table 38). MMR in India is unacceptably high at an average of 450 deaths per 100,000 live births as per the latest World Health Statistics of 2008 released by World Health Organization (WHO) – which is about fifty times that in developed countries. India has progressed rapidly on the socio-economic front but progress in the improvement of maternal health has been slow. Review of safe motherhood efforts in India shows that, despite major initiatives taken by the government in the last ten years, till recently, nearly half of all deliveries take place at home, and the coverage of antenatal care services are low. WHO estimates that 5,36,000 maternal deaths are occurring globally each year – out of which 1,36,000 take place in India, accounting for at least a quarter of global MMR. In addition, millions more women and newborns suffer pregnancy and birth-related ill health. Thus, pregnancy-related mortality and morbidity continues to take a huge toll on the lives of Indian women and their newborns.

The root cause of maternal mortality lies in gender inequality, low access to education for girls; early marriage; adolescent pregnancy; sexual and reproductive health; and other social and economic determinants – so improvement of maternal health is having a direct impact on betterment of maternal and child health (MCH), promotion of gender equality and empowerment of women. Beside all these, one factor that is likely correlated with a high likelihood of maternal death is poverty, which may affect health service infrastructure and women's and men's prospects for education and gainful employment, which in turn affects women's ability to obtain needed prenatal and delivery care. Maternal mortality affects not only women, but also their families and communities. The risk of an infant dying increases significantly with the mother's death. The death of a woman of reproductive age also brings about significant economic losses and setbacks to community development. From human rights, economic and public health perspectives, mobilizing resources to combat maternal mortality is imperative. The National Population Policy (NPP) of 2000 which was framed to reduce the country's 'unacceptable' MMR emphasized the need to contextualize the issue as 'a matter of social injustice' and as an indicator of gender inequity in nutrition and access to health care. The National Policy for the Empowerment of Women (2001) recognizes maternal mortality as a 'sensitive indicator of human development' and labels it a priority concern. The Tenth Five-Year Plan specified that the MMR could be reduced by promoting institutional deliveries and making home deliveries and abortions safer.

Table 38 *Trends of MMR in India: A Profile of the Last 50 Years*

Reference Year(s)	*Maternal Mortality Ratio MMR*	*Data Sources*
1957	1,287	National Sample Survey (NSS),14th Round
1960	1,355	NSS, 16th Round
1963–1964	1,174	NSS, 19th Round
1972–1976	892	Sample Registration System (SRS)
1977–1981	844	SRS
1982–1986	568	SRS
1982–1986	580	PN Mari Bhatt's estimate
1990	570	World Health Report, 1999
1992–1993	437	National Family Health Survey (NFHS) 1
1997–1998	398	1997–1998 retrospective MMR surveys
1997	407	SRS
1998	408	SRS
1998–1999	540	NFHS 2
1999–2001	327	SRS prospective household reports
2000	540	World Health Report, 2005
2001–2003	301	SRS
2005	450	World Health Statistics, 2008

Source: Hazra (2010b).

In recent years, the Government of India has launched the National Rural Health Mission (NRHM) aimed at correcting rural inequities in the matter of health. It seeks to integrate health with those essential inputs in health, namely, sanitation, hygiene, safe drinking water and nutrition. The government is undertaking a wide range of initiatives under NRHM to reduce the MMR to 100 by 2012, giving MMR reduction as one of the top priority. *Janani Suraksha Yojana* (National Maternity Benefit Scheme), launched on 12 April 2005 is one of such major initiatives under NRHM, is providing a comprehensive package of services, geared at reduction of maternal mortality, neonatal mortality, female feticide and gender disparity. Most of these schemes and programmes initiated by the government look good but they usually fail at the implementation level. The infrastructure devised again for rural health delivery has little to find fault with, but the primary health centres and sub-centres are crumbling. The poor implementation haunts practically all our well-intentioned plans and programmes for the welfare of the people. NRHM proposes to empower local communities in the matter of public health; specific health plans are sought to be drawn up for each village by special health committees within the panchayats.

As of 2005, there were 280 million women of reproductive age (15–49 years) in India – one-third more than that of 1992.[19] The challenges of these numbers represent the need for the government to give priority to efforts to reduce maternal mortality and morbidity as it fulfils commitments made at the national and international levels. Maternal health should be seen in the framework of women's health and welfare. The increased political priority, managerial capacity and resource allocation will determine seriousness of our efforts and future of maternal health in India. Health needs to be a priority issue for politicians, and maternal health in particular needs attention. Politicians must ensure that an adequate number of officers with technical competence are looking after maternal health consistently for longer periods. Top politicians, such as health ministers and Chief Minister at the state level and Prime Minister at the national level, should periodically review MMR and maternal health services. Women's NGOs need to take up the issue of high maternal mortality as an important issue to ensure that the government is focused in its efforts to reduce maternal deaths. International development agencies and national-level NGOs need to join hands with professional organizations to make maternity safer in India.

The right to health is a fundamental right and the poorer health indices of half the population is a cause for concern. There is an urgent need for a detailed re-examination of public health statistics for India, disaggregated by gender and region. There is an equally vital need to set up policies and programmes to counter adverse trends. The evidence from such disaggregated data should be used to set targets for action. Progress has to be visible and benchmarks have to be set high. The magnitude of the inequality related to health is often downplayed even within medical circles. The second-class status of women in Indian society persists and women's perspectives continue to be missing, marginalized or ignored. There is a definite need to engage communities and the population as a whole in a debate to challenge traditional stereotypes and accepted social norms. Programmes to achieve gender equality should not only focus on the provision of equal or greater opportunities for women but also concentrate on achieving equality in gender outcomes within a reasonable time frame. Outcomes in general, and health outcomes in particular, are measurable with a much greater degree of accuracy than opportunities.

Women, especially the poor and rural women, are often trapped in the cycle of ill-health exacerbated by child bearing, hard physical labour and deprivation of medicare services. Rural women in India are among the most disadvantaged people in terms of their health status. Access to appropriate health care information, a comprehensive, adequate and affordable health services are still to be achieved for the rural women. Rural women are especially vulnerable to pregnancy and child birth related deaths. Poor health of women and nutritional status in India are inextricably interwoven with social, cultural and economic factors. These factors severely constrain the ability of women and adolescent girls to acquire good health services. Longstanding and entrenched gender inequities affect women's health, their allocation of assets, power, rights, status and opportunities. Women have less access to basic resources such as social, health, educational as well as in other service systems. Though Indian government is committed to improve women's health through various policies and programmes, problems and the inequities in women's health continue to exist in our society. Hence, it is necessary to recognize and to evolve mechanisms to overcome barriers, such as poverty and illiteracy and several socio-economic constraints. There is a need to adopt a justiciable gender sensitive and women friendly approach to the women's health. All plans and projects within community programmes should be assessed using the 'gender lens' in order to achieve gender justice for women. These programmes will have to cover the social context of home, school, workplace, law and politics in order to improve women's health. There is a need to challenge the normalization of gender discrimination in India. The focus should be on public health approaches to change social and cultural perspectives with the aim of primary prevention of discrimination while continuing medical interventions for early diagnosis and management of the medical consequences. There is a need for aggressive gender justice in order that women in India achieve equal health and social status in the foreseeable future.

Tackling Emerging Challenges of Empowering Women

Though India is developing economically and technologically by leaps and bounds but women here still continue to be discriminated and the current status of women in India still causes concern. Although the constitution provides legal equality for men and women but social and economic equality is yet to achieve. This is the fact why Indian women continue to be recipients of welfare and remain at a lower status with low literacy and poor access to resource and facilities. The problem persists despite the vibrant resistance by the women's movement to this over the past several decades. In most parts of India today, women constitute a disproportionate share of the chronically poor population. Indian women face gender discrimination throughout their life within the family, society and at workplace that runs common across the country along all class, caste and religion with varying degrees. Gender division of labour prevails in all sectors of employment. Gender discrimination starts from the foetus, in terms selection of sex, childrearing, feeding, education, employment, control over property and resources, participation and influencing decision-making in public and political spheres, etc. Women need self-confidence to fight against all the atrocities against them and to live self-esteemed life. Hence, boosting the morale and self-confidence of the women is the key to eliminate their inferior complex. Women also have all the potential and empowering women will help to use her full capability and mitigate the economic dependency of women. Empowering women with decision-making aptitude, education and employment will make the society to accept the women as an equal gender like male.

Women's political participation has been considered a major measure of women's empowerment; but in India, attempts to secure political representation particularly in higher political arenas have not been so successful. Fresh impetus is required with a modern approach. Indian democracy is more than 60 years old now, yet the participation of women in politics has actually declined since the days of the freedom movement, both in quantity and quality. Having a high participation of women at the local self-government level can create an environment which is enabling for other women, receptive to the idea of gender-based initiatives and can serve to monitor and implement community and gender-based programmes of the government related to education, nutrition and health. It is also now often pointed out that women's empowerment must be seen as a process wherein we must consider women's awareness consciousness, choices with live alternatives, resources at their disposal, voice, agency and participation. These are all related to enhancement of women's capabilities and decisions they take individually or collectively for themselves. An overview on the role of position of women in these institutions indicates that women have entered these institutions for the first time by introduction of the policy of reservation but, yet they have to go a long way to prove that they are equally capable as men. The policy of reservation provided for women is important not as an end in itself but a step forward in promoting women's participation in the grassroots of democracy.

Dowry has always been an important part of marriages in India, especially of Hindu marriages. Although dowry was legally prohibited in 1961 by Dowry Prohibition Act but it continues to be highly institutionalized. It is ridiculous to notice that even among highly educated sections, the articles of dowry are proudly exhibited in the marriage as a status symbol. In some parts of the country particularly in rural India, dowry still remains the major reason for all the discrimination and injustice shown to women. The most severe form is bride burning, the burning of women whose dowries was not considered sufficient by their husband or in-laws. Most of these incidents are reported as accidental burns in the kitchen or are disguised as suicide. So it is evident that there exist deep-rooted prejudices against women in India. Not only among Hindus, its evil tentacles are now spreading to other religions also. Cultural practices such as these tend to subordinate women in our society. Dowry is one of those social evils that no educated woman will own up with pride; still many are adhering to it, why? Women should be more economically empowered and should be educated properly regarding the various legal provisions such as Section 498A of Indian Penal Code for ensuring protection from domestic violence, etc., then only this evil menace could possibly be eradicated from Indian social system.

The changing socio-economic scenario and the phasing out of the joint family system along with poor community-based protection systems are some of the reasons why women are becoming increasingly prone to violence and abuse. The weak law enforcement and gender insensitivity of the various functionaries fail to check the growing violence against women. At the same time, the extremely poor levels of awareness among women themselves on their rights also perpetuate violence against them. The lack of adequate rehabilitation and reintegration facilities is another crucial factor that finds victimized women further victimized or ostracized by the community. The media too does not reflect gender issues with sympathy and sensitivity; instead, there is a tendency to glorify patriarchal traditions or to depict women as objects of sexual entertainment.

On the other hand, though more than 40 Gender Cells have been set up in various departments and ministries but studies suggested that the following few factors such as: (i) Gender budgeting statement covers only the specifically targeted programmes for women and pro-women programmes, which constitute less than 5 per cent of total budget.[20] The real challenge of gender budgeting is to explore the rest 95 per cent of the budget through gender lens.[21] (ii) Officers of the Gender Budgeting Cell are rarely consulted at the time of formulation of the Annual Plan/Budget of the Department. (iii) There is a significant deviation between the budget allocations and the revised estimates and in turn actual spending. (iv) Unavailability of sex-disaggregated data. (v) The problem of proliferation of too many programmes with too little money continues over the years. (vi) Senior officers involved in policy formulation of the department are still not fully aware of the concepts of gender budgeting as such workshops are generally attended by lower level officers or officers in Gender Budgeting Cells, etc., who are creating obstacles in mainstreaming the gender budget initiatives in India.

Keeping into consideration the hindering factors, there is an urgent need to build the capacity of the Gender Budgeting Cells that have been set up in various ministries. In fact, the Central Government and the Planning Commission should take strong measures for getting the ministries and departments to implement Women Component Plan (WCP) and collect and report gender disaggregated data on their programmes and schemes. Gender budgeting cannot be seen in isolation from the overall economic-political scenario. Identifying and listing resource allocations for women is only a part of the whole approach of gender budgeting. The crux of the issue is the overall economic policy framework in which we operate. If the overall economic framework continues to be driven by a philosophy of withdrawal of the state from important social and economic sectors, its impact on women would be much more harmful than what some additional resource allocations or schemes for women here or there can mitigate. Gender budgeting must be adopted to address socio-economic discrimination against women because many policy commitments can only be achieved if sufficient funds are allocated for their implementation. Women's and men's needs, concerns and priorities differ due to their different roles in society and in case these differences are not recognized – the way a government raises and spends money can have a negative impact on women by perpetuating the existing inequalities. Taking into consideration the contemporary scenario, following initiatives may be effective to provide an impetus to the process of women empowerment in India:

Strengthening Efforts towards Empowering Women: The Tasks Ahead

- Measures to improve the status, role and participation of women must be given high priority both because women have a fundamental right to enjoy equality with men in all aspects of life and because women can play a crucial role in and must fully participate in the sustainable development process. It is therefore essential to integrate gender perspectives in policies, projects and programmes that can be achieved by gender analysis.

- Ensuring proper implementation of existing reservation policies for ensuring women empowerment – be it in political sphere or in employment
- Reservation of seats for women in panchayat or in parliament, however, is only the first step to ensure that a certain number of women will be involved in decision-making process of the government. The very next task and challenge will be to develop their capacity so that they can perform their role properly and can make a difference.
- Women's groups, civil society and government agencies need to push for change in the rules, structures and processes that specify how resources are allocated and how tasks, responsibilities and values are assigned in institutions as well as in the society more broadly.
- Raising gender awareness, especially among adolescent girls, is needed for breaking the silence about issues such as trafficking, sexual exploitation, HIV/AIDS, early marriage and domestic child labour, as well as to create a more open and empowering environment for the girls.
- Need of an increased consultation with women's groups in the planning process, especially at the grassroot level
- Provisioning more financial resources and power to make decisions directly to panchayat to empower them; women representatives at panchayat level should get more autonomy
- Ensuring provision of vocational training in traditional sector, suitable employment and income-generation activities with the ultimate objective of making all potential women economically independent and self-reliant.
- Movement towards experiments in gender responsive budgeting. However, one cannot ignore the challenges that face the process but gender budgeting must be implemented across all ministries and all machineries, including at the state and panchayat levels.
- It is crucial to integrate gender perspectives in policies, projects and programmes that can be achieved by gender analysis. Elimination of gender bias in policies, projects and

programmes; engendering social audits and making gender audits mandatory for all the government schemes are the need of the hour.

- Adopting policies to reduce women's vulnerability to violence; ensure adequate infrastructure and budgets for the Implementation of Domestic Violence Act and for safe environs outside home.
- Adopting a comprehensive life-cycle approach towards women's health and malnourishment; from cradle to the grave, with women-centred health initiatives to reduce the maternal mortality rate.
- There is a marked lack of sensitivity to gender issues at all levels, be it government or bureaucracy or media or the mainstream civil society; these issues need to be acknowledged and should be given due attention in order to be addressed
- Immediate steps need to be taken to control the declining child sex ratio by regulating medical practitioners and giving due emphasis to the implementation of the PCPNDT Act.
- Initiatives should be taken to enact a comprehensive gender-specific law on sexual violence with an expanded definition of rape, with gender neutral provisions to address child sexual abuse.
- Leaders and policy makers seems to require more intense technical expertise and knowledge of how to mainstream gender concerns into development policies and programmes, so suitable provision for their knowledge-building and need-based training regarding this issue needs to be arranged
- Government and non-governmental organizations need adequate funding for direct interventions and to build capacity in collecting data and evaluating programmes and policies for gender equality and women's empowerment.

Expanded policy interventions with effective implementation; awareness building at family, institution and community levels; and better follow-up and intensified efforts for integrating gender dimensions in policy formulation are needed to reduce constraints and to facilitate the participation of women in the mainstream of every societal affairs. Gender-sensitive policies and planning are the keys to bring about changes in women's current status in a positive direction as they are more likely to respond to the deep-rooted patterns of discrimination against women when women themselves will collectively analyse and contribute to policy making and its implementation processes.

Conclusion

Even after over six decades of independence, a significant number of women in India face disparities in access and control over resources. These disparities get reflected in important social development indicators such as health, nutrition, literacy, educational attainments, skill levels, occupational status, etc. In addition, there are a number of gender-specific barriers that prevent women from gaining access to their rightful share in the flow of public goods and services. Unless these gender requirements and their felt needs are incorporated and mainstreamed in the planning and development process of the country, it is likely that the benefits of economic growth will completely bypass a significant section of the country's population (Government of India, 2011). Empowering women is being considered as the basic to the basics of human rights where she wants neither to beg for power nor search for power hierarchy to exercise power against others. On the contrary, she demands that she should be accepted as human first of all. Millennium Development Goal of ensuring women empowerment and to achieve gender equality recognizes the costs to society of continued female disadvantage.

Policy makers should consider direct policy interventions to accelerate social progress, with a particular focus to enhance gender inclusiveness. Major initiatives to increase the role of women can transform society. If more girls had gone to school a generation ago, millions of infant deaths could have been averted each year, and tens of millions of families could have been more educated, healthier and happier. As compared to the other goals of the millennium commitment, the goal to empower women and to reduce gender disparities is unique because it is not specific to any one sector or issue, such as health, education or access to water; instead it cuts across all the sectors and issues addressed in the MDGs and its success depends on the extent to which it is addressed within each of the other sector-specific goals. Moreover, the goal of gender equality is pre-eminent among the MDGs because if it is not achieved, none of the other goals can be met fully.

Notes

1. Kabeer (1999).
2. Sahay (1998).
3. World Bank (2001).
4. WEF (2010).
5. Ibid.
6. Ibid.
7. Coonrod (1998).
8. ADB (2003).
9. WPA (2005).
10. Hazra (2009a).
11. Abu Ghaida and Klasen (2002).
12. Census of India (2001).
13. Hazra (2009b).
14. Ibid.
15. Hazra (2009b).
16. Hazra (2009b).
17. World Bank (1997).
18. Hazra (2010a).
19. Hazra (2010b).
20. Hazra (2010c).
21. Ibid.

References

Abu Ghaida, D., and Klasen, S. (2002). *The Costs of Missing the Millennium Development Goal on Gender Equity*. Discussion Paper 2003–01 (January 2003). Munich: University of Munich.

Asian Development Bank (ADB). (2003). *Combating Trafficking of Women and Children in South Asia*. Philippines: ADB

Census of India. (2001). *India at a glance – Statistics on Demographic and Socio-Economic Characteristics*. Retrieved from http://www.censusindia.gov.in (accessed December 10, 2009).

Coonrod, C.S. (1998). *Chronic Hunger and the Status of Women in India. Condition of Women in India*. Retrieved from http://www.thp.org/reports/indiawom.htm (accessed November 21, 2009).

Government of India. (2007). *Selected Educational Statistics 2004–2005*. New Delhi, India: Ministry of Human Resource Development.

Government of India. (2011). *SAARC Development Goals: India Country Report 2010*. New Delhi, India: Central Statistics Office.

Grown, C. et al. (2005). *Taking Action: Achieving Gender Equality and Empowering Women*. UN Millennium Project Task Force on Education and Gender Equality. London: Earthscan.

Hazra, A. (2009a). Gender Disparity in Education. *Yojana*, Vol. 53.

Hazra, A. (2009b). Educational Status of Women in India. *Social Welfare*, Vol. 56 (6).

Hazra, A. (2010a). Women Reservation Bill: Can We Hope for Gender Equality? *Kurukshetra*, Vol. 58 (8).

Hazra, A. (2010b). Maternal Mortality in India. *South Asia Politics*, Vol. 9 (2).

Hazra, A. (2010c). Gender Budgeting and Development: The Indian Scenario. *A Journal of Social Focus*, Vol. 1 (2).

Hazra, A. (2011). The Challenge of Empowering Women: Exploring The Current Dynamics. *IASSI Quarterly*, Vol. 30 (2).

Hazra, A. (2012). The Need of Right-based Empowerment Approach for Women of Rural India. *Social Action*, Vol. 62 (3).

Herz, B., and Sperling, G.B. (2004). *What Works in Girls' Education: Evidence and Policies from the Developing World*. New York: Council on Foreign Relations.

International Institute for Population Sciences (IIPS) and ORC Macro. (2000). *National Family Health Survey (NFHS-2), 1998–99: India*. Mumbai, India: IIPS.

Kabeer N. (1999). Resources, Agency, Achievements: Reflections on the Measurement of Women's Empowerment. *Development and Change*, Vol. 30 (3).

Narayan, D. (ed.). (2002). *Empowerment and Poverty Reduction: A Sourcebook*. Washington, DC: World Bank.

Planning Commission. *Five Year Plan Documents*. Retrieved from www.planningcommission.nic.in (accessed November 21, 2009).

Sahay, S. (1998). *Women and Empowerment: Approaches and Strategies*. New Delhi, India: Discovery Publishing House.

Shariff, A., and Razzack, A. (2006). "Communal Relations and Social Integration" in *India Social Development Report*. Council for Social Development Report. New Delhi, India: Oxford University Press.

Tilak, J.B.G. (2002). Education Poverty in India. *Review of Development and Change*, Vol. 7 (1).

World Bank. (1997). *Primary Education in India*. Washington, DC: World Bank.

World Bank. (2001). *Engendering Development: Through Gender Equality in Rights, Resources, and Voice*. New York: Oxford University Press.

World Economic Forum (WEF). (2010). *The Global Gender Gap Report 2010*. Geneva, Switzerland: WEF.

World Population Awareness (WPA). (2005). *World Population Awareness: India*. Retrieved from http://www.overpopulation.org/India.html (accessed November 22, 2009).

6 Making India 'Healthy'

Still a Distant Dream

Keeping in view the significance of achieving Millennium Development Goals (MDGs), health is a priority goal in its own right and a central input into economic development and poverty reduction. Among all the goals health assumes centre of the development agenda and a prerequisite for economic growth and social cohesion. The health-related MDGs do not cover all the health issues that matter to poor people and poor countries, but they do serve as markers of the most basic challenges ahead: to stop women dying during pregnancy and child birth, to protect young children from ill-health and death, and to tackle the major communicable diseases, in particular HIV/AIDS. As the health-related goals lie at the heart of millennium commitments, so slackness towards health sector may jeopardize the achievement of other goals, imperilling India's progress towards its millennium commitments. Of all the challenges India faces, improving access to basic health care is perhaps one of the most pressing – from a straightforward human development perspective as well as to ensure a solid foundation for future economic growth. Realizing the essence of making health services available to all, since independence new programmes and initiatives in health sector have been initiated from time to time, as and when it was felt and required.

Table 39 *Major Health Care Initiatives since Independence in India at a Glance*

1943	The Health Survey and Development Committee, was constituted under the chairmanship of Sir Joseph Bhore, was formulated on 18 October 1943 – which was assigned to document the prevailing health conditions in India and to recommend a comprehensive plan for the future. The four-volume Bhore Committee Report was submitted to the government in 1946, emphasizing on the need for a comprehensive and universal health care system, which would push India towards ensuring the right to health for its entire population.

Cont'd...

...Cont'd

It promised health care to all, irrespective of an individual's paying capacity. The report also recognized that poverty and environmental conditions hamper public health systems from achieving the best possible results. It conceptualized a three-tier pyramidal structure for each district to run an integrated health service.

1946 India was one of the first countries to recognize the merits of Primary Health Care (PHC) Approach. PHC was conceptualized in 1946, three decades before the Alma Ata declaration, when Sir Joseph Bhore made recommendations that formed the basis for organization of basic health services in India. The most comprehensive health policy and plan document ever prepared in India was on the eve of Independence in 1946. Following independence reorganization of the health services structure took place in the light of the Bhore Committee recommendations.

1951 India was the first country in the world to launch a family planning programme.

1952 The Community Development Programme was launched for the holistic and integrated development of rural India, which put a special focus on the issues of health and sanitation through establishment of primary health centre and sub-centres. Each Community Development Block comprised approximately 100 villages with a total population of 100,000. For one CDB, one Primary Health Centre was created.

1953 National Malaria Control Programme (NMCP) was initiated. DDT spraying resulted in a sharp decline in the incidence of malaria in all areas under spray. In 1958, NMCP was converted to the National Malaria Eradication Programme (NMEP) with a view to eradicate malaria from the country.

1955 The National Leprosy Control Programme was launched by the Government of India in 1955 based on Dapsone Monotherapy. Multi-Drug Therapy (MDT) came into wide use from 1982 after which the programme was re-named as the National Leprosy Eradication Programme (NLEP) in 1983.

1959 Towards the end of the Second Five-Year Plan, Government of India appointed a 'Health Survey and Planning Committee' headed by Dr A.L. Mudaliar to assess the state of the healthcare field and to measure the progress achieved after implementing the suggestions of the Bhore committee of 1946, which submitted its report in 1962. The Committee recommended that one primary health centre should cater to a maximum of 40,000 people with the improvement in the quality of health care provided by these centres and provision of one basic health worker per 10,000 populations was recommended.

1961 Department of Family Planning created under Ministry of Health

1962 National Tuberculosis Control Programme (NTCP) was launched to control Tuberculosis

1967 The Jungalwalla Committee emphasized on integration of health services and focussed on 'a service with a unified approach for all problems instead of a segmented approach for all different problems'. The committee recommended integration from the highest to lowest level in the services, organization and personnel.

Cont'd...

...Cont'd

1973 The Kartar Singh Committee laid down the norms for health workers. With an aim to ensure proper coverage of health services the committee proposed that one primary health centre should be established for every 50,000 population and each primary health centre to be divided into 16 sub-centres each for covering a population of 3,000 to 3,500. It was also suggested that each sub-centre need to be staffed by a team of one male and one female health worker and the work of three to four health workers to be supervised by one health assistant.

1975 The Shrivastav Committee on Medical Education and Support Manpower focussed on the referral services for strengthening health care system of the country and recommended that the development of a 'Referral Service Complex' by establishing linkages between the primary health centre and higher level referral and service centres, viz., taluka/tehsil, district, regional and medical college hospitals.

1976 National Programme for Control of Blindness (NPCB) was launched as a 100 per cent Centrally Sponsored Scheme with the goal to reduce the prevalence of blindness.

1977
- Taking into consideration, the recommendations of the Shrivastav committee report, Rural Health Scheme was launched, which provided due importance on training of the community health workers, reorientation training of multipurpose workers, and linking medical colleges to rural health care system. With an aim to encourage community participation in rural health care system, the Community Health Volunteer-Village Health Guide Scheme was initiated.
- Renaming of Family Planning to Family Welfare.

1978
- The Alma Ata Declaration provided a dynamic insight into the understanding of primary health care, which viewed health as an integral part of the socio-economic development of a country. The Alma Ata declaration of 1978 launched the concept of health for all by year 2000. It was signed by 134 governments (including India) and 67 other agencies. The declaration advocated the provision of first contact services and basic medical care within the framework of an integrated health services.
- The immunization programme in India was flagged off as Expanded Programme on Immunization (EPI).

1983 The responsibility of the state to provide comprehensive primary health care to its people as envisaged by the Alma Ata Declaration led to the formulation of India's first National Health Policy (NHP) with an aim to provide a universal, comprehensive primary health services across the nation; the policy also emphasized the role of private and voluntary organizations in strengthening the systems of health care service delivery. The National Health policy 1983 also indicated the need to formulate, separately, a National Medical and Health Education Policy.

1985 Universal Immunization Programme (UIP) was launched. Under the UIP, vaccines for six vaccine-preventable diseases (tuberculosis, diphtheria, pertussis (whooping cough), tetanus, poliomyelitis and measles) were made available free of cost to all.

Cont'd...

...Cont'd

1987 The National AIDS Control Programme launched in 1987 established a comprehensive, multi-sectoral programme for the prevention and control of HIV/AIDS in India to prevent HIV transmission; decrease the morbidity and mortality associated with the HIV infection and minimize the socio-economic impact resulting from the HIV infection. The National AIDS Control programme has been decentralized. State AIDS societies have been set up in all the states and union territories to manage state efforts for HIV/AIDS prevention and control, including management of NGO collaboration. The activities of the National AIDS Control Organisation include information, education and communication (IEC) campaigns and social mobilization; condom promotion, blood safety, control of sexually transmitted infections (STIs). In 1999, the second phase of the National AIDS Control Programme (NACP II) came into effect with the stated aim of reducing the spread of HIV through promoting behaviour change. During this time, the prevention of mother-to-child transmission (PMTCT) programme and the provision of free antiretroviral treatment were implemented for the first time.

1992
- Child Survival and Safe Motherhood Programme (CSSM) were launched.
- A national Iodine Deficiency Disorders (IDD) control programme was launched covering all the states and union territories.

1993 National Nutrition Policy was launched for promoting nutritional status for its entire population.

1997
- National Tuberculosis Control Programme could not achieve the desired results, therefore it was reviewed by an expert committee in 1992 and based on its recommendations, Revised National TB Control Programme (RNTCP), which is an application of WHO recommended strategy of Directly Observed Treatment Short course (DOTS) to India, was launched in the country on 26 March 1997.
- The Reproductive and Child Health (RCH) programme was initiated to comprehensively integrates interventions that improve child health and address factors contributing to infant and under-five mortality.

2000 The National Population Policy (NPP) was announced to address the unmet needs of contraception, health care infrastructure, and health personnel, and to provide integrated delivery for basic reproductive and child care services.

2002 The Second National Health Policy was formulated. With its comprehensive and innovative framework of approach it encouraged decentralized public health care system across the nation by establishing new infrastructure in deficient areas and upgrading the infrastructure of existing institutions; it also provided a major boost towards increasing sectoral share of allocation out of total health spending to primary health care.

2003 A comprehensive tobacco control legislation titled 'The Cigarettes and Other Tobacco Products (Prohibition of Advertisement and Regulation of Trade and Commerce, Production, Supply and Distribution) Act, 2003' was notified in the official gazette on 19 May 2003 – with an aim to prohibit smoking in a public place (revised rules have been notified and came into effect on 2 October, 2008) as well as to ban direct and indirect advertisement of all tobacco products.

Cont'd...

...Cont'd

	The National Health Policy 2002 addresses issues relating to access to public health systems especially for the vulnerable sections of the society and aims to evolve a policy structure, which reduces such inequities and allows the disadvantaged sections of the population a fairer access to public health services. Ensuring more equitable access to health services across the social and geographical expanse of the country is the main objective of the policy. It also seeks to increase the aggregate public health investment through increased contribution from the central as well as state governments and encourages the setting up of private insurance instruments for increasing the scope of coverage of the secondary and tertiary sector under private health insurance packages.
2005	• The National Rural Health Mission (NRHM) was initiated with an aim to bring about dramatic improvement in the health system and the health status of the people, especially those who live in the rural areas of the country. NRHM is designed as an umbrella programme – consolidating existing programmes as well as adding some new ones – with a flexible, bottom-up perspective. The mission seeks to provide universal access to equitable, affordable and quality health care which is accountable at the same time responsive to the needs of the people, reduction of child and maternal deaths as well as population stabilization, gender and demographic balance. The mission envisages a synergistic primary health care approach for decentralized health planning and implementation at the village and district level. The mission was made operational from April 2005 throughout the country with special focus on 18 states having weak demographic indicators and infrastructure.
	• Reproductive and Child Health Programme-2 (RCH-2) was launched.

Source: Based on Hazra (2012).

India has also built up a vast health infrastructure and initiated several national health programmes over the last 65 years in the government, voluntary and private sectors, resulting in certain achievement, which is very much evident in the sphere of controlling leprosy, blindness, iodine deficiency disorder, etc. Some of the legislations were also enacted to protect life and personal liberty as the constitution holds the right to health care as a fundamental one. As far as coverage of health care services in India is concerned, an emphasis on decentralization in service delivery is well-reflected in its focus on public health facilities operating at the lowest levels to serve geographically dispersed rural communities, which will be apparent from the existing health service delivery framework (see Table 40). In the public sector, a sub-health centre (sub-centre) is the most peripheral and first contact point between the primary health care system and the community. As per the

Table 40 *A Framework of Existing Organizational Hierarchy in India's Health Care System*

At national level: The organization at the national level consists of the Union Ministry of Health and Family Welfare. The ministry has three departments, viz. Health, Family Welfare, and Indian System of Medicine and Homeopathy, headed by two secretaries, one for Health and Family Welfare and the other for ISM and H. The Department of Health is supported by a technical wing, and the Directorate General of Health Services, headed by Director General of Health Services (DGHS).

At state level: The organization at state level is under the State Department of Health and Family Welfare in each State headed by Minister and with a Secretariat under the charge of Secretary/Commissioner (Health and Family Welfare) belonging to the cadre of Indian Administrative Service (IAS). By and large, the organizational structure adopted by the state is in conformity with the pattern of the Central Government. The State Directorate of Health Services, as the technical wing, is an attached office of the State Department of Health and Family Welfare and is headed by a Director of Health Services. However, the organizational structure of the State Directorate of Health Services is not uniform throughout the country. For example, in some states, the Programme Officers below the rank of Director of Health Services are called Additional Director of Health Services, while in other states they are called Joint/Deputy Director, Health Services. But regardless of the job title, each programme officer below the Director of Health Services deals with one or more subject(s). Every State Directorate has supportive categories comprising of both technical and administrative staff.

At regional level: In the state of Bihar, Madhya Pradesh, Uttar Pradesh, Andhra Pradesh, Karnataka and others, zonal or regional or divisional set-ups have been created between the State Directorate of Health Services and District Health Administration. Each regional/zonal set-up covers three to five districts and acts under authority delegated by the State Directorate of Health Services. The status of officers/in-charge of such regional/zonal organizations differs, but they are known as Additional/Joint/Deputy Directors of Health Services in different states.

At district level: In the recent past, states have reorganized their health services structures in order to bring all health care programmes in a district under unified control. The district-level structure of health services is a middle-level management organization and it is a link between the state as well as regional structure on one side and the peripheral-level structures such as PHC as well as sub-centre on the other side. It receives information from the state level and transmits the same to the periphery by suitable modifications to meet the local needs.

Cont'd...

...Cont'd

In doing so, it adopts the functions of a manager and brings out various issues of general, organizational and administrative types in relation to the management of health services. The district officer with the overall control is designated as the Chief Medical and Health Officer (CM & HO) or as the District Medical and Health Officer (DM & HO). These officers are popularly known as DMOs or CMOs, and are overall in-charge of the health and family welfare programmes in the district. They are responsible for implementing the programmes according to policies laid down and finalized at higher levels, i.e., state and centre. These DMOs/CMOs are assisted by Dy. CMOs and programme officers. The number of such officers, their specialization, and status in the cadre of State Civil Medical Services differ from state to state. Due to this, the span of control and hierarchy of reporting of these programme officers vary from state to state.

At sub-divisional/taluka level: At the Taluka level, health care services are rendered through the office of Assistant District Health and Family Welfare Officer (ADHO). Some specialties are made available at the taluka hospital. The ADHO is assisted by Medical Officers of Health, Lady Medical Officers and Medical Officers of general hospital. These hospitals are being gradually converted into Community Health Centres (CHCs).

At community level: For a successful primary health care programme, effective referral support is to be provided. For this purpose one Community Health Centre (CHC) has been established for every 80,000 to 1 20,000 population, and this centre provides the basic specialty services in general medicine, paediatrics, surgery, obstetrics and gynaecology. The CHCs are established by upgrading the sub-district/taluka hospitals or some of the block-level Primary Health Centres (PHCs) or by creating a new centre wherever absolutely needed.

At PHC level: At present there is one Primary Health Centre covering about 30,000 population. Many rural dispensaries have been upgraded to create these PHCs. Each PHC has one medical officer, two health assistants – one male and one female, and the health workers and supporting staff. For strengthening preventive and promotive aspects of health care, a post of Community Health Officer was proposed to be provided at each new PHC, but most states did not take it up.

At Sub-centre level: The most peripheral health institutional facility is the sub-centre manned by one male and one female multipurpose health worker. At present, in most places there is one sub-centre for about 5,000 populations (3,000 in hilly and desert areas and in difficult terrain).

population norms, one sub-centre is established for every 5,000 population in plain areas and for every 3,000 population in hilly/tribal/desert areas. A sub-centre provides interface with the community at the grassroots level, providing all the primary health care services. As sub-centres are the first contact point with the community, the success of any nationwide programme would depend largely on well-functioning sub-centres providing services of acceptable standard to the people.

In the context of achieving MDGs in health sector, issues such as high maternal mortality rate (as discussed in Chapter 5), soaring infant mortality rate (IMR) and controlling diseases such as HIV/AIDS, TB, malaria, etc., still cause concern for the policy makers which will be quite evident from the following discussion.

Infant Mortality Rate: Still Causes Concern

In the context of the country's overall health scenario, the infant mortality rate often serves as a key development indicator which aptly reflects the combined effects of economic development, technological change, including health interventions and the socio-cultural environment. Infant mortality refers to deaths of children under the age of one year and is measured in terms of the total number of deaths to children under the age of one year for every 1,000 live births. The infant mortality rate is often broken down into two components relating to timing of death: neonatal and post-neonatal. The neonatal mortality rate refers to the number of deaths of babies within 28 days after birth per 1,000 live births. The post-neonatal mortality rate involves the number of deaths of babies from 28 days to the end of the first year per 1,000 live births. As far as the incidences of infant mortality rate in India is concerned, there are wide variations across the states. On the one hand, we have states such as Kerala and Tamil Nadu which have excellent indicators of child health, comparable with those of many developed countries. On the other hand, we have states such as Orissa, Madhya Pradesh, UP, Rajasthan and Bihar whose child health indicators are very poor.

Child Mortality: The Causatives Factors

Malnutrition has been identified as the main factor for retarding improvements in human development and hindering further reductions in infant mortality in India.[1] Although potentially cost-effective and affordable interventions are available, but existing food supplementation and micronutrient programmes in India have not achieved significant reductions in nutritional deficiencies at state or national levels – a factor contributing to the slowing decline of childhood mortality rates. The problem of child malnutrition is multidimensional and multi-sectoral in nature, which very often leads to infant or child mortality. It is estimated that undernutrition and anaemia are contributory factors in over 50 per cent of under-five deaths in the country.[2]

Studies suggest that mother's educational level tends to have a strong effect on the mortality of young children, especially in developing countries like India.[3] Literate mothers usually give birth to healthier babies because they themselves tend to be healthier than mothers who are illiterate. In addition, literate mothers are more likely to provide their children with a healthy environment and nutritious food than are illiterate mothers, even when other conditions are similar. Lastly, literate mothers are likely to have more information about health care facilities and to have more influence within the family in deciding to take sick children for treatment. These traits are likely to result in lower mortality of children at all ages under five (Caldwell, 1994; Cleland and Kaufman, 1993; World Bank, 1993). So, mother's literacy emerges as an important factor associated with child mortality in India during the first five years of life.

At the same time, religion and membership in an SC or ST community is known to affect many aspects of life in India and is likely to affect levels of infant and child mortality as well. Some of the effects of religion and caste/tribe membership on mortality may be due to differences in lifestyle based on traditions and beliefs. Such differences may include customary practices related to childbirth, infant feeding, and health care, and these should have an effect on infant and child mortality independently of other variables. On the other hand, a mother's exposure to radio and television may reduce the mortality of her children because women who are exposed to mass media are likely to have access to information on health-care services and ways of enhancing maternal and child health. Mother's exposure to mass media may also act as an indicator of the economic status of the household.

Therefore, in the context of developing country like India, variables such as place of residence (rural/urban), mother's educational status, household head's religion and membership in an SC or ST community, extent of mother's exposure to mass media, availability of sanitation facilities at household level, etc., are having a direct or indirect impact or influence on the state of child health. Improving female education and nutrition and increasing the use of health services during pregnancy and delivery are all important for reducing childhood mortality rates.

India's Initiatives towards Reducing Infant Mortality

The National Health Policy has prioritized the implementation of the National Immunization Programme and it has been the cornerstone of the child health care system. The Government of India initiated BCG immunization against Tuberculosis in 1948, and it picked up momentum in 1951 with BCG vaccinations conducted in mass campaigns in schools and vaccination centres. DPT immunization of infants and school children against diphtheria, pertussis (whooping cough), tetanus was taken up during the Fourth Five-Year Plan period 1969–1974 (Gaudin and Yazbeck, 2006). The Diarrhoeal Disease Control Programme was initiated in 1978 to prevent death due to dehydration caused by diarrhoeal diseases among children less than five years of age. The Expanded Programme on Immunization (EPI) was started by the Government of India in 1978 with the objective of reducing the prevalence, mortality and disabilities from six vaccine preventable diseases, i.e., tuberculosis, diphtheria, pertussis, tetanus, polio and measles. Immunization against polio was included in EPI in 1979–1980. Tetanus Toxoid (TT) immunization initiated for pregnant mothers in 1975–1976 was integrated with EPI in 1978. Measles vaccine was added to the Indian EPI programme in 1985. As a signatory to the UNICEF declaration in the UN 40th anniversary, India launched the Universal Immunization Programme (UIP) in October 1985. The goal of UIP is to cover 85 per cent of all children and 100 per cent of pregnant women by 1990. All districts in the country were reportedly served by the UIP by 1989–1990 (IIPS, 1995). UIP became part of the CSSM (Child Survival and Safe Motherhood) programme in 1992 and the RCH programme in 1997. India launched the Pulse Polio Immunization (PPI) campaign in 1995 as a vertical programme with a high degree of political commitment. A major component of PPI is the organization of mass immunization on National Immunization Day. Though the campaign mode programme of PPI was led to increased coverage of Oral Polio Vaccine (OPV) it is cited as one of the reasons for the under-achievement of routine immunization goals (Bonu et al., 2003).

India's National Health Policy gives high priority to the health of women and children. There are a number of national initiatives that aim to reduce infant and under-five mortality. The umbrella scheme under which most of the other schemes fall is the Reproductive and Child Health Programme. As a component of Reproductive and Child Health Programme, *Janani Suraksha Yojana* (JSY) has been initiated to address and promote the key issue of promoting institutional deliveries and immunization. Later on, the Integrated Management of Neonatal Childhood Illness (IMNCI) programme was initiated to achieve the National Population Policy's goal of attaining an IMR of 30 per 1,000 by 2010. Under IMNCI, baseline workers are trained in the management of measles, malaria, pneumonia, diarrhoea and malnutrition in a holistic manner with appropriate health facilities. On the other hand, under Mid-Day Meal Scheme of Department of School Education and Literacy, meals are being provided to children in the age group of 6–14 years in the school. At the same time, essential food items have been made available at subsidized cost through Targeted Public Distribution System and *Antyodaya Anna Yojana* by Department of Food and Consumer Affairs.

Reducing Child Mortality: Certain Key Issues

As far as the issue of reducing and controlling infant mortality is concerned, there are certain key issues which need to be tackled with utmost priority. First, there are gender differences in the context of infant mortality across the societies of the nation. Girls have a higher mortality rates than boys during the post-neonatal period to five years. The risk of mortality is higher among girls than boys as their malnutrition levels are higher. Sex differentials in infant and child mortality reflect preference for strong son in many states. Though there is no biological reason for a higher mortality rate in females in the age group of 0–5 years, it is the social causes that adversely affect the mortality rate of girls, and this needs to be tackled. Second, in India, living conditions are generally worse in rural areas than in urban areas, and health care facilities are less readily available and tend to be of poorer quality. These differences usually result in higher infant and child mortality in rural areas than in urban areas. One of the reasons is the lack of accessibility to services either by remoteness of the location and higher proportion of disadvantaged groups. So, bridging the gap between urban and rural child mortality rates and immunization coverage is another challenge to be tackled with. Providing adequate services to specific vulnerable groups and those in the remote areas is the key to bring down the gap. Third, it has been noticed that although concerted global and national efforts have been made to improve child mortality, especially in the post-neonatal phase, less attention has been given to determinants of perinatal and neonatal mortality; as a consequence it is observed that improving child survival still remains a major development task for India. Neonatal mortality accounts for more than two-thirds of IMR in India. Over the last decade, post-neonatal mortality has declined much faster than neonatal mortality. This is mainly due to increased programme interventions focussed on post-neonatal such as immunization, management of diarrhoea and acute respiratory infection (ARI). Policies and programmes should focus on interventions in the sphere of perinatal and neonatal mortality. So, the future child health policies should build on past lessons from child health programmes in India, sustain the achievements that have already been made, enhance quality and efficiency and address specific gaps in perinatal and neonatal care.

Careful monitoring of mother's health and growth of the foetus during pregnancy can identify potential complications during pregnancy, thus improving child survival after birth. Supplemental intake of vitamins and minerals during pregnancy enhances foetal growth and improves survival chances after birth. Furthermore, mother's tetanus immunization during pregnancy can sharply reduce risks of mortality due to neonatal tetanus. Also, timely check-ups of mother and baby after birth can improve survival chances of children. Child malnutrition is another area to be tackled as studies have revealed a synergy between malnutrition and mortality. Now, it is being felt that a single scheme cannot address the problem of malnutrition, rather an updated strategic framework for childhood illness, health and development is needed. Keeping in view these factors, a new strategic framework for child survival is required which will be capable to tackle the emerging issues and causative factors of child mortality.

Table 41 *A Strategic Framework for Promoting Child Survival – Reflecting Options for Reducing Barriers*

Gaps and Barriers in Child Survival	*Possible Policy Options*
The IMR performance gaps	• Focus attention on states with high U5M levels and/or poor relative performance and/or a reduction in IMR declines. Develop state-specific strategies (including advocacy, incentives strategies and increased commitment among stakeholders). • Apply managerial approaches at the state level to identify the main implementation bottlenecks in the health system and the most critical and feasible solutions. • Introduce more efficient, integrated strategies for prevention and management of childhood illness at the community and facility levels.
The neonatal/perinatal determinants	• Introduce or enhance integrated approaches to childhood illness with emphasis on neonatal care and referral services. • Introduce or expand a standard approach to the management of pregnancy and safe delivery; develop strategies for how to increase demand for and use of antenatal services and access to safe deliveries.
The maternal determinants	• Improve female education and nutrition and increase use of health services before, during and after pregnancy and delivery. • Expand successful reproductive health initiatives and develop feasible strategies for increasing antenatal and delivery services.
The gender gap	• Provide supplemental feeding and basic health services to all children, with particular attention to young girls. • Target at-risk girls with health services and supplemental feeding.

Cont'd...

...Cont'd

The nutrition determinants	• Develop an LBW strategy for wide-scale implementation, identifying the most influential factors and cost-effective, feasible interventions, including expansion of supplementary feeding and reduction of maternal anaemia. • Review and revise strategies for micronutrient programmes. Address known constraints such as availability of supplies, and motivating/educating communities. • Include nutrition in integrated strategies for prevention and care of children, including breast feeding counselling, provision of micronutrients and feeding advice.
The urban poor	• Design and expand multi-sectoral approaches for prevention and care in slum areas. • Improve involvement of private sector to increase the reach of quality health care services for the urban poor. • Review and revise protocols and procedures to allow more practical and feasible approaches for private health care providers.

Source: Claeson et al. (1999).

The Government of India needs to reassess the country's current child mortality reduction goals and go forward with enhanced integrated approaches for child health and nutrition. Existing child health programmes and strategies, including initiatives for the eradication and elimination of vaccine-preventable childhood diseases, and specific health and nutrition interventions need to be examined in the context of a broader child health framework that goes beyond disease-specific approaches. A better understanding of the main determinants of the health and nutrition cycle for mothers and children – the life cycle – is central to developing more effective strategies for child survival, health and development. Socio-economic, environmental, behavioural, health and nutritional determinants influence this cycle; the challenges over the next ten years will jointly address the most important determinants and gaps in the cycle with affordable, cost-effective and culturally appropriate interventions. These should take into account both demand and supply factors, and involve local communities in identifying needs and priorities. Because of state differences in infant and child mortality levels and performance in India, stratified child health policies are needed that take into account state-specific epidemiological and demographic patterns and key determinants (Claeson et al., 2000). So it may be concluded that increased access to a minimum package of essential services that would significantly reduce high infant mortality rates are reproductive health services; perinatal care; improved breast feeding practices; proper immunization; home-based treatment of diarrhoea; and timely introduction of supplementary foods.

Controlling HIV/AIDS: Still Remain a Threat

AIDS was recognized for the first time in the United States in 1981. In India, it was identified after five years in May 1986. In October 1985, the health authorities of the Government of India realizing the threat and spread of HIV and AIDS through the Indian Council of Medical Research organized the screening of high-risk groups with the aim of finding out whether HIV infection has reached India. India's first cases of HIV were diagnosed among sex workers in Chennai, Tamil Nadu.[4] It was noted that contact with foreign visitors had played a role in initial infections among sex workers, and as HIV screening centres were set up across the country, there were calls for visitors to be screened for HIV. Gradually, these calls subsided as more attention was paid to ensuring that HIV screening was carried out in blood banks. National AIDS Control Programme was launched to coordinate national responses in 1987. Its activities covered surveillance, blood screening and health education. By the end of 1987, out of 52,907 who had been tested, around 135 people were found to be HIV positive and 14 had AIDS (Kakar and Kakar, 2001). Most of these initial cases had occurred through heterosexual sex, but at the end of the 1980s a rapid spread of HIV was observed among injecting drug users (IDUs) in Manipur, Mizoram and Nagaland – three northeastern states of India bordering Myanmar (Burma).[5] In 2006 UNAIDS estimated that there were 5.6 million people with HIV living in India, which indicated that there were more people with HIV in India than in any other country in the world.[6] In 2007, following the first survey of HIV among the general population, UNAIDS and NACO agreed on a new estimate – between 2 million and 3.1 million people living with HIV.[7] In 2008, the figure was estimated to be 2.31 million.[8] In 2009, it was estimated that 2.4 million people with HIV were living in India, which equates to a prevalence of 0.3 per cent.[9] While this may seem low, because India's population is so large, it is third in the world in terms of greatest number of people living with HIV. With a population of around a billion, a mere 0.1 per cent increase in HIV prevalence would increase the estimated number of people living with HIV by over half a million.

The economic impact of HIV/AIDS results from loss of productivity and efficiency of operations, absenteeism and the cost of care and treatment. In addition, HIV/AIDS also degrades morale and workplace cohesion and forces companies to hire and train substitute workers. Episodes of illness have a negative impact on other members in the work team and on the work process in general that cannot be quantified. Industries that rely heavily on unskilled labour or on labour mobility, such as trucking, are particularly vulnerable.

Table 42 *Populations Considered to Have the Highest Risk of Acquiring HIV*

- **Sex Workers:** Because of widespread poverty throughout India, women often resort to prostitution as a means of making money for their families. Others are forced into sex work due to an underground of violence and disrespect towards women. Finally, women involved in marital break-ups will often begin prostituting themselves as a means of surviving financially after being left with children to feed and a household to support. In some areas of India, it is estimated that one in every two sex workers are HIV infected, many not knowing it.
- **Intra-Venus Drug Use (IVDU):** The recreational use of drugs often overlaps with the sex trade. While IVDU seems to be worse in the northeastern parts of India, it is common throughout the country. Many attribute the widespread problem of IVDU and HIV to government policies that do not support HIV prevention and risk reduction among IV drug users. Because IVDU is a crime and is consistently enforced and prosecuted, getting prevention messages to users is very difficult. There have been instances of prevention workers themselves being arrested while trying to help and educate IV drug users. Official estimates actually report the HIV prevalence among IV drug users to have gone down from 13 per cent in 2003 to 10 per cent in 2005.
- **Truck Drivers:** India's economy depends a great deal on its very large trucking network across the country. While truckers help move goods and services throughout India, they also contribute a great deal to the huge population with HIV and the spread of HIV from one area of India to another. Truckers will pick up sex workers along their route, engage in unprotected sex activity and then drop off the sex worker at the trucker's next stop along the route. This has contributed to the spread of HIV from urban areas into the rural towns and villages. The most damaging fact about truckers and their use of sex workers is that neither party knows they are infected.

Cont'd...

Cont'd...

- **Men Having Sex with Men:** There is a high degree of stigma associated with homosexuality in India. In fact, homosexuality has been criminalized, making HIV education and surveillance very difficult. Outreach workers are often harassed and even arrested for 'promoting homosexuality'. It's estimated that 42 per cent of all men who have sex with men are also married, fuelling the increasing HIV infection rate among women of India.
- **Migrant Workers:** As is the case in the United States, migrant workers in India are very transient and mobile, moving from town to town wherever the work takes them. Unfortunately, they take their risky behaviour along with them, fuelling the spread of HIV throughout India. While there are attempts at HIV education, the variety of languages, dialects and cultures makes HIV education very difficult.

Source: Author's articulation based on Pembrey (2007).

At the beginning of the 1990s, as infection rates continued to rise, responses were strengthened. In 1992, the government set up the NACO (National AIDS Control Organization) to oversee the formulation of policies, prevention work and control programmes relating to HIV and AIDS.[10] In the same year, the government launched a strategic plan, the National AIDS Control Programme (NACP) for HIV prevention. This plan established the administrative and technical basis for programme management and also set up State AIDS Control Societies (SACS) in 25 states and seven union territories.[11] It was able to make a number of important improvements in HIV prevention such as improving blood safety. In 1999, the second phase of the National AIDS Control Programme (NACP II) came into effect with the stated aim of reducing the spread of HIV through promoting behaviour change. During this time, the prevention of mother-to-child transmission (PMTCT) programme and the provision of free antiretroviral treatment were implemented for the first time. In phase two of the country's National AIDS Control Programme, the Adolescent Education Programme (AEP) was launched. The programme aimed to train teachers and peer-educators to educate the student community both in and out of school about life skills, HIV prevention and HIV-related stigma and discrimination.

The third phase (NACP III) began in 2006, with the highest priority placed on reaching 80 per cent of high-risk groups including sex workers, men who have sex with men and injecting drug users with targeted interventions.[12] Targeted interventions are generally carried out by civil society or community organizations in partnership with the SACS. They include outreach programmes focused on behaviour change through peer education, distribution of condoms and other risk reduction materials, treatment of sexually transmitted diseases, linkages to health services, as well as advocacy and training of local groups. The NACP III also seeks to decentralize the HIV effort to the most local level, i.e., districts, and engage more non-governmental organizations in providing welfare services to those living with HIV/AIDS. As a result of these initiatives, there is a huge push to use condoms. Condom machines are being placed in colleges, roadside rest areas, restaurants, gas stations and along truck routes in an effort to promote and increase condom use. However, the stigma surrounding condom use remains, impeding the process. In response, national celebrities are publicly promoting condom use in an effort to remove stigmas surrounding condom use. In an effort to further HIV education, teachers and peer educators are being trained in order to increase the availability and ease of access to HIV education.

Issues and Challenges in Controlling HIV/AIDS

The attributable factors for such rapid spread of the epidemic across the country today are labour migration and mobility in search of employment from economically backward to more advanced regions, low literacy levels leading to low awareness among the potential high-risk groups, gender disparity, sexually transmitted infections and reproductive tract infections both among men and women. The social stigma attached to sexually transmitted infections also holds good for HIV/AIDS, even in a much more serious manner. The effects of stigma are devastating. Discrimination against people living with HIV/AIDS denies them access to treatment, services and support and hinders effective responses. It creates a climate in which decisive action from the government may be side stepped. There have been cases of refusal of treatment and other services to AIDS patients in hospitals and nursing homes both in government and private sectors. This has compounded the misery of the AIDS patients. More often it is mistaken to be a contagious disease and patients are isolated in the wards creating a scare among the general patients. HIV/AIDS-related stigma and discrimination builds upon, and reinforces existing prejudices. They play into and strengthen existing social inequalities, especially those of gender, sexuality and race. They also play a key role in producing and reproducing relations of power and control. They cause some groups to be devalued and others to feel that they are superior. Ultimately, stigma creates and is reinforced by social inequality. HIV/AIDS victims are denied health services and education, or may lose employment on the grounds of their HIV status (UNAIDS, 2002; Wiseman, 1992). In the workplace, there are cases of discrimination leading, on some occasions, to loss of employment. Only clear and candid information about how HIV is and is not transmitted will alleviate unnecessary fear and discrimination.

Efforts need to be made to train all medical and paramedical health care workers to create a congenial environment where HIV/AIDS patients are admitted and treated without any fear and scare. The treatment options are still in the initial trial stage and are prohibitively expensive. While there is no vaccine in sight, multidrug antiretroviral therapy, popularly known as 'cocktail therapy', is not a cure to the disease and may help only in prolonging the life of the patient. Standardization of treatment regimens for these drugs is still evolving and there are fears of patients developing drug resistance and side effects if the therapy is not administered under proper medical supervision. HIV/AIDS is not merely a public health challenge, it is also a political and social challenge. Behaviour change will not occur without a significant change in the social and political environment. Unequal gender and power relations, taboos in frank and open communication about sexual health and stigma and discrimination are particularly significant obstacles to an effective response. The economic impact of AIDS epidemic needs to be acknowledged. The largest economic cost of a death due to HIV/AIDS is usually lost income as those who die from AIDS are generally younger and in their most productive years.

Tackling the Threats of HIV/AIDS: The Way Forward

The greatest need is to educate people to have safe sex by using condoms and avoiding multiple sexual partners. This is done through TV, radio, newspaper and other mass media. It is also required to introduce awareness through course content in the educational institutions. The medical fraternity in our country is prejudiced about HIV/AIDS with the result that patients are denied admission in hospitals and neglected in treatment by not regularly visiting them in the isolation wards. This has resulted in panic reactions. Such rejections are counterproductive. Effective strategies have to be designed and developed which can help the patients in overcoming fear and hysteria. Counselling families, neighbourhoods and members of social-support networks is also an important need because eventually they have to bear a major responsibility for the sick and the survivors. The trained medical staff can impart information about AIDS to the patients and to their relatives. Since persons suffering from STDs are also a significant risk factor it is important to give high priority to the programmes for the prevention and control of STDs. The blood or blood products should be tested for HIV before transfusion. The HIV tests should be made free and confidential for persons who indulge in high-risk activities. The medical staff should ensure the use of disposable syringes and other operation equipment. The condoms should be freely distributed and its use should be encouraged among the sex workers who are the most vulnerable group. The drug users should be persuaded away from using intravenous drug abuse. The voluntary organizations should help spread knowledge on AIDS to different vulnerable groups through innovative and community-based approaches. Nongovernmental organizations working through peer educators with women in prostitution in India have had remarkable success in raising awareness of the basic facts of HIV transmission and AIDS care, promoting condom use, and, not least, empowering marginalized women to take into their own hands the struggle against HIV/AIDS. Thousands of cases of AIDS have been prevented by this work, some of which has been supported financially or in kind by the government. Indeed, the Indian government recognizes officially the effectiveness of peer education as a strategy, the importance of condom distribution in prevention of HIV transmission, and the need to work with women in prostitution. At the same time, NGOs must be included in the design, implementation, and review of national AIDS programme plans. Also, the efforts of AIDS-related NGOs to form national and regional consortia, in order to strengthen their abilities to collaborate with each other and with their respective national AIDS control programmes, must be supported and strengthened. India's plan for dealing with the pandemic so far has focused mainly on prevention of HIV infection. But as it expands treatment, the financial and technical resources required are growing exponentially, putting an enormous strain on its frail public health infrastructure. India has excellent small targeted awareness and successful intervention programmes among high-risk groups. Indian policymakers are still grappling with different approaches to scale up these successful programmes, which can then be implemented country wide with modifications to suit local characteristics.

Tuberculosis: Still a Major Public Health Challenge in India

Tuberculosis is still an epidemic in many regions of the world, annihilating the lives of many millions of people each year. Tuberculosis, better known as TB, is an infectious disease prevalent in many parts of the world. It is caused by a bacterium called mycobacterium tuberculosis. Normally, TB affects the lungs; it can also affect the brain, back, knees, bones and some other organs. TB is airborne. It is spread by breathing the air that someone suffering from TB has coughed, but it requires several such exposures for one to get infected.

Controlling TB in India is a tremendous challenge. Tuberculosis (TB) is one of the major public health problems in India with a significant impact on the health and economy of the country. India is the highest TB burden country in the world, accounting for nearly one-fifth of the global incidence. Annually more than 2,50,000 people die of TB. This is most unfortunate as TB is a curable disease if treated appropriately and adequately. TB remains a stigmatized disease due to the mistaken beliefs about its cause, transmission and treatment leading to discrimination against people with TB. TB is deeply rooted in poverty. Poverty and low socio-economic status as well as social barriers prevent universal access to quality TB prevention, diagnosis, treatment and care (Project Axshya-Programme Management Unit, 2011). The direct and indirect cost of TB to India amounts to an estimated $23.7

billion annually.[13] TB is a disease that has severely affected communities and nations since times immemorial. The disease has brought untold miseries to generations and even today, when newer modalities for diagnosis and treatment of TB have made the disease curable, people are suffering and dying from the disease.

Box 1 *Some Interesting Facts about Tuberculosis*

Fact 1 Tuberculosis is contagious and spreads through air. If not treated, each person with active TB can infect on average 10 to 15 people a year.

Fact 2 More than 2 billion people, equal to one-third of the world's total population, are infected with TB bacilli, the microbes that cause TB. One in every 10 of those people will become sick with active TB in his or her lifetime. People living with HIV are at a much higher risk.

Fact 3 A total of 1.7 million people died from TB in 2009 (including 380,000 people with HIV), equal to about 4,700 deaths a day. TB is a disease of poverty, affecting mostly young adults in their most productive years. The vast majority of TB deaths are in the developing world, with more than half occurring in Asia.

Fact 4 TB is a leading killer among people living with HIV, who have weakened immune systems.

Fact 5 There were 9.4 million new TB cases in 2009, of which 80 per cent were in just 22 countries. Per capita, the global TB incidence rate is falling, but the rate of decline is very slow – less than 1 per cent.

Fact 6 TB is a worldwide pandemic. Among the 15 countries with the highest estimated TB incidence rates, 13 are in Africa, while a third of all new cases are in India and China.

Fact 7 Multidrug-resistant TB (MDR-TB) is a form of TB that does not respond to the standard treatments using first-line drugs. MDR-TB is present in virtually all countries surveyed by WHO and its partners.

Fact 8 There were an estimated 440,000 new MDR-TB cases in 2008 with three countries accounting for over 50 per cent of all cases globally – China, India and the Russian Federation. Extensively drug-resistant TB (XDR-TB) occurs when resistance to second-line drugs develops. It is extremely difficult to treat and cases have been confirmed in more than 58 countries.

Fact 9 41 million TB patients have been successfully treated in DOTS programmes and up to 6 million lives saved since 1995. Five million more lives could be saved between now and 2015 by fully funding and implementing The Global Plan to Stop TB 2011–2015.

Source: World Health Organization WHO (2000).

Table 43 *Socio-economic Impact of Tuberculosis*

- TB primarily affects people in their productive age group.
- Almost 70 per cent of TB patients are aged between 15 and 54 years.
- The disease is more common among the poorest and the marginalized sections of the community.
- While two-thirds of cases are male, TB takes a disproportionately larger toll among young females, with more than 50 per cent of cases occurring among females who are less than 34 years of age.
- In addition, there is a devastating social cost with an estimate of more than 300,000 children forced to leave school because their parents have TB, and more than 100,000 women with TB are rejected by their families.
- On an average, 3–4 months of work time is lost as a result of TB, resulting in an average potential loss of 20–30 per cent of the annual household income.

Source: Tuberculosis Control India (TBC India).

Studies suggest that on an average three months of work time is lost as a result of TB, resulting in an average lost potential earning of 30 per cent of the annual household income. India has more new TB cases annually than any other country. In 2009, out of the estimated global annual incidence of 9.4 million TB cases, two million were estimated to have occurred in India (1 in 5 almost), thus contributing to a fifth of the global burden of TB. The national annual risk of tuberculosis infection rate is 1.5 per cent. The prevalence of TB has been estimated at 3.8 million cases in 2010. However, WHO's most recent estimate puts the prevalence at 3 million. TB accounts for 17.6 per cent of deaths from communicable disease and for 3.5 per cent of all causes of mortality. More than 80 per cent of the burden of TB is due to premature death, as measured in terms of disability-adjusted (Sinha, 2011).

For tackling the threat of tuberculosis, the National TB Control Programme (NTCP) was initiated in 1962; however, due to inadequate ownership of the programme by the states and some inherent flaws in design, it did not make any significant epidemiological impact. In 1992, the Government of India, together with the World Health Organization (WHO) and the Swedish International Development Agency (SIDA), reviewed the national programme and concluded that it suffered from managerial weaknesses, inadequate funding, over-reliance on x-ray, non-standard treatment regimens, low rates of treatment completion and lack of systematic information on treatment outcomes. Around the same time, in 1993, WHO declared TB a global emergency and devised the Directly Observed Treatment – Short Course (DOTS) strategy and recommended that all countries adopt this strategy. The strategy is built on five pillars, viz., political commitment and continued funding for TB control programmes, diagnosis by sputum smear examinations, uninterrupted supply of high-quality anti-TB drugs, drug intake under direct observation and accurate recording and reporting of all registered cases.

The Revised National TB Control Programme (RNTCP) was launched in India in 1997, after extensive field-testing for technical and programmatic feasibility. The RNTCP aims to widen the scope for providing standardized, good quality treatment and diagnostic services to all TB patients in a patient-friendly environment. Recognizing the need to reach to every TB patient in the country, the programme has made special provisions to reach marginalized sections of the society, including creating demand for services through specific advocacy, communication and social mobilization activities. While RNTCP has made great strides in reducing the burden of TB, there are still a large number of TB patients who are not reached by the programme. RNTCP has impressively expanded DOTS treatment in India. India has achieved substantially in bringing down the TB cases in India, however, there are numerous challenges in sustaining the quality across the country and reaching the unreached due to the sheer dimensions of the country and variable capacity of states to tackle the problem.

First, the general health service often does not function optimally. This suggests that patients with tuberculosis can be identified and treated even in a relatively dysfunctional health care system. Second, TB is one of the most common opportunistic infections associated with HIV, i.e., people with HIV/AIDS are more likely to contract TB. TB is also a major cause of death among patients with HIV. So, there is a need to strengthen linkages between TB and HIV services. In developing economies like India, the potential financial burden imposed by TB cases attributable to HIV infection could overwhelm budget and support services. Third, a large and mostly unregulated private sector provides a substantial proportion of outpatient care, and this care is of inconsistent quality. Third, the Indian tuberculosis control programme is now one of the largest public health programmes in the world. The programme has been remarkably successful, although it still faces many challenges. Sustaining this programme in India will require continued financial support, particularly for drugs and contractual supervisors, as well as continued and intensified supervision and monitoring. Fourth, TB-associated stigma is magnified among middle-class Indians, who often deny their condition and fail to seek treatment because they fear losing social standing. There have been increasing calls for celebrities, especially Bollywood stars, to admit positive TB status because their unique social prominence could drastically change Indians' perception of the disease. To wipe out this stigmatized view regarding TB from the mind of common people remains one of the major tasks for the government in the context of combating and controlling TB. So, creating awareness about TB forms the backbone of the efforts taken to eradicate this dreadful disease which poses a huge challenge before the policymakers.

It is essential to overcome these barriers, diminish peoples' vulnerability to TB and ensure an effective response to TB as part of a broader development agenda aimed at achieving the MDGs. It has become imperative to act now in order to ensure India's success in reaching towards these goals. High burden countries such as India need to increase their investment in TB research and TB control programmes. Resource allocation to the national TB control programme should be increased to bring innovation and conduct research, and strengthen the recording and reporting systems. Since the challenges of TB care and control are multidimensional, it is important to strengthen the community response and make the community voice heard against the threatening TB epidemic of the country through meaningful and effective participation of the civil society organizations (CSOs). With the shift to universal access of TB care, the role of CSOs will become more critical in terms of consolidating and scaling up those key community linkages with the essential services, especially in the underserved, difficult-to-reach areas and with marginalized, criminalized and migrated population groups across the country. There is also huge task and challenge to link the non-formal and private health care providers effectively to the National TB Programme.

Controlling Malaria: Still Need Attention

Malaria and six other diseases, viz., diarrhoea, HIV/AIDS, tuberculosis, measles, hepatitis B and pneumonia account for 85 per cent of global infectious disease burden.[14] Malaria is one of the serious public health problems in India. Under the country's National Vector Borne Disease Control Programme (NVBDCP), malaria was believed to have infected 1.53 million and killed just over 1,100 in 2009. However, World Health Organization (WHO) has estimated over 15,000 deaths.[15] Currently, the states of Orissa, Jharkhand, West Bengal, Northeastern states, Chhattisgarh and Madhya Pradesh contribute bulk of malaria. Urban areas contribute about 15 per cent of the total malaria cases reported in India and are primarily associated with construction activities and migrant population. Most of the malaria attributable mortality is reported from Orissa and other forested areas occupied by ethnic tribes in the country. The true burden of malaria in India is not known (Kumar et al., 2007). A real picture of burden is important on two counts. First, it enables to set priorities right in the planning and resource allocation for malaria control, and second, it provides evidence that enables international donor agencies to assess financial need for operational research and disease control (Amexo et al., 2004).

The Global Malaria Eradication Programme of WHO launched in the 1950s was a huge success in India as the incidence declined from estimated 75 million cases and 800,000 deaths in 1947 to just 49,151 cases (annual parasite incidence [API] per thousand: 0.13; slide positivity rate [SPR]: 0.38 per cent and *Plasmodium falciparum* [Pf]: 34.9%) and no deaths in 1961 and malaria was thought to be on the verge of eradication (Sharma et al., 1996). At the time of independence malaria was contributing 75 million cases with 0.8 million deaths every year prior to the launching of National Malaria Control Programme in 1953. A countrywide comprehensive programme to control malaria was recommended in 1946 by the Bhore Committee report that was endorsed by the Planning Commission in 1951. The national programme against malaria has a long history since that time (Dash et al., 2008) which will be more evident from Table 44.

Table 44 *Malaria Control Activities in India since Independence at a Glance*

- Prior to 1953 – Estimated malaria cases in India – 75 million estimated deaths due to malaria – 1 million
- 1953 – Launching of National Malaria Control Programme
- 1958 – Launching of National Malaria Eradication Programme
- 1966 – Cases reduced to 0.1 million
- Early 1970s – Resurgence of malaria
- 1976 – Malaria cases 6.46 million highest in post-DDT era (one of the reasons for resurgence was insecticide resistance in malaria vectors)
- 1977 – Modified Plan of Operations Implemented
- 1984–1998 Annual reported incidence within 2–3 million cases
- 1994 – Resurgence of malaria in some states
- 1997 – World Bank Assisted Enhanced Malaria Control Project (EMCP)
- 2005 – Global Fund Assisted Intensified Malaria Control Project (IMCP) – 100 million population in 94 districts of 10 states being covered from 2005 to 2006
- 2006 – World Bank Assisted Enhanced Vector Borne Diseases Control Project (EVBDCP) – 189 million population in 191 districts in 13 states
- 2006 – Artemisinin Combination Therapies (ACT) introduced in areas showing Chloroquine resistant falciparum malaria.
- 2008 – ACT extended to high-risk Pf districts covering about 80–90 per cent Pf infection.

Source: Dash et al. (2008).

Since independence, though India has designed and implemented several programmes towards controlling malaria but these initiatives have so far failed to bring the desired result as expected by the policymakers. So, there is need to adopt strategic approach which would help in meeting MDGs in halving the malaria morbidity and mortality by the year 2015. As far as the issue of malaria control is concerned, there are numerous challenges. No single individual method can be used to achieve a successful malaria control programme. Strategic control methods must involve some combination of effective clinical control, vector control, reduction in contact of the mosquito with its human host, improved sanitation, and better health education and malaria prevention programmes. Most of the rural areas do not have access to good health care systems. Usually there are no accessible roads to the health centres, which in turn are poorly equipped and have inadequate drugs for malaria treatment. Drug-resistant malaria is common and antimalarial drugs are becoming less effective as the plasmodium parasite develops resistance to affordable drugs. This poses a serious threat to clinical management and treatment of malaria. Policy makers need to aggressively pursue malaria control strategies.

Factors that are also responsible for the increase in the resurgence of malaria must be addressed in malaria transmission control. These factors include the large-scale resettlement of people usually associated with ecological changes, increasing urbanization disproportionate to the infrastructure, drug-resistant malaria, insecticide-resistant mosquitoes, inadequate vector control operations and public health practices. Vector control is significant in the light of increasing drug-resistant malaria, as well as for cost-effective reasons. Insecticide-treated bed net trials are being conducted in some parts of Nigeria and the results so far have been promising for the reduction in severity and prevalence of malaria in children. The cost-effectiveness of using insecticide-treated bed nets in reducing paediatric admissions also reduces the personal costs that family and friends bear during a hospital admission. Such costs include out of pocket expenses, travel, family input into treatment and productive time lost by mothers who have to take their children to the clinic or stay with them in hospital. A trusted method of controlling the mosquito is spraying breeding sites with insecticide such as DDT. Although some studies have reported the presence of DDT resistant mosquitoes, it is still one of the most effective and economical forms of insecticide in the control of malaria (Carringto, 2001).

Accessibility to primary health care centres and affordability must be guaranteed. Units within primary health care centres should be set up to diagnose, treat and monitor malaria cases. These centres will need the basic equipment required to check blood films for malaria parasites and a full blood count. Epidemiological surveillance is highly essential in any control strategy and is

Table 45 *State of Health in India: An Assessment with Some Major Health Indicators*

Key Health Indicators		*Year*	*Data Sources*
Total expenditure on health as per cent of gross domestic product	5.0	2005	WHS 2008
Infant mortality rate (per 1000 live births)	57	2006	WHS 2008
Maternal Mortality Ratio (per 100,000 live births)	450	2005	WHS 2008
Total Fertility rate (live births per woman)	2.9	2005	SRS 2005
Average life expectancy at birth	63	2006	WHS 2008
Crude Birth Rate (per 1000 population)	23.8	2005	SRS 2005
Crude Death Rate (per 1000 population)	7.6	2005	SRS 2005
Access to improved drinking-water sources	89	2006	WHS 2008
Access to improved sanitation	28	2006	WHS 2008
Mother and Child Health			
Births assisted by Doctor/Nurse/ANM/LHV/MPW/ other health personnel:	48.2%	2005	NFHS III
Institutional births	40.7%	2005	NFHS III
Anaemia among pregnant women (15–49)	57.8%	2005	NFHS III
Mothers covered at least three Antenatal check-up	50.7%	2005	NFHS III
Children Underweight (below 5 years)	46%	2005	NFHS-III
Every third malnourished child in the world lives in India		Source: MWCD Report, 2007	
Four out of every five children are anaemic		Source: NFHS-III	
Mortality/Death Rate			
Early Neonatal mortality rate (per 1000 live births)	28	2005	SRS 2005

Cont'd...

...Cont'd

Neonatal mortality rate (per 1000 live births)	37	2005	SRS 2005
Post-neonatal Mortality Rate (per 1000 live births)	22	2005	SRS 2005
Perinatal mortality rate (per 1000 live births)	37	2005	SRS 2005
Under-five mortality rate (U5MR) (per 1000 live births)	85	2005	MDGR India 2005
Adult (15 to 60 years) mortality rate (per 1000 population)	241	2006	WHS 2008
Non-communicable diseases deaths (% of total deaths)	53	2005	CCS India, WHO
Tuberculosis death rate (per 100,000 population)	33	2003	MDGR India 2005
Malaria death rate (per 100,000 population)	0.09	2004	MDGR India 2005
Cancer death rate (per 100,000 population)	49	2004	NCMH 2005
Cardio-vascular diseases death rate (per 100,000 population)	188	2005	NC MH 2005
Human Resources			
Doctors of modern system (per 10,000 population)	7	2005	HII 2005.
Doctors of alternative systems (per 10,000 population)	7	2004–05	HII 2005
Nurses (per 10,000 population)	8.0	2004	HII 2005
Midwives (per 10,000 population)	4.7	2004	WHR 2006
Dentists (per 10,000 population)	0.6	2004	WHR 2006
Pharmacists (per 10,000 population)	5.6	2004	WHR 2006
Public and Environmental Health Workers (per 10,000 population)	3.8	2004	WHR 2006
Community Health Workers (per 10,000 population)	0.5	2004	WHR 2006
Lab Technicians (per 10,000 population)	0.2	2004	WHR 2006

Cont'd...

...Cont'd

Prevalence of Diseases			
Diarrhoeas (per 1000 total population)	9	2005	IHSP 2005
Acute respiratory infections (per 1000 total population)	22	2005	IHSP 2005
Anaemia (6–35 months) (per 1000 total population)	792	2005–06	NFHS-III
Tuberculosis (pulmonary) – reported cases (per 100,000 population)	79	2005	HII 2005
Malaria incidence (per 100,000 population)	29	2005	IHSP 2005
Filaria (per 100,000 population at risk)	239	2004–05	HII 2005
Leprosy (per 100,000 adult population)	13	2004–05	IHSP2005
HIV (per 100,000 total population) in 15–49 years	910	2005	NACO
Cardiovascular diseases (per 100,000 population)	3422	2005	NCMH 2005
Diabetes (per 100,000 population)	2792	2005	NCMH 2005
Cancer (per 100,000 population)	19	2004	NCMH 2005
Blindness (per 100,000 population)	1120	2004	NCMH 2005

Note: CCS = Country Cooperation Strategy, India, 2006–2011; HII = Health Information of India; IHSP = India Health System Profile, Ministry of Health, India; MDGR = Millennium Development Goal Report; SRS = Sample Registration System, India; MWCD = Ministry of Women and Child Development, Government of India; NCMH = National Commission for Macroeconomics and Health, India; WHO = World Health Organization; WHR = World Health Report; National AIDS Control Organization; NFHS = National Family Health Survey; WHS = World Health Statistics of WHO.

Source: Hazra (2010).

an essential guide in developing a multidimensional approach. The malarial control units set-up should keep data on the epidemiological surveillance and the information should be sent to the national malaria control centre. It should also be taken into account that mass health education campaigns and training in malaria prevention are important. People should be educated on the importance of not providing conducive dwelling and breeding places for the mosquito. Refuse dumps should not be located near houses. Collection of rainwater in discarded waste such as old tires and empty cans should be prevented. Draining all stagnant water, clearing bushes around the house and eliminating pot holes on the roads are methods of depriving mosquitoes of their breeding grounds. Domestic water should be stored in containers that can be covered and should not be left open. To avoid non-compliance, it is important that people are sensitized and mobilized prior to the initiation of the programme. Acceptance of the various malaria control strategies by the community is important; therefore, local chiefs, community leaders and women should be involved in education and mobilization campaigns. The cost of controlling malaria, as expensive as it may be, cannot outweigh the benefits when morbidity, mortality, pain and suffering, and the economic consequences of malaria are taken into consideration.

Health Sector of India: The Emerging Issues and Challenges

As a result of the numerous initiatives taken by the government from time to time in the last six decades, significant achievements are noticeable in the sphere of health parameters, health legislation, health research and technology and disease control. India has made significant progress in the past several decades in improving the health and well-being of its people (Table 45). Despite these significant strides, the country continues to bear a heavy burden of both communicable and non-communicable diseases. Furthermore, India is experiencing a slow epidemiological evolution from infectious and parasitic diseases to non-communicable diseases.

While the health sector has made significant progress in the years since the country's independence, India still faces significant challenges. The major challenges for the health sector include accessibility and coverage in rural areas, ineffective management of existing infrastructure, and inadequate number and quality of health care professionals. Although India's health care system has gradually improved in the last few decades, it continues to lag behind those of its neighbouring countries. The poor state of health care in India may be attributed to the lack of government funding on health care initiatives, as estimates reveal that the per capita spending on health care by the Indian government is far below international recommendations.[16] Therefore, while there has been considerable success in developing physical infrastructure and coverage of primary health care provision, significant challenges remain across the country in health care provision, especially in terms of accessibility, coverage, rural areas, ineffective management, and inadequate quality and availability of health care professionals. Despite a steady increase in the number of medical establishments in the country, there still remains a severe shortage of sub-centres, primary health centres and community health centres. Lack of adequate healthcare is also reflected in the low density of healthcare personnel. While India has made significant gains in terms of health indicators – such as demographic, infrastructural and epidemiological – it continues to grapple with newer challenges. Not only have communicable diseases persisted over time but some of them such as malaria have also developed insecticide-resistant vectors, while others such as tuberculosis are becoming increasingly drug resistant. The 1990s have also seen an increase in mortality on account of non-communicable diseases arising as a result of lifestyle changes. The country is now in the midst of a dual disease burden of communicable and non-communicable diseases. This is coupled with spiralling health costs, high financial burden on the poor and erosion in their incomes. A study conducted by the World Bank explores that around 24 per cent of all people hospitalized in India in a single year fall below the poverty line due to hospitalization.[17] At the same time, health gaps exist between rich and poor, well-educated and less-educated, rural and urban – even between impoverished and marginalized groups. Malnutrition among children is rampant; one in every three of the world's malnourished children lives here and about 50 per cent of all childhood deaths in India are attributable to malnutrition.[18] The proportion of low-birth-weight babies remains high at one-third of all births. The promotion of early and exclusive breast feeding is a well-recognized strategy for child survival. It is estimated that in India 28 per cent of mothers initiate breast feeding within one hour of delivery and only 39.7 per cent practice exclusive breast feeding till six months.[19]

Steady declines have been noted in fertility, maternal, infant and child mortalities, and the prevalence of severe manifestations of nutritional deficiencies, but the pace has been slow and falls short of national and MDG targets. Substantial unmet need for contraception remains, adolescent pregnancies are common and access to safe abortion is inadequate. Increases in the numbers of deliveries in institutions have not been matched by improvements in the quality of intrapartum and neonatal care. Infants and young children do not get the health care they need; access to effective treatment for neonatal illness, diarrhoea and pneumonia shows little improvement; and the coverage of nutrition programmes is inadequate. Absence of well-functioning health systems is indicated by the inadequacies related to planning, financing, human resources, infrastructure, supply systems, governance, information and monitoring (Paul, 2011). On the other hand, the expansion of India's economy has, no doubt, greatly affected the lives of its citizens. Higher levels of work-related stress, increasing time constraints and more sedentary lifestyles have increased Indians' consumption of alcohol, tobacco and fast foods/prepared foods. This behaviour, combined with higher levels of pollution, has led to an increase in obesity, cardiovascular disease, diabetes and certain types of cancer. At the same time, however, one would also suspect that more money and attention is being paid towards healthcare (Boston Analytics, 2009).

India's achievements in the field of health have been less than satisfactory and the burden of disease among the Indian population remains high. Infant and child mortality and morbidity and maternal mortality and morbidity affect millions of children and women. Infectious diseases such as malaria and especially TB are re-emerging as epidemics, and there is the growing spectre of HIV/AIDS. Many of these illnesses and deaths can be prevented and/or treated cost-effectively with primary health care services provided by the public health system. An extensive primary health care infrastructure provided by the government exists in India. Yet, it is inadequate in terms of coverage of the population, especially in rural areas, and grossly underutilized because of the dismal quality of health care provided. In most public health centres which provide primary health care services, drugs and equipments are missing or in short supply, there is shortage of staff and the system is characterized by endemic absenteeism on the part of medical personnel due to lack of oversight and control (Bajpai and Goyal, 2004). Current delivery of health services in India has substantial gaps, including inadequate physical infrastructure, ineffective management, limited availability and lack of qualified health care professionals. Unlike primary health care, where public facilities are generally underutilized (especially at PHC level), the secondary and tertiary public health facilities (hospitals) are in high demand. Public hospitals are unable to meet the growing demand, and the infrastructure is either inadequate or unable to cope with the pressure of demand. In addition, quality of services provided in secondary and tertiary care and improved efficiencies are also much desired. At the same time, healthcare indicators vary widely across states, partly reflecting the differing levels of resources available to state governments, but one trend that is totally consistent is that indicators are much worse in rural areas than in urban ones. Due to demand outrunning supply, and with constraints on public expenditures, there is need for innovative public-private partnerships (PPP) to improve efficiencies and quality, and address financing gap in secondary and tertiary health care.

While overall mortality has declined considerably, living standards are still among the poorest in the world. The major constraints facing the health sector are lack of resources, lack of an integrated multi-sectoral approach, insufficient Information, Education and Communication (IEC) support, poor involvement of NGOs, inadequate laboratory services, a manually operated health management information system (HMIS), poor disease surveillance and response systems, and the heavy investments needed in dealing with non-communicable diseases. The problems of gender disparity still manifest themselves in various forms, as evidenced by the declining female to male population ratio, social stereotyping, violence at the domestic and social level, and continuing open discrimination against the girl child, adolescent girls and women.

Tackling the Challenges of Health Sector in India: The Way Forward

With health recognized as a central part of a wider development agenda we have a chance to push past the conventional target-based public health approach and to re-ground health policy in the most critical debates of the day, including globalization, human security, equity, human rights and poverty reduction. To many health policymakers, the health system seems forbiddingly complex, like a spider's web that will lure in, tangle up and paralyse even the best-intentioned initiatives. This wariness has contributed to the tendency, especially among donors, to favour initiatives that can go around the facility-based public health system and deliver services in vertical programmes deploying their own insulated infrastructure and resources. Many family planning and immunization programmes, for example, are designed this way. Such programmes have often yielded relatively rapid success for the targeted outcome, although their sustainability is less clear and their long-term impact on the health system questionable.

In India, to achieve equitable and sustained improvements across health services and outcomes, efforts would be required for systems strengthening in essential components: policy, financing, human resources, supply systems, service provision and management, and information and management systems.[20] The decentralized district-based planning envisaged in the NRHM needs to be rolled out throughout the country by 2012. Methods for situation analysis and planning need to be disseminated, and the capacity developed to use them. The National Health Systems Resource Centre has provided useful support to fill this gap. Since districts are so large, decentralized governance needs to go a step further. Health and nutrition policies need to be based on biological, epidemiological and operational evidence that is applied in the appropriate socio-cultural contexts and programmes. Strategies should, however, be designed to take into account best practices and evidence, and they should promote equity. Rigorous monitoring and assessment should be built in and the initiatives should not be allowed to imply political generosity. On the other hand, rampant and unremitting child under-nutrition is restricting future human potential and intellectual capital. India needs to aim at prioritization of action for its future human capital. The National Child Nutrition Mission should focus on children in the age group 0–2 years. Nutrition of pregnant and lactating women should be included in this mission, but the main focus should be indicators of child nutrition (Paul, 2011).

Portraying the Priorities in Health Sector: The Felt Needs

- There is a felt-need for quality management and quality assurance in health care delivery system so as to make the same more effective, economical and accountable. No concerted effort has been made so far to prepare comprehensive standards for the sub-centres. The launching of NRHM has provided the opportunity for framing Indian public health standards.
- Concerted efforts are required towards making health services and facilities accessible and available to the people, especially the underprivileged, through the regionalization of health services, rational transfer policies, incentives and career development opportunities, and minimizing inter and intrastate differences.
- Communicable diseases such as TB are still the major killers. Though these have been given special attention under NRHM, but spending has not increased significantly. There is urgent need to step up spending on communicable diseases.
- Gender-sensitive policies are a must and gender budgeting must come with a perspective wherein the patriarchal values and their penetration into programme strategies has to be consciously eliminated.
- The sexual and reproductive health of young people is pivotal to address India's ability to achieve the health MDGs. Reproductive health of young people has profound implications for maternal health, child survival and the nation's ability to combat HIV/AIDS. Most young women have little autonomy to make decisions about health, including contraception, care surrounding pregnancy and post-natal care. The content and coverage of initiatives for adolescent health should be strengthened. Innovative ways to provide counselling to young people about sexual and reproductive health, services and supplies are urgently needed.
- In addition to developments in allied sectors such as water, sanitation and education, and development of infrastructure, communications, science and technology, a transformed health and nutrition sector will enhance the lives of children, adolescents and women in India.

- There is marginal increase in capital expenditure. In a situation where rural health services are at the blink of collapse, extra initiative should be given in this regard. Additional resources need to be put at both the centre and the states to augment rural health services.
- There is a need to ensure equitable distribution of health facilities, especially in underserved areas, and promote autonomy in the use of allocated funds for maintaining buildings, equipment and supplies.
- Though the government is primarily responsible for public health, it alone cannot deliver public health. Engaging the private sector through public-private partnerships can potentially strengthen human resources required for improving service delivery in underserved areas and thus reducing gaps in the supply, needs and demands for human resources, and achieving national public health goals.
- It is also necessary to review the current human resource policies and organizational structures and the capacity to develop and manage health manpower.
- Reaffirmation of the highest political commitment and game-changing initiatives are required to address the emerging priorities of health sector.
- More efforts should be given towards strengthening of inter-sectoral coordination for implementing preventive and promotive health in an integrated and comprehensive manner, and strict and effective enforcement of available legislation relating to health and the environment.
- Build inter-sectoral collaboration for strengthening and maintaining infrastructure in the health and related sectors that would benefit mothers, newborns and children.
- A long-term effort is now required to rebuild the public health workforce; this will require major support from national and a wide variety of international agencies. A strengthened public health workforce will be in a better position to ensure that evidence on the effectiveness of health interventions and the new resources coming into the health sector lead to improvement of the health of all populations, not just the most advantaged. However, it will require large resources both

financial and technical. Though National Health Policy, 2002 has indicated enhancement of resources for public health but the same may not be available. Therefore, international support should be sought to revamp the public health system.

- The NRHM must work towards building an integrated service as accepted by the Alma Ata declaration. That is possible only with strengthening of the PHC, referral systems and linking up secondary hospitals with tertiary institutions. The overemphasis on tertiary sector with hi-tech services for diseases of the rich must not be allowed to hijack the system.
- Attention is needed on conducting study on need-assessment to identify existing gaps in human resources in health sector in collaboration with the local government, increase deployment of appropriate skilled health providers, especially at the primary care level. Operational efficiencies should be enhanced by task-shifting.
- Health professionals and health workers need strong, integrated health systems at both national and local levels to support the delivery of universal care and services. Proven, affordable interventions, provided within an integrated network of care, from community to referral centres, can prevent millions of needless deaths and disabilities.
- Identify innovative strategies and good practices with regard to development and management of health workforce within the states.
- Referral services need to be strengthened between different levels of services and this does need good public transport systems to support patient movement. Innovative schemes could be tested in this sphere
- Given a vast private sector, its regulation and monitoring is critical. Standardization of treatment, its price and compulsory pooling of data for national monitoring systems must be the minimum requirement
- Establishment of AIIMS-like institutions or the Population Foundation of India (PFI) should not be at the cost of primary health services.
- There is the urgent need to generate additional resources for health sector. Several options can be thought of. To start with

a direct health tax in the line of professional tax can be imposed; additional levies can be imposed on consumption of health hazardous substances.

- India's existing disease burden and the changing demographic and disease profile reflect a critical need for adding more health workers in order to achieve even modest coverage for essential health interventions. The need for more health workers have been envisaged under the NRHM which has made the estimates of such requirement.
- Despite tremendous improvements in interpersonal and mass communications, India has not harnessed their potential to create awareness of health and nutrition issues, change norms and practices, and persuade individuals, families and communities to make positive behaviour changes. Through culturally appropriate behaviour-change communication, delivered through several complementary channels, health and nutrition messages need to reach every household repeatedly. Key themes should include family planning, safe abortion, safe practices for sexual intercourse, antenatal care, diet and supplements in pregnancy, birth and emergency preparedness, deliveries in institutions, breastfeeding, immunization, complementary feeding, hygiene and care seeking.
- Therefore, the overall challenge for the Indian policymakers is to find ways to improve upon the existing situation in the health sector and to make equitable, affordable and quality health care accessible to the population, especially the poor and the vulnerable sections of the society.

The above measures are very elementary and may not be adequate for developing comprehensive public health system for all. The need for a radical transformation of entire health care system and the way it is financed today is imminent if we really want to change this regressive system of finance where people have to pay heavily, borrow and sale their assets in order to tide over their health emergencies to one where every Indian have access to comprehensive health care services. Unfortunately, as of now, there is hardly any positive step on the desired direction, radical transformation remains a far cry.

Despite India's dazzling recent economic performance, persistent widespread poverty means that malnourishment and communicable diseases remain serious problems. Immediate medical relief and preventing major outbreak following disasters is another area to fight with. There are some challenges to face with such as population stabilization, to reduce infant and maternal mortality, mobilization of funds on health, to increase manpower, to increase female literacy and so on. Control of some diseases such as HIV/AIDS, vector-borne ones, cancer, cardiovascular diseases, diabetes, trauma-related injuries and mental disorders is another point to improve the service delivery system in the sphere of health care and management and to meet these emerging challenges, the way forward has to be multipronged, focusing on finance, manpower, research and social factors such as sanitation, drinking water availability, female literacy, etc.

Conclusion

The current very high burden of disease in India is a barrier to its economic growth and poverty reduction efforts. With the threats posed by TB and other lifestyle and infectious diseases, the future burden of disease is expected to increase dramatically. If unchecked, it has the potential of wiping out past development achievements as has been the case in many Sub-Saharan African countries. The cost of investing in people's health is much less compared to the cost of paying inadequate attention to it. Following the adoption of the MDGs at the Millennium Summit of the United Nations in September 2000, the Report of the Commission on Macroeconomics and Health in 2001 argued that poor health was one of the most important determinants of poverty and urged the governments of developing nations to upscale their health systems and commit to the improving and investing in their people's health (Bajpai and Goyal, 2004). The initiation of the MDGs brings new energy and resources to the development agenda, with a strong emphasis on health outcomes. However, ensuring that such goals are met in an equitable manner, with the worst-off groups benefiting at the same or greater rate as the better-off groups, is a central challenge.

Notes

1. Measham and Chatterjee (1998).
2. Arnold, Choe and Roy (1996).
3. Govindasamy and Ramesh (1997); Hobcraft, McDonald, and Rutstein (1984); Mosley and Chen (1984); United Nations (1985).
4. Simoes et al. (1987).
5. Panda (2002).
6. UNAIDS (2006).
7. UNAIDS (2007).
8. UNAIDS (2008).
9. UNAIDS (2010).
10. Kakar and Kakar (2001.)
11. Ibid.
12. UNAIDS (2008).
13. Sinha (2011).
14. Murray and Lopez (1997).
15. Sinha (2011).
16. Boston Analytics (2009).
17. Hazra (2012).
18. UNICEF India (2005).
19. Gupta and Gupta (2003).
20. WHO (2000).

References

Amexo M, Tolhurst, R., Barnish, G., and Bates, I. (2004). Malaria Misdiagnosis: Effects on the Poor and Vulnerable. *Lancet*, Vol. 364.

Arnold, F., Choe, M.K., and Roy, T.K. (1996). *Son Preference, the Family-Building Process and Child Mortality in India*. Working Papers, Population Series No. 85. Hawaii, USA: East-West Center.

Bajpai, N., and Goyal, S. (2004). *Primary Health Care in India: Coverage and Quality Issues*. CGSD Working Paper No. 15. In Working

Papers Series (ed. Development CoGas). The Earth Institute at Columbia University. Available at: http://www.earthinstitute.columbia.edu (accessed December 10, 2009).

Bonu et al. (2003). The Impact of National Polio Immunization Campaign on Levels and Equity in Immunization Coverage: Evidence from Rural North India. *Social Science & Medicine*, Vol. 57.

Boston Analytics. (2009). *Healthcare in India: Report Highlights*. Boston: Boston Analytics.

Caldwell, J.C. (1994). How Is Greater Maternal Education Translated into Lower Child Mortality? *Health Transition Review*, Vol. 4.

Carringto, A. (2001). Malaria: Its Human Impact, Challenges, and Control Strategies in Nigeria. *Harvard Health Policy Review*, Vol. 2 (2).

Claeson, M., Bos, E., and Pathmanathan, I. (1999). *Reducing Child Mortality in India: Keeping up the Pace*. Washington, DC: The International Bank for Reconstruction and Development/The World Bank.

Claeson, M., Bos, E., Mawji, T. and Pathmanathan, I. (2000). Reducing Child Mortality in India in the New Millennium. *Bulletin of the World Health Organization*, Vol. 78 (10).

Cleland, J., and Kaufmann, G. (1993). *Education, Fertility and Child Survival: Unraveling the Links*. Paper presented at a workshop of the International Union for the Scientific Study of the Population (IUSSP), held in Barcelona, Spain, 10–14 November.

Dash, A.P., Valecha, N., Anvikar, A.R., and Kumar, A. (2008). Malaria in India: Challenges and Opportunities. *Journal of Biosciences*, Vol. 33.

Gaudin, S., and Yazbeck, Abdo S. (2006). Immunization in India 1993–1999: Wealth, Gender, and Regional Inequalities Revisited. *Social Science & Medicine*, Vol. 62 (3).

Govindasamy, P., and Ramesh, B.M. (1997). *Maternal Education and the Utilization of Maternal and Child Health Services in India*. National Family Health Survey Subject Report, No. 5. Mumbai, India: International Institute for Population Sciences; and Calverton, MD: Macro International.

Gupta, A., and Gupta, Y.P. (2003). *Status of Infant & Young Child Feeding in (49 districts) of India: A National Report of the Quantitative*

Study. Delhi: Breastfeeding Promotion Network of India. Available at: http://www.bpni.org (accessed March 16, 2005).

Hazra, A. (2010). State of Health in India: The Current Scenario. *Kurukshetra*, Vol. 58 (4).

Hazrd, A. (2012). The Challenge of Keeping Rural India Healthy. *Kurukshetra*, Vol. 60 (10).

Hobcraft, J.N., McDonald, J.W., and Rutstein, S.O. (1984). Socio-economic Factors in Infant and Child Mortality: A Cross-national Comparison. *Population Studies*, Vol. 38.

International Institute for Population Sciences (IIPS) and Macro International. (2007). *National Family Health Survey (NFHS-3), 2005–06: India*. Mumbai, India: IIPS.

International Institute of Population Sciences (IIPS). (1995). *National Family Health Survey (MCH and Family Planning)*, India 1992–93. Bombay, India: IIPS

Kakar, D.N., and Kakar, S.N. (2001). *Combating AIDS in the 21st Century Issues and Challenges*. New Delhi, India: Sterling Publishers Private Limited.

Kumar, A., Valecha, N., Jain, T., and Dash, A.P. (2007). Burden of Malaria in India: Retrospective and Prospective View. *American Journal of Tropical Medicine and Hygiene*, Vol. 77.

Measham, A., and Chatterjee, M. (1998). *India Wasting Away: The Crisis of Malnutrition in India*. Health, Nutrition and Population Unit, South Asia Region, Report No. 18667. Washington, DC: The World Bank.

Mosley, H.W., and Chen, L. (1984). "An Analytical Framework for the Study of Child Survival in Developing Countries" in Mosley, H.W., and Chen, L. (eds.). Child survival: Strategies for research. *Population and Development Review*, Vol. 10 (suppl.).

Murray, C.J.L., and Lopez, A.D. (1997). The Global Burden of Disease 1990–2020: Alternative Projections of Mortality and Disability by Cause for Eight Regions. *Lancet*, Vol. 349.

Panda, S. (2002), "The HIV/AIDS Epidemic in India: An Overview" in Panda, S., Chatterjee, A., and Abdul-Quader, A.S. (eds.) *Living with the AIDS Virus: The Epidemic and the Response in India*. New Delhi: Sage.

Paul, V.K. et al. (2011). Reproductive Health, and Child Health and Nutrition in India: Meeting the Challenge. *Lancet*, Vol. 377 (9762).

Pembrey, G. (2007). *Who Is Affected by HIV and AIDS in India*. India: Avert.

Project Axshya-Programme Management Unit. (2011). *Tuberculosis: Challenges for India*. Policy brief series: No. 12; February-March. New Delhi, India: Centre for Legislative Research and Advocacy (CLRA).

Sharma, R.S., Sharma, G.K., and Dhillon, G.P.S. (1996). Intervention measures for Transmission Control; in *Epidemiology and control of malaria in India*. New Delhi: National Malaria Eradication Programme.

Simoes, E.A. et al. (1987). Evidence for HTLV-III infection in prostitutes in Tamil Nadu (India). *Indian Journal of Medical Research*, Vol. 85.

Sinha, K. (2011, 23 April). India's malaria figures grossly underestimated? *The Times of India*.

Sinha, K. (2011, 24 March). 70 per cent TB patients in India are Under 50. *The Times of India*.

Tuberculosis Control India. *Socio-Economic Impact of Tuberculosis*. Retrieved from http://www.tbcindia.org. (accessed April 20, 2011).

UNAIDS. (2002). *Report on the Global HIV/AIDS Epidemic*. Geneva: UNAIDS.

UNAIDS. (2006). *2006 Report on the Global AIDS Epidemic*. Geneva: UNAIDS.

UNAIDS. (2007, 6 July). *2.5 Million People in India Living with HIV, According to New estimates* (Press Release). India: UNAIDS.

UNAIDS. (2008). *2008 Report on the Global AIDS Epidemic*. Geneva: UNAIDS.

UNAIDS. (2010). *Report on the Global AIDS Epidemic*. Geneva: UNAIDS.

UNICEF India. *India Health*. Retrieved from http://www.unicef.org/india/health.htm (accessed March 17, 2005).

United Nations. (1985). *Socio-economic Differentials in Child Mortality in Developing Countries*. New York: United Nations.

Wiseman, T. (1992). NGOs and AIDS: The Benefit of a Consortium Approach. *AIDS and Society*, Vol. 3 (1).

World Bank. (1993). *World Development Report 1993: Investing in Health*. New York: Oxford University Press.

World Health Organization (WHO). (2000). *The World Health Report 2000*. Geneva: World Health Organization.

Index